The Collected Poems of Barbara Guest

Wesleyan Poetry

THE

COLLECTED POEMS

OF

BARBARA GUEST

Barbara Guest

Edited by Hadley Haden Guest

Wesleyan University Press

Middletown, Connecticut

Published by Wesleyan University Press, Middletown, CT 06459
www.wesleyan.edu/wespress
© 2008 by the Estate of Barbara Guest
Introduction copyright © Peter Gizzi, 2008
Printed in the United States of America
5   4   3   2   1

Library of Congress Cataloging-in-Publication Data
Guest, Barbara.
[Poems]
The collected poems of Barbara Guest / Barbara Guest.
    p.   cm. — (Wesleyan poetry)
Includes index.
ISBN 978–0–8195–6860–1 (cloth : alk. paper)
I. Title
PS3513.U44   2008
811'.54—dc22   2008020147

Frontispiece: Early photo of Barbara Guest on a train © Fred W. McDarrah

NATIONAL
ENDOWMENT
FOR THE ARTS
A great nation
deserves great art.

Publication supported by a grant from the National
Endowment for the Arts.

green
press
INITIATIVE

Wesleyan University Press is a member of the
Green Press Initiative. The paper used in this book
meets their minimum requirement for recycled paper.

Contents

The Location of Things · Archaics · The Open Skies (1962)

The Blue Stairs (1968)

I Ching (1969)

Moscow Mansions (1973)

The Countess from Minneapolis (1976)

The Türler Losses (1979)

Biography (1980)

Quilts (1980)

Musicality (1988)

Fair Realism (1989)

Defensive Rapture (1993)

Stripped Tales (1995)

Quill, Solitary APPARITION (1996)

If So, Tell Me (1999)

The Confetti Trees (1999)

Rocks on a Platter: Notes on Literature (1999)

Symbiosis (2000)

Miniatures and Other Poems (2002)

Dürer in the Window, Reflexions on Art (2003)

The Red Gaze (2005)

1

New Poems

Introduction: Fair Realist

When Barbara Guest passed away in the winter of 2006, America lost one of its most fiercely independent and original artists. She had been writing poetry for sixty years. One might call her commitment to the art "heroic" but her primary task was rather, in her words, "to invoke the unseen, to unmask it." Hers is a poetry of revelation and of mystery. When Guest arrived on the scene in the mid-1950s, her work was characterized by an advanced lyricism that must have seemed already full-blown to her contemporaries. Yet as this volume attests, over the decades that followed, her poetry kept pushing the limits of the art with astonishing urgency, complexity, and daring. With only sporadic recognition along the way, most of it late, her work remained at the vanguard of the genre throughout her career.

Guest's poetry, like all great art, makes us reconsider tradition—not as a fixed canonical body that exists behind us or bears us up but as something we move toward. We find it reading back through those very works that were ahead of their own time, their readers, and even their authors—in the poems of Emily Dickinson or William Carlos Williams, for instance. If this model of discovery teaches us anything, it is that tradition is, in fact, always just ahead of us. It is an occasion we rise to.

In her essay "Wounded Joy," Guest writes: "The most important act of a poem is to reach further than the page so that we are aware of another aspect of the art. . . . What we are setting out to do is to *delimit* the work of art, so that it appears to have *no beginning and no end, so that it overruns the boundaries of the poem on the page*" (*Forces of Imagination*, 100). "The Türler Losses," one of her most adumbrated and yet literal poems, about the loss of a wristwatch, suggests the double bind of keeping and losing time, and the wonder of poems as timepieces. It is only, it seems, in reiterating temporal markers that one feels time expand within the poem, extending forward and looping back, incorporating and re-imagining the relation of future and past—and the difficult role of the poem in negotiating between them.

This desire to "delimit" the poem spatially and temporally has characterized Guest's work from the very beginning. Strictly speaking, her poems are not abstract; rather, they locate us always exactly where we already are, at the edge of meaning in an already impacted, developing world. Her poems begin in the midst of action but their angle of perception is oblique. In this way, the poem, like the world, exists phenomenally; it is grasped as it is coming into being, and she records the outer edges of the context of this movement, placing the poem at the horizon of our understanding.

Her early poem "Parachutes, My Love, Could Carry Us Higher" is a classic example of Guest's facility with paradox in the context of a complex emotional clarity. Suspension is the chief conceit of the poem: the suspension of disbelief, the suspension of a locatable time and place, the suspension of a shared amorous attachment, and the suspense of not-knowing—not knowing how to proceed and not-knowing as a human condition. It's a poem about being adrift but also about being alert to the elements, the medium of transport, willing to reconsider the terms of perception at each turn, as each line launches us into a variable reality.

Throughout her career, a contrapuntal tension between location and un-locatability would permeate her work. Guest was born in Wilmington, North Carolina, in 1920, the daughter of James Harvey and Ann Pinson. As a child, she moved to Florida and to California, living at various times with her aunt and uncle and with a grandmother. Guest wrote, "I never really had a 'home.' That was hard and it created unnecessary anxiety." Perhaps the indeterminacy and expansiveness of her voice were an answer to the necessity of establishing a lived space within the work of art.

Guest attended UCLA, then UC Berkeley, receiving her BA in 1943. After the war she moved to New York, marrying Stephen, Lord Haden-Guest in 1949, and Trumbull Higgins, a professor of military history, in 1954. She raised two children: Hadley Guest and Jonathan Higgins. She wrote art criticism and was an editorial associate at *Art News* from 1951 to 1959.

Her first book of poems was published by the Tibor de Nagy Gallery in 1960. It was titled *The Location of Things*, and, in fact, it located her within the New York poetry nexus in ways that both have and have not served the reception of her work. In that same year, her Berkeley classmate Donald Allen placed her among the New York School in his seminal anthology *The New American Poets*. Of the 65 contributors in the period's two major anthologies of American poetry (one edited by Allen in 1960 and the other by Donald Hall in 1962), she was one of only five women.

In the coming years she would publish *Poems* (1962) and *The Blue Stairs* (1968), followed by *Moscow Mansions* (1973), *The Countess from Minneapolis* (1976), and *The Türler Losses* (1979). Guest also wrote several plays, which were produced in New York in the Artists Theatre and the American Theatre for Poets, and a novel entitled *Seeking Air* (1978).

In a 1996 interview with the *American Poetry Review*, Guest described her process as similar to that of the abstract expressionists who believed in "letting the subject find itself." Reading her art writing, it becomes clear that her understanding of painting derived from—and in retrospect serves to elucidate—her own processes of composition. She wrote that Helen Frankenthaler's paintings are "landscapes of the interior" and positions them "on the margin of her universe." Disturbing the conventional relations of subjects and objects, of reality and imagination, is one of Guest's signature gestures. She writes that Frankenthaler "forces Nature to copy Art" (*Dürer in the Window*, 8).

In Guest's hands, art can say something about itself without becoming pedantic; it can be absorbed in the quandaries of perception without getting lost. Her poems more often evoke the joy of being found. There is a tenderness in Guest's ability to view experience as a composition in its own right, taking it in at a respectful distance as one might view a work of art; or as lived experience might be triangulated and compounded *through* a work of art, as in a poem like "Roses," with its gestures to both Gertrude Stein and Juan Gris or in her masterful poem "The Nude."

Her poems bespeak a long engagement with literary and artistic tradition, less by establishing allusive signposts than by exposing and exploring the difficulties that acts of imagination have always presented. She would find herself at home in modernism, influenced by H.D.'s imagism and by other manifestations of the high modern, including surrealism and Dada. Guest drew from imagism a sense of the impacted history of objects and of words and how they can be "set" within a poem. In a sense, Guest's work reflects a natural progression of imagism into literary abstract expressionism. That is, if an image is but a fragment of a larger field, it has already become abstract. It bears the traces of a human context but is not immediately locatable within a specific time or place. For Guest, "the poem begins in silence," not noise, and it is quietly drawn into polyphony with its own echoes (*FI*, 20).

She had an integrity that predisposed her for telling the truth as she saw it, and writing poetry as she understood it, even when it ran contrary to popular trends. As the women's movement was gaining strength and might have offered her a sense of context, Guest eschewed overtly polemical and political poetry—though it is worth noting that at this time she spent close to a decade writing the definitive biography of her great modernist precursor, H.D.: *Herself Defined* (1984).

Her later poems were often characterized by the bridging of antagonistic dualities, as expressed in two of her most influential books, *Fair Realism* (1989) and *Defensive Rapture* (1993). Even a title like "Wild Gardens Overlooked by Night Lights" implies a frisson between the forces of nature (wild) and the cultivated (gardens). In its brilliant control of framing and juxtaposition to build emotional intensity through narrative compression, the poem exemplifies the heights of contemporary lyric practice. One doesn't think of Guest as a narrative poet, but her poems are laced with dramatic tensions and an engagement with invisible, imaginary, phantasmagorical elements, inexplicable turns in the path, and a mysterious sense of inevitability. Her most recent poems in *Rocks on a Platter* (1999), *Miniatures* (2002), *The Red Gaze* (2005), and after, take the reader quietly from one realm to another, as evidenced in one of her last poems, "Shelley in the Navy-Colored Chair" (dedicated to her editor Suzanna Tamminen). As in Wallace Stevens's late poems, the relation between reality and imagination has become seamless.

Guest spoke eloquently—and defensively in the sense of Shelley's "Defence"—about mystery, about poetry and its spiritual dimension, a theme that permeates her recent collections of prose, *Dürer in the Window: Reflexions on*

Art (2003) and the magisterial *Forces of Imagination: Writing on Writing* (2003). She wrote that "vision is part of the poet's spiritual life of which the poem, itself, is a résumé" (*FI*, 27). The poem "should not be programmatic, or didactic, or show-off"; rather, one should "go inside the poem itself and *be in the dark* at the beginning of the journey" (*FI*, 80). Her statements on poetics were direct ("Respect your private language") and, at times, as practical as a survival manual ("When in trouble depend upon imagination") (*FI*, 78, 79). Implied always was a sense of poetry's charge—its energy and intensity but also its responsibility—and the understanding that writing was, in many ways, playing with fire:

> The forces of the imagination from which strength is drawn have a disruptive and capricious power. If the imagination is indulged too freely, it may run wild and destroy or be destructive to the artist. . . . If not used imagination may shrivel up. Baudelaire continually reminds us that the magic of art is inseparable from its risks. . . . " (*FI*, 106)

She was fearless and, to those who knew her, sagacious and outspoken.

Her last book, *The Red Gaze*, ends with a sentence by Theodor Adorno: "In each genuine art work something appears that did not exist before." This is the Promethean power of which Guest's poems never lost sight and which have thus, in their own way, changed our world.

—Peter Gizzi

Timeline

1920: Born Barbara Ann Pinson on September 6 in Wilmington, North Carolina, to James "Harvey" Pinson and Anna Mae Pinson during a brief stay in town while Harvey looked for work as a probation officer.

1921–30: Alternated between the home of her grandparents in Charleston, West Virginia, and various towns around Miami, Florida, with her parents. Her mother gave birth to two boys, Jimmy and David, and two girls, Nancy and Mary Patrice. Barbara was educated in Miami and "backwoods" one-room schoolhouses. She learned to read at age three.

1931–37: Barbara was sent to live with her aunt, Mary Louise Hetzel Pelzel, and uncle by marriage, John Pelzel, who were childless and lived in Los Angeles, at the urging of her grandmother in West Virginia, Mary Lilian Cundiff Hetzel, in order for Barbara to receive a better education. She attended Virgil Junior High School and Beverly Hills High School, both in Los Angeles.

1938: Graduated from Beverly Hills High School.

1939: Attended the University of California, Los Angeles as an English Literature major. Met her future husband, the sculptor and painter John Dudley, a roommate of the writer Henry Miller, for whom Barbara was a typist. Barbara's father, Harvey Pinson, died.

1940: Unsatisfied with the English Department at UCLA, Barbara took a leave of absence for a year to attend a junior college where she felt the faculty had a better understanding of modern poetry.

1941: Returned to the University of California, Los Angeles.

1942: Transferred to the University of California, Berkeley and moved to a Leroy Street apartment in Berkeley.

1943: Graduated from the University of California, Berkeley with a bachelor of arts degree in English Literature.

1943–45: Returned to Los Angeles and took a job as a social worker for the city. Worked with Air Force flyers recuperating from bombing missions during World War II. Married John Dudley.

1946:	After living briefly with John Dudley's parents in Kansas, the couple moved to New York City where they lived in a Greenwich Village apartment and became friends with several artists, some of whom would later become members of what John Bernard Myers called in his 1969 book "The Poets of the New York School," a tongue-in-cheek designation that set the little-known group of young poets apart from the well-known and appreciated abstract expressionist artists of the "New York School." Barbara and John Dudley were divorced later in the year.
1947:	Met Stephen Guest (later known as Lord Stephen Haden Haden-Guest) who came to New York in the 1930s from London. They lived together in a Greenwich Village apartment where Stephen Haden Haden-Guest introduced Barbara to the poet H.D. (Hilda Doolittle).
1948:	Married Stephen Haden Haden-Guest and took the pen name "Barbara Guest."
1949:	Daughter Hadley Haden-Guest born on March 22 in Pinehurst, North Carolina, while Barbara visited her sister Mary Patricia Pinson Howe. Lived briefly in Washington, D.C., in an apartment with her mother, brother David, and daughter.
1950s:	Became a central member of "The Poets of the New York School" along with Edwin Denby, Frank O'Hara, James (?) Schuyler, Kenneth Koch, John Ashbery, Kenward Elmslie, and others.
1952:	Wrote art reviews for the publication *Art News*.
1953:	*The Ladies Choice*, a play written by Barbara, staged at the Artists Theater in New York.
1954:	Barbara and Stephen Haden Haden-Guest were divorced. Barbara and the World War II historian Trumbull Higgins were married soon after.
1955:	Son Jonathan van Lennep Higgins born.
1958:	Received the Yaddo Fellowship.
1960:	*The Location of Things*, a book of poetry edited by John Bernard Myers and featuring a collage by Robert Goodnough, published by the Tibor de Nagy Gallery in New York.
1961:	Moved to a rental house in Washington, D.C., with her son, daughter, and husband while Trumbull worked for the Institute for Defense Analysis.

1962:	*Poems: The Location of Things, Archaics, The Open Skies* published by Doubleday in New York. The artist Grace Hartigan created two lithographs inspired by poems from the book.
1963:	*The Office: A One Act Play in Three Scenes* produced and directed by John Bernard Myers; staged at Café Cino in New York.
1965:	*Port: A Murder in One Act* produced and directed by John Bernard Myers; staged at the American Theater for Poets in New York.
1966:	Wrote a play entitled *The Diving Board;* never staged. Friend and fellow New York School poet Frank O'Hara died.
1967:	Wrote a play entitled *Chinese Ghost Restaurant;* never staged.
1968:	*The Blue Stairs* published by Corinth Books in New York featuring cover art by Helen Frankenthaler. Received Longwood Award for *The Location of Things.*
1969:	*I Ching* published by Mourlot Graphics in Paris featuring lithographs by Sheila Isham. *Barbara Guest Reading Her Poems with Comment in the Recording Laboratory* recorded at the Library of Congress.
1971:	Essay "Jeanne Reynal" published in *Craft Horizons.*
1973:	*Moscow Mansions* published by the Viking Press in New York. Awarded the Poetry Foundation Prize.
1975:	Served as Editor of the *Partisan Review.* Essay "Helen Frankenthaler" published in *Arts Magazine.* Wrote a play entitled *The Swimming Pool;* never staged.
1976:	*The Countess from Minneapolis* published by Burning Deck in Providence, Rhode Island.
1978:	*Seeking Air: A Novel* published by Black Sparrow Press in Santa Barbara, California, featuring cover art by Robert Fabian. Received a National Endowment for the Arts grant and the Fund for Poetry Award.
1979–83:	Rented the back section of a house in Long Island for her family in addition to a cottage behind the main house where Barbara worked on a biography of H.D.
1979:	*The Türler Losses* published by Mansfield Book Mart Ltd. in Montreal, Canada.
1980:	*Biography* published by Burning Deck in Providence, Rhode Island.

1981: *Quilts* published by Vehicle Editions in New York.

1982: Exhibition "Poets and Artists" at the Guild Hall Museum in Long Island featured Barbara's poem "Tessera" with a painting by Fay Lansner.

1983: Served on The Poetry Society of America Board of Governors for two years.

1984: *Herself Defined: The Poet H.D. and Her World* published by Doubleday and Quill in New York. Essay "A Reason for Poetics" published in *Ironwood*.

1985: *Herself Defined* published by Collins in Great Britain. Essay "Leatrice Rose" published in *Arts Magazine*. Essay "June Felter at 871 Fine Arts" published in *Art in America*.

1986: *The Nude*, published by The Arts Publisher in New York featuring etchings by Warren Brandt. Essay "Mysteriously Defining the Mysterious: Byzantine Proposals of Poetry" published in *How(ever)*.

1988: *Musicality* published by Kelsey St. Press in Berkeley, California, featuring art by June Felter.

1989: *Fair Realism* published by Sun & Moon Press in Los Angeles, California, featuring cover art by Leatrice Rose. A Grace Hartigan lithograph entitled "The Hero Leaves His Ship," inspired by Barbara's poem of the same name, appeared in *Universal Limited Art Editions: A History and Catalog*. Began service on the Poets Advisory Committee in New York, a position she would hold for the next ten years.

1990: Trumbull Higgins died. Essay "The Vuillard of Us" published in *Denver Quarterly*. Awarded the Lawrence J. Lipton Prize for *Fair Realism*.

1991: *The Countess from Minneapolis*, second edition, published by Burning Deck in Providence, Rhode Island. Essay "Shifting Personas" published in *Poetics Journal*.

 The Altos published by Hank Hine Editions in San Francisco, California, featuring art by Richard Tuttle. Received the Jerome J. Shestack Poetry Prize for poems appearing in *The American Poetry Review*. Recorded *Barbara Guest Reading Selections from Her Poetry* for the Poetics Program in Buffalo, New York.

1993: *Defensive Rapture* published by Sun & Moon Press in Los Angeles, California. Received the Poetry Center Book Award.

1994: Festchrift held at Brown University to honor Barbara. Received the Fund for Poetry Award and the Jerome J. Shestack Poetry Prize for "Motion Pictures," appearing in *The American Poetry Review*. Barbara and daughter Hadley moved to Berkeley, California.

1995: *Stripped Tales* published by Kelsey St. Press in Berkeley, California, featuring art by Anne Dunn. *Selected Poems* published by Sun & Moon Press in Los Angeles, California, featuring a 1950 collage by Barbara entitled "Ninth Street, New York." *Fair Realism*, paperback edition, published by Sun & Moon Press in Los Angeles, California. Received the San Francisco State University Poetry Center Book Award for *Defensive Rapture* and the America Awards for Literature in the Best Poetry category for *Selected Poems*.

1996: *Selected Poems* published by Carcanet Press in Great Britain. *Quill, Solitary APPARITION*, published by The Post-Apollo Press in Sausalito, California. Served as Judge for the America Awards and the Columbia Book Award. Received the Josephine Miles Award for Poetry for *Selected Poems;* the Fund for Poetry Award, and the America Awards for Literature in the Best Poetry category for *Quill, Solitary APPARITION*. Gave the Gertrude Clarke Whitthall Lecture at the Library of Congress. Recorded *Barbara Guest Recording Her Poems in the Mumford Room* at the Library of Congress and *Barbara Guest Reading Her Poems* for the Lannan Foundation.

1997: *Seeking Air: A Novel* is reissued by Sun & Moon Press in Los Angeles, California, featuring cover paintings by Robert Fabian. Played the sister of Claus von Bulow in *Island of Lost Souls*, a play written and directed by Kevin Killian, staged at The Lab in San Francisco, California.

1998: *Etruscan Reader VI* (with Robin Blaser, Lee Harwood, Barbara Guest) published by Etruscan Books in South Devonshire, England. Two poem-cartoons by Barbara and Joe Brainard exhibited at the University Art Museum in Berkeley, California. Received Poetry Foundation Award.

1999: Received the Frost Medal for Distinguished Lifetime Work from the Poetry Society of America. *Outside of This, That Is* published by Z Press in Vermont, featuring art by Trevor Winkfield. *If So, Tell Me* published by Reality Street Editions in London, England, featuring cover art by Anne Dunn. *Rocks on a Platter: Notes on Literature* published by Wesleyan University Press in Middletown, Connecticut, featuring a 1951 collage by Barbara entitled "Awakening." *The Confetti Trees* published by Sun & Moon Press in Los Angeles, California, featuring art by Max Beckman and June Felter. *Strings*, fifteen copies handmade by artist Ann Slacik.

2000: *Symbiosis* published by Kelsey St. Press in Berkeley, California, featuring art by Laurie Reid. *Often*, a play co-written by Barbara and Kevin Killian, and *Three Plays by Barbara Guest* produced by Small Press Traffic and directed by Kevin Killian and Wayne Smith; both staged at the California College of the Arts and Crafts in San Francisco, California. Served as Judge for the Frances Jaffer Award of Kelsey St. Press and for the Jessica Nobel Maxwell Memorial Prize of the *American Poetry Review.*

2001: *Often* published by Kenning in Buffalo, New York.

2002: *Miniatures and Other Poems* published by Wesleyan University Press in Middletown, Connecticut, featuring a 1950 collage by Barbara entitled "East Ninth Street, New York."

2003: *Herself Defined* reissued by Schaffner Press in Tucson, Arizona. *Forces of Imagination: Writing on Writing* published by Kelsey St. Press in Berkeley, California, featuring art by Laurie Reid. *Dürer in the Window, Reflexions on Art* published by Roof Books in New York featuring the poem-painting "Honey or Wine?" by Barbara and Mary Abbott.

2005: *The Red Gaze: Poems* published by Wesleyan University Press in Middletown, Connecticut.

2006: Died on February 15 in Berkeley, California.

Works by Barbara Guest

Poetry:

The Location of Things. New York: Tibor de Nagy, 1960.

Poems: The Location of Things, Archaics, The Open Skies. Garden City, N.Y.: Doubleday, 1962.

The Blue Stairs. New York: Corinth Books, 1968.

Moscow Mansions. New York: Viking Press, 1973.

The Countess from Minneapolis. Providence, R.I.: Burning Deck, 1976, reprint 1991.

The Türler Losses. Montreal: Mansfield Book Mart, 1979.

Biography. Providence, R.I.: Burning Deck, 1980.

Quilts. New York: Vehicle Editions, 1980.

Fair Realism. Los Angeles: Sun & Moon Press, 1989, reprint 1995.

Defensive Rapture. Los Angeles: Sun & Moon Press, 1993.

Selected Poems. Los Angeles: Sun & Moon Press, 1995.
Cover collage by Barbara Guest.

Quill, Solitary APPARITION. Sausalito, Calif.: Post-Apollo Press, 1996.

Rocks on a Platter: Notes on Literature. Hanover, N.H.: Wesleyan University Press, 1999.
Cover collage by Barbara Guest.

If So, Tell Me. London: Reality Street Editions, 1999.

The Confetti Trees. Los Angeles: Sun & Moon Press, 1999.

Outside of This, That Is. Calais, Vt.: Z Press, 1999.

Miniatures and Other Poems. Middletown, Conn.: Wesleyan University Press, 2002.
Cover collage by Barbara Guest.

The Red Gaze. Middletown, Conn.: Wesleyan University Press, 2005.
Cover art by Barbara Guest.

Novel:

Seeking Air: A Novel. Santa Barbara, Calif.: Black Sparrow, 1978; reprint, Los Angeles: Sun & Moon Press, 1997.

Biography:

Herself Defined. The Poet H.D. and Her World. New York: Quill, William Morrow, 1984.

Herself Defined. The Poet H.D. and Her World. Garden City, N.Y.: Doubleday, 1984.

Herself Defined. The Poet H.D. and Her World. London: Collins, 1985.

Herself Defined. The Poet H.D. and Her World. Tucson, Ariz.: Schaffner Press, Inc., 2003.

Collaborations:

Robert Goodnough, Painter. (With B. H. Friedman.) Paris: Georges Fall, 1962.

I Ching: Poems and Lithographs. (With artist Sheila Isham.) Paris: Mourlot Art Editions, 1969.

The Nude. (With watercolors by artist Warren Brandt; includes Barbara Guest's poem "The Nude".) New York: International Editions, 1986.

Musicality. (With artist June Felter.) Berkeley: Kelsey St. Press, 1988.

The Altos. (With artist Richard Tuttle.) San Francisco: Hank Hine Editions, 1991.

Stripped Tales. (With artist Anne Dunn—see also her cover for Barbara Guest's *If So, Tell Me.*) Berkeley: Kelsey St. Press, 1995.

Etruscan Reader VI. (With Robin Blaser and Lee Harwood.) South Devonshire, England: Etruscan Books, 1998.

Strings. (With artist Ann Slacik.) St. Denis, France: 1999: Limited, handmade copies by Ann Slacik.

The Luminous. (With artist Jane Moorman—see also Barbara Guest's poem "The Luminous" in *If So, Tell Me.*) Palo Alto, Calif.: 1999. One copy, handmade.

Often. (With Kevin Killian.) Produced in San Francisco by Poets Theater, California College of the Arts and Crafts, 2000.

Symbiosis. (With artist Laurie Reid.) Berkeley: Kelsey St. Press, 2000.

Art Criticism:

Dürer in the Window, Reflexions on Art. New York: Roof Books, 2003.

Essays:

Forces of Imagination: Writing on Writing. Berkeley: Kelsey St. Press, 2003.

Plays:

The Ladies' Choice, produced in New York at Artists Theater, 1953.

The Office, produced in New York at Café Cino, 1963.

Port, produced in New York at American Theater for Poets, 1965.

Port, produced in San Francisco by Poets Theater, California College of the Arts and Crafts, 2000.

Collages:

Ninth Street, New York (1950). On cover of Barbara Guest's *Selected Poems.* Los Angeles: Sun & Moon Press, 1995. Note: in 1950 Barbara Guest was living in a rental apartment on East Ninth Street, Manhattan, New York.

East Ninth Street, New York (1950). On cover of Barbara Guest's *Miniatures and Other Poems.* Middletown, Conn.: Wesleyan University Press, 2002.

Awakening (1951). On cover of Barbara Guest's *Rocks on a Platter: Notes on Literature.* Middletown, Conn.: Wesleyan University Press, 1999.

Wheel (1951). Following page (page 97) to Barbara Guest poem "Leaning Structures," in *American Letters & Commentary,* Winter 2007; Anna Rabinowitz, Executive Editor; Catherine Kasper and David Ray Vance, Co-Editors.

The Red Gaze (2003). On cover of Barbara Guest's *The Red Gaze.* Middletown, Conn.: Wesleyan University Press, 2005.

Notes and Acknowledgments

The poems collected here include all of the work that Barbara Guest had elected to publish in book form, along with the handful of poems she completed after her final book, *The Red Gaze* (Wesleyan, 2005). It was her stated wish not to include in this book any poems published in magazines or journals but not subsequently collected in one of her books. Because certain discrepancies in the published versions of some of these poems have not been resolved, minor changes have been made, without comment, in punctuation, spelling, and line spacing. This book is organized chronologically by collection. Given the nature of a collection of this size, some spacing issues have needed to be resolved. For instance, in texts like *Symbiosis*—a continuous poem that, in the original, prints only a few lines per page—page breaks in the original are indicated by a bullet. Please note that the poem "The Time of Day" appears only in the 1960 edition of *The Location of Things* (Tibor de Nagy, 1960). The final poems are arranged chronologically—insofar as this can be established—according to the date they were completed.

Grateful acknowledgment is made to the publishers of the original editions of Barbara Guest's books. Special thanks go to Mae Klinger, the editorial intern at Wesleyan University Press who prepared the manuscript for production.

—Suzanna Tamminen
Wesleyan University Press

Poems

THE LOCATION OF THINGS

ARCHAICS

THE OPEN SKIES

THE LOCATION OF THINGS

The Location of Things

Why from this window am I watching leaves?
Why do halls and steps seem narrower?
Why at this desk am I listening for the sound of the fall
of color, the pitch of the wooden floor
and feet going faster?
Am I to understand change, whether remarkable
or hidden, am I to find a lake under the table
or a mountain beside my chair
and will I know the minute water produces lilies
or a family of mountaineers scales the peak?

Recognitions

On Madison Avenue I am having a drink, someone
with dark hair balances a carton on his shoulders
and a painter enters the bar. It reminds me
of pictures in restaurants, the exchange of hunger
for thirst, art for decoration and in a hospital
love for pain suffered beside the glistening rhododendron
under the crucifix. The street, the street bears light
and shade on its shoulders, walks without crying,
turns itself into another and continues, even
cantilevers this barroom atmosphere into a forest
and sheds its leaves on my table
carelessly as if it wanted to travel somewhere else
and would like to get rid of its luggage
which has become in this exquisite pointed rain
a bunch of umbrellas. An exchange!

That head against the window
how many times one has seen it. Afternoons
of smoke and wet nostrils,
the perilous makeup on her face and on his,
numerous corteges. The water's lace creates funerals
it makes us see someone we love in an acre of grass.

The regard of dramatic afternoons

through this floodlit window
or from a pontoon on this theatrical lake,
you demand your old clown's paint and I hand you
from my prompter's arms this shako,
wandering as I am into clouds and air
rushing into darkness as corridors
who do not fear the melancholy of the stair.

Piazzas

for Mary Abbot Clyde

   In the golden air, the risky autumn,
leaves on the piazza, shadows by the door
on your chair the red berry
      after the dragonfly summer

we walk this mirroring air our feet chill
and silver and golden a portrait
by Pinturicchio we permanently taste the dark
grapes and the seed pearls glisten

      as the flight of those fresh brown birds
an instant of vision that the coupling mind
and heart see in their youth
with thin wings attacking a real substance
      as Pinturicchio fixed his air.

After all dragonflies do as much
in midsummer with a necessary water
there is always a heaviness of wings.

To remember
now that the imagination's at its turning
how to recall those Pierrots of darkness
(with the half-moon like a yellow leg of a pantaloon)
I would see you again (like the purple P
of piazza).

    Imagination
thunder in the Alps yet we flew above it
then met a confusion of weather and felt
the alphabet turning over when we landed
in Pekin. I read the late Empress's letters
and thought they were yours,
that impeccable script followed by murders

    real or divined
as the youth leaning over the piazza
throwing stones at his poems. He reads
his effigy in the one that ricochets
he weeps into the autumn air
and that stone becomes golden as a tomb
beware the risky imagination

    that lines its piazzas
with lambswool or for sheer disturbance
places mirrors for Pinturicchio
to draw his face at daybreak
when the air is clear of shadows
and no one walks the piazza.

All Grey-haired My Sisters

All grey-haired my sisters
what is it in the more enduring
clime of Spring that waits?
The tiger his voice once prayerful
around the lax ochre sheen
finally in withering sleep
its calendar,

Relatives
delicious plumages your scenery
has a black musical depth
the cardinal flies into
he learns to repeat on an empty
branch your distillations. Sombre
mysteries the garden illumines
a shape of honey hive
the vigorous drones lighting
up your face as fortunes pour
from your cold pockets into the heat
and glaze, fortresses
for those memories brisk
in the now doubling air,

Adventuresses
guided by the form and scent
of tree and flower blossoming
the willow once frail now Image
cut of stone so to endure,

My darlings
you walked into the wars
with wreaths of pine cones, you lay
by the sea and your sweet dresses
were torn by waves as over each receded
and pebbles were lifted at your feet
in the foam,

Ancestress
with blond boating hair
as daisies drop at your wrists
which flight are you making?
down the lime aisles
I see your sashes disappear.

Why should I count you more equinoctal, sun?
Smoothly the oars into the bay
the ultramarine fast as a castle, or rock
its soul plunged to craters virginal
the rapid twist of spume to all-forgetting
wrecks, intensely now that story's done.
Mermaids your hair is green. I recognize
the powerful daylight heat. My savages
a cooling torpor rearranges,
as at its southern margins, the oak.

From your journals
He said: "In nymphic barque"
She replied: "A porcupine."
And later,
"Reason selects our otherness."

In the broad strange light,
a region of silences. The delphic
clouded tree knows its decline,
if you were to forget animosities, girls,
and in the pagan grass slide heedlessly
blossoms would return such songs
as I've sung of you, the youthful ashes
fling upward settling fragrant
brightness on your dusky marquetry,

All grey-haired my sisters
this afternoon's seraphicness
is also fading. Linger while
I pass you quickly lest the cherry's
bloom changed to white
fall upon my head.

Windy Afternoon

Through the wood
on his motorcycle piercing
the hawk, the jay
the blue-coated policeman

Woods, barren woods,
as this typewriter without an object
or the words that from you
fall soundless

The sun lowering
and the bags of paper
on the stoney ledge
near the waterfall

Voices down the roadway
and leaves falling over there
a great vacancy
a huge leftover

The quality of the day
that has its size in the North
and in the South
a low sighing that of wings

Describe that nude, audacious line
most lofty, practiced street
you are no longer thirsty
turn or go straight.

Russians at the Beach

The long long accent
    the short vowel
that thing wrapped around a palm tree
    is it this water, or this jetty?

The blue, in air dismal
    to the face further than sand
then green rolling its own powder
    you will provide you stranger

The cargo intimate cargo
      of lashes and backs bent like a crew
the miles are vast and the isthmus
      shows five-toed feet
erect thunders all afternoon

You have traveled
more than this shore where
the long bodies
    wait
      their thin heads
do not understand

They are bent
    the breeze is light
    as the step of a native is heavy
you are tired
    but you breathe
    and you eat
and you sleep where the stream is narrow
    where the foam has left off
      ascending
    the day meets your borders
      so easily
    where you have discovered it.

The Hero Leaves His Ship

I wonder if this new reality is going to destroy me.
There under the leaves a loaf
The brick wall on it someone has put bananas
The bricks have come loose under the weight,
What a precarious architecture these apartments,
As giants once in a garden. Dear roots
Your slivers repair my throat when anguish
commences to heat and glow.

    From the water
A roar. The sea has its own strong wrist
The green turf is made of shells
    it is new.

I am about to use my voice
Why am I afraid that salty wing
Flying over a real hearth will stop me?

       Yesterday the yellow
Tokening clouds. I said "no" to my burden,
The shrub planted on my shoulders. When snow
Falls or in rain, birds gather there
In the short evergreen. They repeat their disastrous
Beckoning songs as if the earth
Were rich and many warriors coming out of it,
As if the calm was blue, one sky over
A shore and the tide welcoming a fleet
Bronzed and strong as breakers,

       Their limbs in this light
Fused of sand and wave are lifted once
Then sunk under aquamarine, the phosphorous.
Afterwards this soundless bay,
Gulls fly over it. The dark is mixed
With wings I ask if that house is real,
If geese drink at the pond, if the goatherd takes
To the mountain, if the couple love and sup,

       I cross the elemental stations
from windy field to still close. Good night I go to my bed.
This roof will hold me. Outside the gods survive.

Les Réalités

It's raining today and I'm reading about pharmacies
       in Paris.
Yesterday I took the autumn walk, known in May
       as lovers' walk.
Because I was overwhelmed by trees (the path from the playhouse
leads into a grove and beyond are the gravestones),
squirrels and new mold it is a good thing today
to read about second-class pharmacies where
mortar and plastic goods disturb death a little
and life more. It is as if perpetual rain
fell on those drugstores making the mosaic brighter,
as if entering those doors one's tears
were cleaner.

As if I had just
left you and was looking for a new shade of powder
orchidée, ambre, rosé, one very clarified and true
to its owner, one that in a mirror
would pass for real and yet when your hand falls upon it
(as it can) changes into a stone or flower of the will
and triumphs as a natural thing,
              as this pharmacy
turns our desire into medicines and revokes the rain.

In the Middle of the Easel

My darling, only
a cubist angle seen after
produces this volume in which our hearts go
(tick tick)

      I see you in a veil of velvet
      then I'm quiet because you've
      managed the apples, you've arranged
      to sit. You are twice clothed
      in my joy, my nymph.

Painters who range up and down
Mont hill or Mont this, disarray
in the twilight those boulevards,
make every stroke count and when one of the Saints
(in the dark apse tonal) quits,
I'm with you.

      Together we'll breathe it,
      you and I in the sleeve forgiving requiem,
      in the priest tinted air.
      In the gaslight that ridiculous plume
      reminds me of hawks, I admire
      their arc, I plunge
      my everyday laughter into that kimono wing
      what a studio soar! What rapture!
      The gifted night, the billowing dark!

The heroine Paint sobs

"No one who has ever loved me
can tell me why
there are two birds at my wrist
and only one flies."

On the Way to Dumbarton Oaks

The air! The colonial air! The walls, the brick,
this November thunder! The clouds Atlanticking,
Canadianing, Alaska snowclouds,
tunnel and sleigh, urban and mountain routes!

Chinese tree
your black branches and your three yellow leaves
with you I traffick. My three
yellow notes, my three yellow stanzas,
my three preciousnesses
of head and body and tail joined
carrying my scroll, my tree drawing

This winter day I'm
a compleat travel agency with my Australian
aborigine sights, my moccasin feet padding
into museums where I'll betray all my vast
journeying sensibility in a tear dropped before
"The Treasure of Petersburg"

and gorgeous this forever
I've a raft of you left over
like so many gold flowers and so many white
and the stems! the stems I have left!

Cape Canaveral

Fixed in my new wig
the green grass side
hanging down
I impart to my silences
operas.

Climate cannot impair
        neither the grey clouds nor the black waters
the change in my hair.

Covered with straw or alabaster
I'm inured against weather.
The vixen's glare, the tear on the flesh
covered continent where the snake
withers happily and the nude deer
antler glitters, neither shares
my rifled ocean growth
            polar and spare.

Eyes open
        spinning pockets
for the glass harpoons
        lying under my lids
        icy as summers

Nose ridges
        where the glaciers melt
into my autumnal winter-fed cheek
hiding its shudder in this kelp

            glued
            cracked as the air.

Sunday Evening

    I am telling you a number of half-conditioned ideas
    Am repeating myself,
    The room has four sides; it is a rectangle,
    From the window the bridge, the water, the leaves,
    Her hat is made of feathers,
    My fortune is produced from glass
    And I drink to my extinction.

    Barges on the river carry apples wrapped in bales,
    This morning there was a sombre sunrise,
    In the red, in the air, in what is falling through us
    We quote several things.

I am talking to you
With what is left of me written off,
On the cuff, ancestral and vague,
As a monkey walks through the many fires
Of the jungle while a village breathes in its sleep.

Someone stops in the alcove,
It is a risk we will later make,
While I talk and you bring your eyes to the fibre
(as the blade to the brown root)
And the room is slumberous and slow
(as a pulse after the first September earthquake).

Parachutes, My Love, Could Carry Us Higher

I just said I didn't know
And now you are holding me
In your arms,
How kind.
Parachutes, my love, could carry us higher.
Yet around the net I am floating
Pink and pale blue fish are caught in it,
They are beautiful,
But they are not good for eating.
Parachutes, my love, could carry us higher
Than this mid-air in which we tremble,
Having exercised our arms in swimming,
Now the suspension, you say,
Is exquisite. I do not know.
There is coral below the surface,
There is sand, and berries
Like pomegranates grow.
This wide net, I am treading water
Near it, bubbles are rising and salt
Drying on my lashes, yet I am no nearer
Air than water. I am closer to you
Than land and I am in a stranger ocean
Than I wished.

The Crisis

Not to be able to carry mice to your room
when you have walked the boulevards
with rain at your tail and umbrellas
opened an edifice of dragoons
preparing to ascend when the park was hungrier,
its bursting branches were loaves
under the yellow sky. Alas the great days
of desire have passed.

Prepare for bulbs and minor grasses; seize on
imported mauves, ivory cutlasses prepared
in Switzerland for sailors whose white eyelashes
will curtain the whim of captains and make
graceful the long Cape trip. You will sail
upon mats of periwinkles, if you prefer.

Why tramp now the marshes where the expert mice
rest on borders and sit
with their pierced hearts? They have grown fat
under the discipline of raiders who need in the night
corridor a lawful pillow, in the black watches

a slim straw purchased for a mouse, a hat
to cover the dark marches and the small
confidences laid on cushions before daybreak
when fountains plash and mirrors reflect
the thick mud where armies have passed.

Upside Down

> Old slugger-the-bat
>   don't try to control me
> I've a cold in my head
> and a pain in one side
>
>   it's the cautious climate
>   of birds.

Where the bitter night shows
fat as an owl the skeleton
            not counting the skin.

            This species can't bite,
but it has a hurt. We've all got birds
            flying at us

little ones over the toes.

The hand that holds is webbed
no knuckles
            but the bone grows.

Seeing You Off

            Bracketed in my own barn
                        where ignorant as those armies
I flash my light upon the Hudson
                        and shout continental factories
take fire! Send navies out from Jersey
            let there be more edens
            of soap and fats

            Such splendors make rigid a democracy
                        define its skeleton
permit the night to cleanse its air
            with moving vans
                        olympic as dawn

            Upon the big liner
                        moored at last
by little landscape poems
            frail as lifeboats
settling down to rest

            While we kiss in the saloon
                        far above the cries
from plows and auto parts
                        sending up goodbyes

as ugly as those waifs of paper
        on the pier
or that truck profiled into gloom
        his whole insides protest

Departures make disgust into a cartoon
        of rose Nabiscos and I digest
the sinking afternoon in a fleet
        of taxicabs dead sure as you

        and Carthage after?
        we'll float on that wine-dark sea

Safe Flights

To no longer like the taste of whisky
This is saying also no to you who are
A goldfinch in the breeze,
To no longer wish winter to have explanations
To lace your shoes in the snow
With no need to remember,
To no longer pull the two blankets
Over your shoulders, to no longer feel the cold,
To no longer pretend in the flower
There is a secret, or in the earth a tomb,
And no longer water on stone hurting the ear,
Making those five noises of thunder
And you tremble no longer.
To no longer travel over mountains,
Over small farms
No longer the weather changing and the atmosphere
Causing delicate breaks where the nerves confuse,
To no longer have your name shouted
And your birthmark again described,
To no longer fear where the rapids break
A miniature rock under your canoe,
To no longer repeat the mirror is water,
The house is a burden to the weak cyclone,
You are under a tent where promises perform
And the ring you grasp as an aerialist
Glides, no longer.

Sadness

We were walking down a narrow street.
It was late autumn. In my hotel room
the steam heat had been turned on. In the office
buildings, in the boutiques, coal was lit.

That morning I had been standing at the window
looking out on the Tuileries. I had been crying
because the yellow tulips were gone and all the children
were wearing thin coats. I felt an embarrassing pain
distributed over my arms which were powerless
to order the leaves to blossom or the old women
on the stairs to buy shoes to cover their feet.

Then you took my hand. You told me that love
was a sudden disturbance of the nerve ends
that startled the fibres and made them new
again. You quoted a song about a man running
by the sea who drew into his lungs the air
that had several times been around the world.

A speck of coal dust floated down and settled on my lapel.
Quickly with your free hand you rubbed out the spot.
Yet do you know I shall carry always
that blemish on my breast?

Jaffa Juce*

This orange bric-a-brac has a paper luster very decadent.
Crossing Hyde Park I am brimming
with sad thoughts of the Royal Bank of Scotland
when the shepherd calls to his sheep
and daylight crisps my hands in streaks.

The primroses are lying in thin groups of threes
transparent as the fool's stammer
when the old king came wailing to his pool

---

*Jaffa Juce is an orange drink high in vitamins, low in price, bottled and drunk in
Britain.

and vagabonds clustered
to the guard's hall
hoping to see

a burning palace. Then the family
sat down to tea.

There's a lady in a macintosh
trying to climb a wall. Her tears
her broken tears,
more fabulous for their tumult caused

(by moonlight assembling pears,
a Jericho harp for the guests)

she has heard the museum mating chairs,
seen the varnished fragments of the bomb
meeting in a closer circle.

Reginald after the battle!
What a cry for a miner, alas he's lost
his keys and can't locate the platter.

The silver cooking geese have left the plain,
no one shoves the tin

My darling
Weymouth sands are green

There's drought in the wind
there's ash in our eye
the poor dead hands are clean

Sing derry down
the hospital shakes its leaves

For the players
and their laughing daughters, the morning is bright
upon the square, the air shows its face
like a powdered Indian, the fog
is braced with sun; over the setting
heyday toasts there's a ring of moon
for tomorrow.

A crown lies
under the cake. They're borrowing streamers
for the race and white candles with tartan crests
burn in the cellars below the streets. The Crescent
has an Egyptian hue. Everyone is civil.
Buns in the oven, cider in the hall,
            pleasant sings our land

Who frets above the stair with sour eye in glove?
Is it the Marvellous Boy? Someone crept from a grove?
Who carries the axe with sharpened blade,
not that wraith of laureates under the hill?
The prisoner or the emigrant horde?

Ho for the emigrant's song!

"In this autumn's double grace from war
I watch the housefronting plummets of cream

            wear echoes of sinks
            and banners of choice portals

when I ride my sorrel to Marble Arch
praying for the liquidating
skin to melt

            into a victory column
            built like a ship

bonded for New Plymouth where my fortune
            (folios of bent seed)
will take root on the first wave
            will take root."

In Dock

We are living at an embarkation port
            where the gulls
            and the soft-shoed buoys
            make Atlantic soundings

This air of ours is photographing fish

and the rice and the white antelope pelts
are asleep in the dark orchid hold
where old women have sent their black lids to be parched
and young bronze boys are tying knots in their limbs
while the spume and the salt
        send thick-painted pictures to the hatchway

O Thracian! O Phoenician!

        Vergilian harbors are wearing laurels
yet our hideaways are empty
as your camphor bottles, the scent
the wild scent has fled the hills
to couple under thyme beds
and the nectar of honey, it too has faded.

        Fleeting rivers, your robberies
have paved our zones, you're alive in our hearts
as yesterday or tomorrow
or the ghost ship from Athens
plying its shuttered bark
crying Zeus! Zeus!

        as it shatters this pier.

People in Wartime

        Attilio, the minor Hun,
        Rose with the sun.
        Washed his face
        In a little grape
        And cried, This is I.

        This is one who would
        Conquer
        The fever
        And the world outside.

        With this he took a stride
        Across his hall bedroom,
        Faced the broken glass
        And into the mirror sighed,
        Such was I.

Now am I to become
This singular juxtaposition
Between the man
And his decision
Am I history, or am I a plot?

Or such was his reflection
For
He was not interested
In
Art
Or politics
Or women
Or even getting ahead,

I have said
He was a minor character
And his misery
Was not Alpine,
But extremely particular,
Was he history, or was he not?

Landing

This afternoon I am very careful.
I watch myself. I watch the egg
Unhatched. I am the sight
Over the egg, like an aviator
Unknowing, but confident
That the instrument will behave.
The window outscaped
Brings the climate indoors.
The eye is free, adorned
By that which is becoming.
What is near, prevalent, adored
By the inner is echoed
By the ear. My conscience
Is receptive. I sight the cause
Of the exterior and so I hear
What is sounded in the interior.
Yet the break is this:
The germinal is split.

Not content with eye and sphere,
I race the continual
And drift to the absurd,
The conjugal, from which
The flight is only heard.

History

for Frank O'Hara

Old Thing

    We have escaped
    from that pale refrigerator

       you wrote about

Here

    amid the wild woodbine landscapes
    wearing a paper hat

I recollect

    the idols
    in those frozen tubs

       secluded by buttresses

when the Church of

      Our Lady cried Enough

and we were banished

    Sighing

      strangers
      we are

   the last even breath

     poets

Yet the funicular
was tied by a rope

    It could only cry
    looking down

      that midnight hill

My lights are
    bright
the walk is
    irregular

    your initials
    are carved on the sill.

Mon Ami!

    the funicular
    has a knife

      in its side
Ah allow these nightingales to nurse us

Oriental Movie

Lady your orange back
is waving at Foujita
we're all in a canoe
sipping the light drink of the tamarind bark
while the white-eyed paddles
whisper orange
    and blue
and the solemn wall says
    orange and blue
to your cunning slant-eyed rind
of a rainstorm shining
    in the gloom
like the lights
    of Hong Kong brewed
    on the hill
and tomorrow there'll be another
thin brush a thinner brush

The Crisis

After the white-collared boats
    the smithies will return
    then we shall hear
    the ding dong.

After the laundries, the lavatories of trains
        when velvet returns
        we shall see the snails
        making their own ding dong
        when it rains.

After the rich seas, the closed stations,
the plumed clocks, the long balconies,
        a quiet vista of snails.

In the time of great kings
I hid this knife with a friend
to cut off the trail (silver)
which led to my house.

        Ding dong
        without a shell.

Having to wait until it was over
I stayed on a sofa
when Madame returned
        she discovered
a frieze on the wall and she exclaimed
        in horror
        (it was over)

You have murdered our friend!

        Ding dong
        from now on.

West Sixty-fourth Street

for Miriam and Mitchell Ittelson

The room isn't as white as you'd suppose
        (accustomed to a cube of ice
        or a flake of eiderdown in Pekin
        after the palace was closed; the warriors
        in thin shirts tried to open the door
        they found a message written in clear ink
        forgetting to describe the tracks on the Yangtze floes)

There's a sign of Work and Joy
     facing the brave night whose shoulders
     are covered with primary colors
     under which we succumb with a smile

Permitting the glass blowers to thicken their bottles
     while candelabra melt into forests
     gathering their heartache
     into bouquets of grass

Yet wicker is impermanent as these burning lights
     when at daybreak it is said
     "the painter has dropped his brush in the canal"

So afterwards we'll go on to the Villa
I'll play you its record the next time we go for a walk
in Central Park the hour the statues say "yes."

The Time of Day

Or when I see a sailor in front of my house on the
                                     sidewalk
     He is hurrying, the church bells are ringing:
     « Okay! » says the man who takes the money.

Or when two nuns enter the library, one of them is
                                going to smile
     She is not thinking of what is ahead:
     « Okay! » says the man who takes the money.

Or the mannequin who opens a closet full of hats
     His arm holds his elbow and the hand caresses the
                               face while he selects:
     « Okay! » says the man who takes the money.

Or when someone addresses me who is not a regular
                            member of the Army
     And I answer, good afternoon Major:
     « Okay! » says the man who takes the money.

Or when I go into the room and close my door
     It is the hour for decisions and I am going to take
                               a little nap:
     « Okay! » says the driver.

Heroic Stages

for Grace Hartigan

I had thought you were disappearing
under the desperate monuments of sand
I discovered you were leaning on grass
which after green is noble.

In the sunlight each morning
        is delivered to your table
        among the oranges and white bottles
        the Quest.

If ever after Valhalla should proclaim
a string of knights (usually seen wandering)
this grey silent space would be orchestrated
for their maneuvers. And way over there
shining by itself in the blue twilight
a misunderstood Chalice.

Grand breaks!
        the forest is growing too high
        (the waves are longer, there is no sound)
        the river has turned from its bed
        rocks have no moss they have plumes
        the chiaroscuro results in serpents.

Danger!
        where only the poets
        held to the routes by the tender-eyed peasants
        and you painters
        who have drawn those deep lines on the globes
        are without anger and starvation.

My penitent self sing when you perceive
        it is a kindergarten
of giants where grapes are growing.
        The wind is southerly.
You face a park. There are wings in this atmosphere,
sovereigns who pour forth breezes to refresh
your atlas.

Rulers
have exacted fares, the former slope was icy.
Now in the Spring air with leaves posed above benches
the waterfall as hesitant as ever,
Biography removes her gauntlet
            to cast care from your brow.

In America, the Seasons

            You in the new winter
                stretch forth your hands

            they are needles,
            the sun quivers,

                    the landsman translates
                    epine

            False starter,
            regretter of seasons,

            you are tomahawking
            summer
                    and
                    I incline toward you
            like dead Europe
            wrapped in loose arms.

            Yet on this plain
            who would hesitate?

            seeing the funeral of grass
            the thin afternoon
            plundering the rocks,
            the broken leaves

            and silence incontinently snapped.
            Who hears Piers calling now?

                    It is the face
                    under the blanket
                    we watch.

Belgravia

I am in love with a man
Who is more fond of his own house
Than many interiors which are, of course, less unique,
But more constructed to the usual sensibility,
Yet unlike those rooms in which he lives
Cannot be filled with crystal objects.

There are embroidered chairs
Made in Berlin to look like cane, very round
And light which do not break, but bend
Ever so slightly, and rock at twilight as the cradle
Rocks itself if given a slight push and a small
Tune can be heard when several of the branches creak.

Many rooms are in his house
And they can all be used for exercise.
There are mileposts cut into the marble,
A block, ten blocks, a mile
For the one who walks here always thinking,
Who finds a meaning at the end of a mile
And wishes to entomb his discoveries.

I am in love with a man
Who knows himself better than my youth,
My experience or my ability
Trained now to reflect his face
As rims reflect their glasses,
Or as mirrors, filigreed as several European
Capitals have regarded their past
Of which he is the living representative,
Who alone is nervous with history.

I am in love with a man
In this open house of windows,
Locks and balconies,
This man who reflects and considers
The brokenhearted bears who tumble in the leaves.

In the garden which thus has escaped all intruders
There when benches are placed
Side by side, watching separate entrances,
As one might plan an audience

That cannot refrain from turning ever so little
In other directions and witnessing
The completion of itself as seen from all sides,

I am in love with him
Who only among the invited hastens my speech.

In the Alps

Where goes this wandering blue,
This horizon that covers us without a murmur?
Let old lands speak their speech,
Let tarnished canopies protect us.

Where after the wars, the peaceable lions,
The forests resting from their struggle,
The streams with loads upon their icy backs,
Is this a reason for happiness,
That one speaks after such a long time,
That the hand one holds leads one far away?

Is this a fairy tale then?
This new-discovered place where one can dream
Of tigers with fair hair and houses whose hearths
Are tended by knights lingering there?

Riding down to Venice on borrowed horses
The air is freed of our crimes,
Lovers meet in the inns of our fathers
And everywhere after dusk the day follows.

The Past of a Poem

Do you remember as I do,
the beautiful dressing that covered
the old poem?

There it lay not quite dead,
nor even suffering, but so quiet
the linen didn't stir

and all that heartache, the way
water runs in sewers
and you walk over them
sometimes twisting your heel

knowing how dirty the river
under the slender neat street

You might even refuse
to put a bird in it
if the feathers
weren't too moist and stained,
a difficult color

The cold water flat that June
night you put your hands on the radiator

crushed by your fingers
yet still fresh that poem
from its bewildering year

Come close to it now
and listen, don't you hear
"septic sighs of sadness"?

ARCHAICS

Atalanta in Arcadia

Atalanta who paces the roadway
January wind in her tresses
throws leaves against the wall,
only her lover waits in the shade
adoring his thin magnetic ankles.

On Arcadian nights the eager moon
has two fellows who hold the balloon,
that's all they have to do,
until day cast in bronze
makes Atalanta angry and they fall
beside a stream of air
arms flailing at her strenuous leap,

so fair when she promenades
Venus proclaims her a glorious follower,
if the path her lover takes is steep, perhaps
he shall slip and she will bury her tears
in his garments,

then other nymphs will laugh with her
for briefly the promises of mortals
are cheerless.

Careless Atalanta,
that boy once continual shadow prepares
for the age of athletes, the ritualistic
grass uncovers his apple and bees
are stumbling in your sacred pasture.

> Who is there to warn Atalanta
that her huntress days are over?
> Who will tell her

of the famous youth pursuing her?
                    And the speed with which her girlhood
will be consumed?
                    The sweetness of the capture?
                    If one kind god hiding in the thicket
would change that last strophe!

"From Eyes Blue and Cold"

From eyes blue and cold
the nymphs drink
                    your snow

Olympus

                    There on watchful
heights dawn prepares her lesson
as the groves thicken with
one's first song

                    See now its wing arch
over the valley and the brisk toot
of the satyr no longer limping

From eyes blue and cold
out of the abandoning water
                    another goddess

Again Olympus
from your delicate forgeries
                    a naïve daybreak

Hoof, reed, horn
will bring to the sandy river
a far-off coastal lithesomeness
                    when she awakes
with seaweed in her arms
from eyes blue and cold
                    shares that beauty

Dido to Aeneas

I love you
I have permitted myself to say choirs
(as if the late birds sang in branches) when for them
in the dusk at wind set
the garage eave yields its water cup.

Not for us the paling light
the white urn at the driveway,
nor for us the palmettos and the squeak
of tiles. The fountain at noonday cries,
"You are not here" and the sea at its distance
calls to a single path flanked by hibiscus,
the sea reminds itself each day
that it is solitary and the bather gambles
in its waves as a suicide who says "tomorrow is
another" an hour in the wrecker foam.

I love you
I am writing your name as if I were a Trojan
who expected someone else to smooth the shore
of souls who said
to the great reaches of wave and salt,
"I am replenishing as a light falling on a single tree"
and it is wonderful like ice on a floe,

I love you
miracle, mirror, word, all the same
you come, you go
I love you
(on my rioting lawns the plaster flamingos
endure your wonder)

Green Awnings

Leander walked over with a basket of peonies.
He was eating grapes he had picked by the old
cottage where he stayed and where there was a door
hung with vines. He was living on grapes, training
his muscles for that solitary climb. Somedays the tower
seemed higher and he felt a little blue twinge
in his arm.

She was sewing a white heron into her gown.
Messages came each day from her father, but
she ignored them, preferring to think of the pale
autumn legs of her bird.

She put water in a vase and wished for flowers.

It was half-past three, but the Latin sun
stayed in the room. How she longed to bathe
in the river. How piteous to be a prisoner
when one was as young as she knew herself to be
in her mirror. She was as earnest as her parents
and nightly prepared her body. She was hopeful
and prayed to the stars who liked her.

She went to the window.

Games need companions, he decided, and sat on the grass.
He had pretended that tree was the armor of his friend, Catylus,
and used up his arrows. The river urged him
to practice his stroke. Later floating on his back,
looking up at the tower, he saw an arm pulling
at an awning strap. What was his surprise when
the green canvas loosed, a girl's hair fell after it.

Palm Trees

What an arch your
        heavy burlap branches
        decide they'll go into!
(the first plunge did not destroy
that green youth hid itself)
And now freshly you start to go upward
You want to reach a curve that will draw
    the sky to yourself and say blue
        here is your arabesque!
    The woman walks near you
    Under the sea a fern resembles you
    The heat stops and waits
        and you give nothing.
Calm fan no one touches

In the Campagna

"It was kind of you to ask"
you there at the entrance.

The cave looked even darker,
darker than the covering leaves

A suspicious person would say
they guarded.

You wanted to know if we wished
to throw off our shields and rest

Lay our heads in the shade
and take from the dripping roof water

A cupful to drink.

Your heart was visible
your hand open

Why did we stare
and group our pikes?

Why are we cautious whom the forests
had refused comfort?

Stones on the hillside
bruised our feet

And the well had been empty.

Why are we shy of your pillow
your twin black eyes?

The thunder came nearer
it made a road in our ears

Rain fell yet we lingered
at the cave's door

Waiting for familiar torrents
expecting an ordinary storm blast

As a nephew might stop
at our house his shoulders loaded

With town purchases
vegetables and dress stuffs

This nephew who was often troublesome
who was stealthy at equinox

Yet of our sister's blood
all the same.

You, are you Cerberus, four-footed
who halts us this night

While lightning
pitches straw about

And trees glitter strangely?

We, four men lost
on a starless mountain

In the middle of the year,

Your question: "Will you enter?"
What does it mean?

"Who will accept our offering at this end of autumn?"

to Seferis

That shock of hair in the white morning

We were up early while the grain was heaviest
and the earth was taking leaves to its stairwell

We, our arms in the heat, felt a chill
while the sun turned over, went around our shoulder

It was a cold glare; honey in the jars
clasped and unclasped the shell.

You of the thick twist, like an earring
your hair, pendulous and coarsely welded,

As if walking toward the gate one had stopped
and picked up this object, shouted "archaic"

To the tombsman who had accompanied the discoveries,
neither literate nor blind, whose weight

Bore down on the sand like a helmet
pressing his curls.

This fruit of the land remembers
the warmth of the braziers on its marbles

The dew on its columns
and in its branches the wind

Tossing into the cistern
the strength-bearing seeds,

Vengeful the storms and afterwards
the pines meagre as they are,

Slowly goes the animal
up the mountain edge,

For us carrying the bronze,
who will not be there at harvest.

THE OPEN SKIES

The Voice Tree

Of Anger and Sorrow

Growth

the parallel vines

from you to me
a white shadow, a break

on the window, a cast

To my tears that fall straight
as the birch, thick and round

as bulbs at your base.

Seasons, horizons,
natal days and those

that are dark

I celebrate wisely
or with terror or watch
the leaves as they fall
minutely and crack
the wide underground.

Raven and bird from far-off

. . . at your neck
feathers of sea tern

tree of iodine and blue . . .

When you are spine
and leafless branch

how you will rage

you will force me
in the garden packed with snow

to surround you with fire
to pad your roots with ash

the red flames to your green throat

the wild spark to your open mouth

Then your voice in the smoke
leaping and shouting

the icicles melting, melting.

Lights of My Eyes

Lights of my eyes
            my only
they're turning it off
                while we're asleep on this shore
and the thick daffodils
            are crying
lights of my eyes
don't be afraid of me
what we saw
rivers and roads
            ruins
the cast of the sculpture in winter
They will return your voice
and I'll go on singing *"adieu"*

Snow Angel

The storm's threat and ache
Angels are in peril there on the rooftops
Angels are grey ·
Sticks the prancing
sticks to give them shelter it rained and webs
broke wings shrank the branch-bearing river
shook
bewildered as a sun
Magister who brings
thunder the firs are ready for their burden
underground fires are lit
in the dark sits
the first Angel of snow
tomorrow in the outraged
sky
his form

Santa Fe Trail

I go separately
The sweet knees of oxen have pressed a path for me
ghosts with ingots have burned their bare hands
it is the dungaree darkness with China stitched
where the westerly winds
and the traveler's checks
the evensong of salesmen
the glistening paraphernalia of twin suitcases
where no one speaks English.
I go separately
It is the wind, the rubber wind
when we brush our teeth in the way station
a climate to beard. What forks these roads?

Who clammers o'er the twain?
What murmurs and rustles in the distance
in the white branches where the light is whipped
piercing at the crossing as into the dunes we simmer
and toss ourselves awhile the motor pants like a forest
where owls from their bandaged eyes send messages
to the Indian couple. Peaks have you heard?
I go separately
We have reached the arithmetics, are partially quenched
while it growls and hints in the lost trapper's voice
She is coming toward us like a session of pines
in the wild wooden air where rabbits are frozen,
O mother of lakes and glaciers, save us gamblers
whose wagon is perilously rapt.

Nocturne

Toi, Seine, tu n'as rien. Deux quais, et voilà tout . . .
                                        VERLAINE

Do you know what silence means?
Deux quais, et voilà tout.

My dear, my dear,
The skaters tremble.

In the grey there is no void.
The grey resembles ice as the stairs
This city. The voice begins
Like the ice to tremble.

Oh! foreign vase
On the mantel your force
Is tremendous as if the ice were soft
And you immovable.

Or the white statue,
Statue of lace
Moved even her hand or her face
Leaned backward into the past.

So my mysterious, unbroken calm,
This fortitude you have kept for an hour.

Do you know what silence means?
Deux quais et voilà tout.

The First of May

My eye cannot turn toward you
Night
because it has Day watching.

(A spoon heated over the fire,
a cup with milk in it
shadows at its brim.)

I would like to go for a walk
in the dark
without moonbeams

down that path of mushrooms
in my nightdress
without shoes,

I would like to sit under your wall
and you fortify me
as you did once on the road,
a stranger.

I would like to steal
and take it to you.

I would like to go to a hotel
with you.

Turn out the lights!

Your arms, I feel them,
your eyes, I cannot see them.

Day is watching me
from over the transom.

Day whose light is blinding me,
as lightning on the firebreak
of a mountain,

who brings me a quail
caught in the smoldering underbrush

where the smell is of yucca
and sage.

Day brings me this bird.

I must go and feed it
with milk from the cup,
a few drops on the spoon.

The sirens are screaming
in the streets.
It is an order to take cover.
And I, I
must bring this bird to shelter.

I must not be caught out
in the night
unless I am willing

to give you up Day forever,
when I join the guerrillas,

who would like my cup
and spoon,

who would roast my bird
and eat it.

Dardanella

Those forms in gauze
        we see as arches
the tile replaces with mountain
the script says: As water this life
poets go to the mountain
followed by girls in white

The king of the heavy mustache
"like buffaloes these men"
cannot find dawn in his sleep

So agents prepare the morning mosquito
it must be noisy yet not alarming

Those who hear it across the valley
in their ears closed with honey
will feel the sting of bells

in the palace only one vase need splinter

from his arms only the virgin need struggle

the boy knows now to kiss

he will ride horses to the blue dome.

        Twenty-four veils in a pile
        and hatchoutchoui houri
        for hours and hours and hours
        the patient needy camel lifts his neck
        over the sun brick petals catch
        that is all . . . no vines . . . no miles
        . . . no hills . . . no caves in the hills . . .

        women walk to the fountain

        Pasha is with the Consul
        the French woman writes letters a violet eye
        toward the boy who has peed on the tile
        she forgets the name for raisin says plum

        Milk say the heavens regarding the white sand

        Bosphorus click of eel in your wave off Egypt
        tow-ridden plain of Kilid Bahr
        trees and risk where ancient bouncing flat
        is war land of the tomb otherwise lids

        Air in the arch is black
        as sighs from vessels cast
        on the shut-off tide.

The Brown Studio

Walking into the room
        after having spent a night in the grove
        by the river
its duskiness surprised me.

The hours I had spent under foliage,
the forms I had seen were all sombre,

even the music was distinctly shady, the water
had left me melancholy, my hands I had rinsed
were muddy. I had seen only one bird with a bright
wing, the rest were starlings,

      the brownness alarmed me.

I saw the black stove, the black chair,
the black coat. I saw the easel, remembering it as
an ordinary wood tone, rather pale, I realized
it was inky, as were the drawings.

Of course you weren't there, but a photograph was.
Actually a negative. Your hair didn't show up at all.
Where that fairness had lit the open ground,

      now there was an emptiness, beginning to darken.

      I believed if I spoke,
if a word came from my throat
and entered this room whose walls had been turned,

it would be the color of the cape
we saw in Aix in the studio of Cézanne,
it hung near the death's head, the umbrella,
the palette cooled to grey,

if I spoke loudly enough,
knowing the arc from real to phantom,
the fall of my voice would be,
a dying brown.

All Elegies Are Black and White

To Robert Motherwell

      When Villon went to his college
      he wore a black gown
      he put his hood up when
      he went out on the black streets.

      He ate black bread
      and even drank a kind of black wine,
      (we don't have any longer)
      it wasn't that good Beaune
      his skill taught him how to steal,
      a disappearing drink also.

The sky was white over Paris,
until it fell in the streets,
like a sky over mountains,
disturbing and demanding.

When you are in Spain
you think of sky
and mountain where the forest
is without water.
You think of your art
which has become important
like a plow
on the flat land.

There are even a few animals
to consider.
And olives.

Do you regard them separately?
The forms of nature,
animals, trees

That bear a black burden
whose throat is always thirsty?

I know of Seville of black carriages
one factory
one river
the air is brown.

Alas we have fair hair, are *rojo*.

Throw a mantilla over your face
rojo of the light,
walk only in the white spaces.

The trains that cross back and forth
the borders of Elegy
sleep all afternoon, at night
lament the lost shapes.

I think when you oppose
black against white,
archaeologist you have raised a dream
which is bitter.

The white elegy
is the most secret elegy.

One may arrive at it
from the blue.

The sky in Spain is high.
It is as high as the sky
in California.

When one begins with white and blue
it is necessary for one's eyes to darken.
One may have fair hair in Spain,
yet the trouble of blue eyes!
Unless one can always live
sparsely as in Castille.

(How wise you are to understand
the use of orange with blue.
"Never without the other.")

And what courage to allow oneself
to become black and blue!

It is necessary that eyes be black
so the white may deepen
in them the white may sink,
it can then be constant, as music
is constant, or a marriage, or fountains,
or a palace whose shadow is constant.

To make an Elegy of Spain
is to make a song of the abyss.

It is to cut a gorge into one's soul
which is suddenly no longer private.
This privacy which has become invaded
straightens itself up, it sings,
"I am proud as a cañon."

Can you imagine the shock over the world

against which two enormous black rocks roll

this world that looks like a white cloud

shifting its buttocks?

                    When the guitar strikes

A procession of those tasters of ecstasy
the thieves of dark and light

beginning with Villon

whose black songs are elegies
whose elegies are white

Dios!

The Open Skies

I

Molluscs in their shell

the skies

Breathe up and down

unspiraling

Open skies

seeded with light and stone

II

Pattern of drift   Is eye of air
stray ephemeral visible   hand from sky   form?

III

Revolving day prisoner in the openness

Smiling lips daylight fair
unbreakable you seem

Hitched to me as I
window thrust to you

IV

Cloudless

you take

My happiness
rising in the morning

Light descends to me
buoyantly   I stare

A tremor on this hand
light has touched

I pass into your frailness

Noiseless hour
span of float and flight

Sky without lever or stress

V

Tough the cone to shelter

Ecstatic harking to upward dome

VI

Ash and ember
creature and skin

Soft body of unprotected gilt

VII

Sky whose fancy
sways and swings above

All quick airiness
and slow guide

Without you I cannot see.

Hurricane

The house. The pictures there on the wall
and the rug I slept on it as a child
near the dining table, drowned while they ate.

Now a threat, a dawn of horse hooves, a manger
where the straw is blown and hens in the yard,
their tail feathers high, and cat with open eyes.

I wonder before it strikes from the low clouds, I
not yet to bed near the steps where leaves lie,
how far the water will rise?

If the storm only a few miles from here,
if its white cheek and wet arm,
its eyelash curled
and its wrist angry and at last free

will touch this house, will caress
the old furniture and names erase them,

         if the roof, all the chambers
will be lifted from our faces, will we
go gladly into its barn, magnified by wet
and rain and drops that slope
increasingly to that eave where we wait

for darkness, or thunder, or night
         on the drenched tile
to lead us away?

His Jungle

Recognized only its hands
That monkey face is known later
      and the wind accompanying it.

Torrents replace the usual seasons
    conquest by variety
A handsome thunder, a thaw
Out of the earth comes another air
    smoky as animal.

      He lifts his hands to his face.

The stone he must roll it.
He must rub the flakes without
Being shaken.
He must break down the door
Behind it.

That tree how many leaves
Strain it. He wonders
If a four-legged beast
Will find the flower

And eat it. Rather it than him.

If that place going round
Beyond the trees if the door's most
Difficult inscription will be lost
In the whirl

                Will escape him,

Will be too mashed will remind
Him of mold will have gone
Too far and he dislike
Black as he fears green,

A chatter in the grass,
Wind replacing ivory
With a tusk makes him drop
His tools.

                It is the headsman,
Earth's fragile runner who is caught
In his trap who describing pain
Plaits a monkey face
Arc and area wide enough

                For both to fire.

Timor Mortis, Florida

White foam tide
            waves descending
line of blue and white
            blue submarine
where the dark sweel of thrust
            retched water

Gulf whose eye is bluest screen

Aii the width of it settling
and frozen fish warming

Aii the width of it settling

A near palm leans, frond chilled
arched breeze and frontal cold

North Ice

       sweep across a bright lateral

all plumes peaked, riders wary

risked sails   the ride

          hot and cold

a headland wilderness

           odd winter, a dismay

to treat as cemetery. Wind.

In gardens, in snow, in flurry and flake
the bird wren, bare tree, to follow.

Desire at the stake of palmetto
Desire the empty marina   tideless

Sands

         Oars in the fronds

through bullrushes

Sunset the backland washes   gates

While silt as light as dawn

over the threshing sea

Sand

        The distance
           see
        the miles produce
             reckoning,
      water
           extending

      Sand

        while
      the sky airs itself
          requests
      clouds remain
         in numbers

far off
also
      the hand,
eyes, limbs
sand tests
      coolness and heat
      body levels

      . . . Remain flat
planes fly over you
under a belly
      prone side
of earth end

      Neutral
to haughty black land and sea
      that swank of blue
clammering
      greed of ear
and rapacious its thunder,
or even the mild wave at
dawn's edge
      a honey
when youthfully it begins to boil
and foam wildly spilled
      . . . noonday

      Salt throat
the tongue clasps the swell,
releases sends monitoring ceaseless
thirst back to ocean depth
      tides return to dark

      The skeleton
shock of wave lift, a column
on the shore its profile ever foreign
its ruin permanent   recurs

The bowl has changed color
gulls flown inland,
Poets walk across you their footprints
cannot shock your softness, on you
shells, pearls, weeds
discards as on a mountain top
is found record of horizon

as Patmos is an isle,

As you are mouth and sable skin
range of the sandle-footed

Rejoice
in ancient nothingness

Wave

i

And   preparing a net

Wave

whose arm is green
         your
half-wayness I, too, would meet you there

                    in foam

Borders

the rip slices   turns   backwards
swimmers this treachery is cast by mirrors
once in profile only this multiplied

                    the arrow backstroke sent to bliss

we cry deepest and turn not daring to spy
full-face on ocean crest that carries on

              on

space now azure fullest where the depth

is danger

                    long roll

Again   the ride

              And equinoctal plunge

it dares   beach   the   horizon

              with you

                    wailings

(that drift shrieks at low tide)

          bubbling

the loose and soggy shelf

       Bell

ii

the eye tolls as burnished as Bell
on coral the wave breaks or here
cold zone of equal blue and grey

        Tritons' throng appears

              where zephyrs
cast skyward by the spume glance down
on islands of the deep mermaids
we'll never see   or hear   yet each

wave rolling brings in brightest
phosphorescence their hair

          a lyre

sweet voice of brine

    other secrets

in the tease and stress of wave song

         Sun

multipowered it brushes

thins and splays

        burns

wild-lidded over foam   in air   to touch

      Remembering the violence
we turn on house pillow and let
dolphins surmise us (dreams) the lap
of shore water enter our heads as ponds
forced from sea are inlets, we are
islets become soft   become grassy
turning   swaying   to each and yet

      the angry

         it calls

Noon
    the crab walks

Night
     small fish

Rock and dawn

         Fog

iii

I would walk from this porch to your farthest

        do I dare

Lights without you the house is ghosty
          the pier is broken
          its points are webbed

cricket and bird song about   alas

     until morning   the great sea and ledge

from which pines such low soundings   pines

that are green   and sea that is swelling

sea whose earth is sandy who in sleep

     changes as the pilot arm beckons

the arm we lie on shifts

         early the stir

to crease from night close   to begin

to gather   to fall   as Wave

        Bountiful and Bare

Geography

    cold

    Moon track across the snow field
    a saddle I ride its rope
    into the light

the flank is soft
a fine departure the snow
bears my weight

to the mosses

the ripest blossoms fall
turn black in water
so dependency on sun is error

rather blue milk fields skimmed
and grass shod of twilight plain

than urn water swamp

on however

the swamp leaves at horse's neck
a chatter of owl and bird fright

the rope loosens
the hand is moist with vine leech

a journey wince of cowhide
shriek and storm where weather

suddenly

warms

we reach the pole
of earth statues

heat

visibleness decreases
immaculate as a heron
without rust
I shine

the snow in the wound
becomes stucco
the magnificent sun
waves a flag above it

The Blue Stairs

The Blue Stairs

There is no fear
in taking the first step
or the second
or the third

        having a position
        between several Popes

In fact the top
can be reached
without disaster

        precocious

The code
consists in noticing
the particular shade
of the staircase

        occasionally giving way
        to the emotions

It has been chosen
discriminately

To graduate
the dimensions
ease them into sight

        republic of space

Radiant deepness
a thumb
passed over it

        disarming
        as one who executes robbers

Waving the gnats
and the small giants
aside

        balancing

How to surprise
a community
by excellence

somehow it occurred

           living a public life

The original design
was completed
no one complained

In a few years
it was forgotten

           floating

It was framed
like any other work of art
not too ignobly

           kicking the ladder away

Now I shall tell you
why it is beautiful

Design: extraordinary
color: cobalt blue

           secret platforms

Heels twist it
into shape

It has a fantastic area
made for a tread
that will ascend

Being humble
i.e. productive

Its purpose
is to take you upward

On an elevator
of human fingerprints
of the most delicate
fixity

Being practical
and knowing its denominator

To push
one foot ahead of the other

Being a composite
which sneers at marble

                              all orthodox movements

It has discovered
in the creak of a footstep
the humility of sound

Spatially selective
using this counterfeit
of height

To substantiate
a method of progress

Reading stairs
as interpolation
in the problem of gradualness

                              with a heavy and pure logic

The master builder
acknowledges this

As do the artists
in their dormer rooms

                              eternal banishment

Who are usually grateful
to anyone who prevents them
from taking a false step

And having reached the summit
would like to stay there
even if the stairs are withdrawn

Turkey Villas

At night I sometimes see
those wooden villas
as if they were shacks
caught in an avalanche
and I crossing the Alps

Or
to make a shorter story
and relate in truth
to my life
as if it were San Francisco
1937
and a waterfront strike
the houses on the hills
were wooden and grey
tilted

Those ordinary houses
in which a few people
preserved the art
of pipe playing . . . A.D.

It is a vast smooth dream
this uncrippled Bosphorus

I don't like to consider
what goes on at the bottom
or the galleons and risks
that plunged
as ever so often a canoe

It is a shade
a window shade also
one that can be drawn if the
curtain is working
like a vat of oil

Now to be a proper historian
of my dreams
I must relate
the sidereal action

Of a ship seen from
A Hotel Hilton balcony
Think of that
Balcon Hilton!

Enough of this dizziness
let us apply the oars

Not to freeze
in a mosaic
not to be fooled
by a Mosque

What an idea!

I am spinning with ideas
to the top of the Mosque
I am an ice cream cone
Muzzein

I am drenched
with Blue

Fevered with ideas
I heat them in my pocket
these beads of ideas
and when they have cooled
what I shall have to exist on

I shall be able to escape the seraglio
I shall go on collecting pottery
yet it shall be blue

as an edifice
blue as the diagram
of a prince watering his horse

I shall be medieval and slim
at once!

Blue canopy
unmodernized
and empty

Blue windows
to let in the grey

Blue metaphysics
of the ultra refined center

I shall be able to paint
blue
those wooden villas

What sylvan blues
have I dreamed

What half-oriented eyes
have I opened

forcing them to see
the blue heavens

Effacing the mud
wracking myself with blue
coughs

And rising to walk
in my blue veils
over the Bosphorus

to my villa
my wooden peg

where I can advocate
successful blue Crusades

Yet I am always sleepy
and troubled
when the moon
is at its Crescent

I am not sure
of the color of these shutters

My dreams
are stupidly turbulent
I am in a boat
and the tourist guide
says
Regard those grey houses

Mohamet
I wake
with a cold toe.

Walking Buddha

Should I forget your scales
in confirmation of your knighthood

        or voice what is petal-soft
        in the cracked eye-lift?

Not circular or fleeting
but *swinging*

        pushed forward by your idiom
        like a giantess opening a window sash

you refuse to remark
the offering below your building

        you refuse to go downstairs
        because your gait is forward
        we must go around you

Brilliant decision!

        a frangipane rewards you
        with color streak

in the wet season

        that coloring protects

better than ghee, better than opium

A metal eye that cannot open

stretched as far as elephant, yet firm
in its enclosure

Diadem head!

The masons have finished their research

not a cubic inch more

There is:

The arm whose elongation

the open hand

the chest measurements

Rough cement ruled

an original of *Art Brut*

unrailed staircase

a smash knee surface

to conceal the bronze asperity

essentials of being classical
in a violent world before the decline

under slip-shoe palm

Colonial Hours

The year of the hurricane
(we are speaking)
bay roadway
the drenching
leaves flattened to echo
dry velvet before
hush

All quarrelsome
of whether hibiscus
shut

Tender magnificence

Land in wake of Prospero

with splayed tendrils
        washed

        Now
Episcopal bells
        shudder
as when you placed water pails

Think what justice the liberty bells
        peal on moon base
in a peculiar climate
        and rusting

Rhapsody of helmet
        it also chants
a head burden to catch
        sun granaries
legacies the sea strokes up
        dried as weed cemetery
or blue ballooning stingarees
        thrown

Night temples of palms
        the rain blows *tropique*
as ceiling fans
        you go in your orphan feet
        crossing the tiles

You are two sinister people
        in your oleander suit
        your scorpion shoes
        your eyeglasses ground from sand

You whisper it is so silent
under the mosquito net
remembering the prisons from which you sprang
        the machinery of coral walls
        your bamboo crest
the stockade that encircles you

as day the fresh water river
flowing from brow to throat
it cuts this salt thong
          you are released
          to the jointure of others

an amulet that is a beetle
to be fed by palmetto and cane

          cherished by the thrice blue seas

you shall reconnoiter

          As a shell your dynasty

          you are a porch with screens

You are a lucky person who hears
          the wild the luxurious birds
their scream is like yours
          when you fear the cold

they sing in the heat draughts
          they sip from the fountain

joy in their male coloring is yours
          and the neck reach

          the colonial language
          of tern sibilancy

Today you sit on the cropped grass
today looking at the map
          you blink

          Magnified world
          my education
          my craft

My fruit my oranges

Saving Tallow

Visible tallow of the hurricane night
thin fair candle
a yacht cradling
the room's deep water
                              where the wave
raises
                              its sail
a procession
                              of shoulders
the falling olives
                              on yellow knees
and cities
                              drowned
in their comet clothing
                              dragged from the sea

                              Candle!
lone palm tree   lonely diver
covered with sea lice
                              most vertical
the room dedicates its curves to you.

                              There was once a shadow
called Luis; there was once an eyebrow
whose name was Domingo. Once there
were children, grown-ups, organs;
there were moving legs and there was
speech. In the daylight there were
small whimpers made by the African cat;
in the candlelight there were couplings
of such sonority evening callers
merely left their cards; no one drew back
the curtains; there were no curtains
the candlelight fell on grass and
like a candle up stood the water hose.

                              There were many mathematical
forms
                              the obliquity of a painting
                              her mouth drawn by a corner

transverses on the arrow light
                                    where the smile flies off
at the room's center a hair part
                              the nose of a window
                              louvered as coral rock
                              where a person walked

                         was sleepy
                         must be awakened
for adorations and questions

                              is marine
related to the diving fish

                         Take me on your dolphin skin!

                         I shall be absent soon!

Saving the tallow with capable hands
seizing with the loyal closed eyes of foliage

                         Puff

The Return of the Muses

So much goes away

Forms are now shades,
those solid weights, how empty they are,
mere boxes,
the whispering voice,
the ankle bone only an arch.

Peasants once sowed this valley
there isn't any wheat here or oats
there almost isn't a valley,
only a dent.

This morning was all concaveness,
the clouds drew back into themselves,
the clouds went so far away leaving it blue,
now we're quite convex
and the rain is emptying itself out on me

The rain that took weeks to return,
the rain that left us on Wednesday
after tears, after dark, after that sluicing
about in memory, fishing up

The rain is here now.

"It makes for change and a certain disagreeableness
this coming and going makes one nervous"

The farewells to buildings
and then to the hole in the ground

This hello on one's lips
to a new perspective
finished by the end of the week,
completed a fresh horizon line

The earth is old, no longer fragrant
those planets are promising,

Goodbye, hello.

Yet you who had vanished
you trailing your garments
who went away in that last March stanza
not liking the violins
or standing around waiting
your arms circling each other's waists
or the salt in your mouth
where the sea was whipping itself up in the corner
and foam falling like ash

You departed divine Muses
without warning

And I went on a diet
I stopped eating regularly,
I changed my ways several times

"strict discipline, continuous devotion,
receptiveness"

were mine.

Here you are back again. Welcome.

Farewell, "strict, continuous, receptive"—

There's that old shawl in the corner
looking like a wave

There's a ringing in my ears
as if a poem were beating on stone

The room fills now with feathers,
the birds you have released, Muses,

I want to stop whatever I am doing
and listen to their marvelous hello.

A Reason

That is why I am here
not among the ibises. Why
the permanent city parasol
covers even me.

      It was the rains
in the occult season. It was the snows
on the lower slopes. It was water
and cold in my mouth.

      A lack of shoes
on what appeared to be cobbles
which were still antique

      Well wild wild whatever
in wild more silent blue

      the vase grips the stems
petals fall   the chrysanthemum darkens

      Sometimes this mustard feeling
clutches me also. My sleep is reckoned
in straws

      Yet I wake up
and am followed into the street.

Direction

Let us give up our trips
to pace to and fro here as easily
the foreignness of these leaves
the untranslatable silences, the echoes
of a tower, difficult winds,
as well here sail our barges.

Friend of the static hour
I take your hand across the borders.

Haven't we with our skills
lost important elements
of our luggage performing in lonely
hotels? The seacoasts are cruel
in winter the sand is a waste
cry to my tongue the sand it is like
my heart which I have buried in it
now there is a posture lying there
you can recognize it. I have only
two hearts, I need this orphaned
one here at home which is
the Scandinavia of all Russias.

The light is not idle, it is full of rapid
changes we can call voyages
if we like, moving from room to room.
How representative of us this thoughtful
weather that has travelled the water
to reach us, the touch of a certain side
of the skin when we open the window.

Our eyes are viewing monuments
constantly, the angry sculpture
of the facade it is also a journey
to the center where the rock is uncut.
Climbing it tests our strength, our bruises
are so many cities, the blood we shed
is ours, so I say we can belong
nowhere else, here is the counter
of our wounds and our delicacies.

On our own soil that is an excavation
desolate as the place whose name
we must never pronounce.

Barrels

Y otras pasan; y viéndome tan triste,
toman un poquito de ti
en la abrupta arruga de mi hondo dolor.
CESAR VALLEJO

I won't let anybody
take a drink
out of this barrel of tears
I've collected from you.

Least of all another woman.

I see her coming along.
I know the type.
I can tell you what she'll
be wearing.

I know the type
I won't like it.

She'll look at that barrel
she's had a few in her day.

Not that she's ever filled one.

She'll remark casually,
"Sweet water,
good to wash my hair."

And who doesn't know
tears are purer
than rain water
and softer on the hair.

Just as she steps toward it
and makes for the cup,
I'll see phantom you
and what you were
brought up by the sea.

And scraps of paper
from this ditch of my brain
will float on the water
and choke her.

East of Omsk

I am living in the Siberia
of your rose
there is a family of us
and we laugh
when the petals fall
in our house
there is a festival every night
called frozen

Which is actually a tree
you cannot recognize
through its icicle burrs
at the last station
to Vladivostok
before taking the boat
to Yokohama

       Where it rains
and our memory snow
       melts
       Only the beast fur
shines in this light of twelve tones
       Radiant as a warm
skeleton whose profile
       in Yokohama
will be drawn to endorse
the acacia weather
       of your rainbow homecoming

Better known in the south
where Yalta reproduces those skiffs
on a soft threshing
coast of pineapple waves

        Russia! a natural tribute
to have sent this wordgram
        so far
translating "flowers"
        from under a pelt cap

Parade's End

The most that can be said
for following the parade
is that the Head was red.

Liking grotesque the architect
went along with it,
the balloons and the bellies
enlarged.

He had a craze for size,
so he said.

Looking at it from the sidelines
we weren't so amused
as chilled by the snow wind,
our feet getting smaller
in unadaptable leather

our eyes formed truly gigantic tears

we dropped when the last
soldier had passed and the confetti
was buried in the ash can.

It was quite a day. I brought home
an unopened poem. It should grow
in the kitchen near the stove
if I can squeeze out of my eyes
enough water. Water.

Clouds Near the Windmill

Counting you as one of us
                        among the rushes
the difficult pebbles, these stones . . .
Quiet the water, it can do more,
we prefer it still and birds not chattering.
We like your voices because they have more portent.

We like the armor of your skin
the wisdom of your life line
hesitating from window to windowpane
and the exhaustion of your bare feet
climbing the sand.
                        Even as you turn
in the wind woodenly I catch a different sound,
enough to separate you from them
bringing, as you do, the bandages
from tree to wounded tree.

These are known as digestive moments
and the pear wearing its wrinkles
tunes down. Abiding calm
as light less curious now
and even less significant. That chair
it is moving closer to the pond.

Later we will watch the shadowless
birdwing and those straight lines
harsh without a tremor,
resembling pagoda field,
resembling stalks with your imagination.

The land is rutted with carriages,
they have their hoods pulled down.

Fan Poems

I

Who walks softly causes mutiny among the lilies
as a chateau is perverse refusing wings,
refusing a colder climate for its rooms;
and the blossoms fall repeatedly, exciting

those unique flower beds when at morning's edge
they hasten to lift themselves to a cautious heel print.

II

Windows, Melissa, they contain what is best
of us, the glass your arm has arranged
into crystal by spinning eye, by alarms
taken when the rain has chosen a form
unlike the universe, similar to ups and downs
which vary or change as cowslips
in the meadow we cross have a natural tint,
the panes reflect our hesitations and delight.

III

Repeatedly striking, i.e., to strike the imagination
another blow, neither heat nor cold,
but the power in the wing, the chill
smothering feather outlined narrowly
by vertebrae extended for an instant;
it makes one shudder, the quick umbrella
unfurled near the tearful statue.

IV

Traditional service to and from
like elastic. It covers ten moments
and maybe twenty. The wound is safely
succored, the branch spared from storm.
I have covered a hundred miles on vibrating
tires, they hum a safe tree.
The highway oaks are undisturbed
their age protects adventure, giving
visual shelter encouraging voices
to clear themselves from stanza to mute stanza.

V

Classically perchance am I your robin
or rossignol, not hirondelle, that dark
word ending in dress? At the top of stairs
stands the Marquis wearing a burnt
ribbon, wearing an "air," so they say,
I wonder at its quaintness, I wonder also
at my hoops, my stays are "pinching,"
let us take the night air in an ice.

VI

Why not make a perspective of ancient allée
so that it can promenade? You'd probably
end with muslin, catching the lion's curve
as he backs into pond, seconds before the wet tail lashes;
As this hour presents us with what it knows best,
as this hour wishes to retire rather than wander.

VII

What I recall of your romance
is: "sleep is milk."
Saluting the gypsies and always thirsty.

A Way of Being

There we go in cars, did you guess we wore sandals?
Carrying the till, memorizing its numbers,
apt at the essential such as rearranging
languages. They occur from route to route
like savages who wear shells.

"I cannot place him." Yet I do.
He must ascend indefinitely as airs
he must regard his image as plastic,
adhering to the easeful carpet that needs
footprints and cares for them.
as is their wont in houses, the ones we pass by.

Such a day/or such a night
reeling from cabin to cabin
looking at the cakewalk or merely dancing.
These adventures in broad/or slim
lamplight,

                    Yet the cars
do not cheat, even their colors perform in storm.
We never feel the scratch, they do.
When lightning strikes it's safer to ride
on rubber going down a mountain,
safer than trees, or sand, more preventive
to be hid in a cloud we sing, remembering

The old manse and robins. One tear,
a salty one knowing we have escaped
the charm of being native. Even as your glance
through the windshield tells me you've seen
another mishap of nature

                        you would willingly forget,
prefer to be like him near the hearth
where woodsmoke makes a screen of numbers and signs
where the bedstead it's not so foreign as this lake.

                    The plateau, excursionist,
is ahead. After that twenty volumes
of farmland. Then I must guide us
to the wood garage someone has whitened
where the light enters through one window
like a novel. You must peer at it
without weakening, without feeling
hero, or heroine,

                    Understanding the distances
between characters, their wakeful
or sleep searchingness, as far from the twilight ring
the slow sunset, the quick dark.

Four Moroccan Studies

(after Delacroix)

1

Who knows why they enter the gate of Mekenès
with their sand banners. It is enough
that they speculate before the big rush,
that they are riding good horses, not the maddened
ones of Revolution. Perhaps it is the return
of a desert patrol delighting in theatrics
and in their audience seated on the baked walls.
There may have been an issue; there may have been
a document read that morning, yet it was
a sublime sort of exercise, the dune play,
the descent on admiring townsmen.

2

Beliah. Moorish girl
comment you delight the painter.
Not so much you as your blouse,
your striped robe, those billowing pants
tied at the knee, the girdle at your bosom
and those turquoises. I have made
a note for each color. Keep your head in profile
Beliah and your feet wide apart
so I can draw your heavy sexy legs.

3

Since the last holiday the room has been empty.
Enjoy it, if you please. The doors have been opened
by horses. Servants have climbed the tile steps.
And so have I, liking to lean from the balcony.
Regard. There are no shadows. How somber it is,
yet the walls light up. It is a chamber of ambiguity
where two equals may meet before disappearing.

4

Can this courtyard which is myself
inspire me? Indeed those vigorous pillows
have felt my heel tap. I have had several dreams
this century attired in colors
and my arms have opened each time
the window revealed a pipe stem.
I am a marauder returning with what is my own;
I will repay you in horses and pictures.

20

Sleep is 20
        remembering the
insignificant flamenco dancer
in Granada
        who became
important as you watched
the mountain ridge
        the dry hills

What an idiotic number!

Sleep is twenty

it certainly isn't twenty sheep
there weren't that many in the herd
under the cold crest of Sierra Nevada

It's more like 20 Madison Ave. buses
while I go droning away at my dream life
Each episode is important
that's what it is! Sequences —
I've got going a twenty-act drama
the theatre of the active
the critics are surely there
even the actors
even the flowers presented onstage
even the wild flowers
picked by the wife of the goatherd
each morning early (while I sleep)
under the snow cone
of Sierra Nevada

> yellow caps like castanets
> I reach into my bouquet   ·
> half-dreaming
> and count twenty
> yellow capped heads

flowers clicking twenty times
because they like to repeat themselves

as I do as does the morning
or the drama one hopes
will be acted many times

As even these dreams in similar
people's heads

> 20

> castanets

A Handbook of Surfing

I

It is time to find the peak the rosy trimmings are sliding up

toward you whose fingers reach over the balcony the flowers

and trees are damp morning up breaks differently each sibilant

wavering the night closet shut   seeks . . .

A circular moon continued; ideal these conditions a
settled air on its five or six feet the wave rocks
early over the coast foam line spews as once at her lightest
the goddess washed goats tumbled into the brine mark their forks
body erect and facing the shore margin he of the water sign considers

. . . Bottom what is there under the shell determining size and type
those coral rocks an idiot glance from crevice to crevice they watch
the smooth wave. Why did Columbus the Navigator
select the reef? Its products are strong even off the simple isle.
Sand bottom more fickle rippling sand roulette, a dusty
depth and shifty, an unknown alphabet whose squeaky
letters as apt to let one down or forget to lift us up, we
cannot always climb the sand horn or blowing
hot then cold erratic it sometimes sleeps in the dovecote water.

Domestic requisites (agricultural, manufactured, urban,
                    non-urban, marital or no)
have placed you here sun-struck and geared
with your ocean plan for a soupy ride
right or downside
eyewash of roar speech saltness he thinks less thus
is better to concentrate the hash of whether/or

                    . . . No one has gentled this leash
                    Not you marbled H's

In the wave wilderness wily wild
cuckoo strength bearers as rapists
knee songs and thigh grippers

foam slashers bone knockers
surf kindlers in the riddle splash

                t   wit   ter   woo
like a long legend

II

Since there are probably no two surfers in the world who
will agree one hundred percent on the techniques of
advanced surfing, we would like to deal only with
the basic principles of learning to surf . . . we would
like to tell here about paddling, standing and turning,
straightening out or pulling out, we shall discuss
the effect of tides and bottom conditions . . .

Paddling is prone or kneeling or sitting
Standing and Turning mean exactly that plus some wisdom
as when you go down a hill on your heels and up one
on your toes. Everyone knows how to turn or turn about
or make a reverse these are daily decisions both
politic and poetic and they have historic sequences
in the surf they are known as Changing Directions

                as is seen a darting fish

                yet we deserve reunion

                    it soothes

this peak mounting even in ruffled calm
to search this way and that on the desert a palm
a white car to guide swiftly
as quoted my paddling self you have veins in your hands

Ardent days! Golden backs! The pier
at your peak helmeted one   hot dogging
the shore break   well there are many types of
waves they all fall (differently) you must assume
the General Positions:

                on nose
                spinning
                driving down
                head dips

Duke Kahanamoku

Makaha

Excellencies on the woodless sands

　　　　your emblem of polyurethane

Today I shall walk the board my teak sandals
on the wax the surf's down waterwheel furled
the monkey figure of moustached shiverless scale
we are also goons with our bent backs
not so turbulent in the shallows, but boring
as after prayers and feasting the sleepy travellers

III

Paddling out:　　Tributes must be paid that this
　　　　　　　　waterway be freed

and further:　　I think I see you blink in Iceland
　　　　　　　　top pole of wave
　　　　　　　　your midnight eye at crest　there
　　　　　　　　Viking foam . . . barriers the pine seed

Rolling through:　On the way to line up it's under the soup
　　　　　　　　you with your immaculate verb sense the
　　　　　　　　indicative clause so under control and
　　　　　　　　the novel how much you understand of
　　　　　　　　character plot action not to
　　　　　　　　mention vice or the splitting sensitivity of
　　　　　　　　Balzacian Frabrizio and those days in
　　　　　　　　so long Trevio　I remark your courage when
　　　　　　　　you decide the form is exactly at its crest of
　　　　　　　　sequence as in England the forty long spins
　　　　　　　　take us to India and back or within
　　　　　　　　a wearisome reach so tiring this spin on
　　　　　　　　top of water　Now roll your board under
　　　　　　　　you go the big spume breaks you're safe
　　　　　　　　with your underwater cartilage it's only
　　　　　　　　a quaint mishap to be thrown by imagination
　　　　　　　　and never if you're careful. While you wait
　　　　　　　　the longest while the first chapter, never
　　　　　　　　fear your head will roll on top. Not even

depth, but spun ivy tickle water
you're up then you're on top. A hard
way to it and the only. Just the beginning
Mister Tom. I mean master of swallows.

the dynamite crest

(Where are the childish waves the lappings
eschewed as to the lighthouse balloons
against a window your narrow partings)

IV

Wondering if this day fills you with ennui as it does me
in your bunnyhood so busy on the beach opening tops
six package I'm told. Where is your yellow long
veiled anger where is your passion diphthong?
On the beach with only vulture gulls can you
forget your dislike of bibliothèque?

Go
orange volume sandy named a windy
nomenclature suitable or yours pensioned

Lo your glossy tunics the simple wrap around
or take off always one shoulder the porous
statues on the hill stanced seaward sunstruck
withered frequently headless only the bosoms
upholding strict maidens courageous also
so many storms and tribal wars so much murder
to remain unburied . . . the warrior torso
over whom you keep watch remembering this beauty
especially at full moon one hand disjointed
severed reaches still to you as on the waveboard

a girl takes the wing position the surfer's arm
upholds so at Samothrace so will capture
Boreas all bunnies the wind speaks finally
air braided of wind is your upward tether
not these duplicate days you expend
. . . your mosaics
will they survive the dolphin's flight?

V

Questing the oracles en route to wave line-up
what did the breezes sing whisking the vases
the stern crones at idle nine o'clock did they repeat
flat or uncommon sea surf down or up
we'll know soon enough when the obituaries are out
each year another statesman backwash to our policy
our double daring life dips   owl not gull
be wise tell us when the necessary pull out

        this one yonder at its peak if too grand
        bail out you can't get away with everything
        even in your detective clothes sometimes
        as now one can continue the turn a right
        or left motion dependent on guerrilla wave strength

Dashed if I didn't flub it . . . remember
"All can transform the ugly wipeout
into a thing of beauty"
can save face even in oceanic pratfall
recognizing superior strength takes moral
courage once gained on a really critical turn
later made the pipeline but don't
expect each year to
                cop the Kangaroo crown

You with your lease on World Championship

VI

        Surfari . . .

        if you travel the water ways
in a moment you find the sluice gates
as if/ the shut of a book when
before your eyes you study its rhyme
I can remark the seconds before sunset
when vaporizing the smoke night
            sets its teeth
I'd rather a more vigorous selection
            two stanzas at twilight
            you hear ringing the columns

VII

Hélas! "In closeout conditions no one surfs"
There is a point beyond which big storm surf is unrideable
The four fathom five you hope to squire

sweet gauzy weeds to be coronals
on oceanic floor swaying they've learned their dance
they have a habit of performing without audience;
yet greed, for they are penniless, makes them desire a swimmer.

Am called Cassandra in these summer days
when in the soft illness of heat I'm ready
to talk of battles

        He rides in the heat
        he never squeaks
        he is ready for shore order

whether/or the village cong cough
like a leaky board when the surf is rough
Cassandra thinks of a child whose muscles
are thin; she weeps at the motorboard cost
the reef he'll hit young as Wordsworth's Lucy
in the quick clime of bomb

        Protest!

Nobody rides in closeout!

VIII

In the polyandry green of life there's a rule you stride

        quick to the whip before the foam
        the complexion of green
        shadows under the sandcove eyes
        the slim waistline of coast

to be adored as you glide spookless
this rhythm ancient as self the muslin shore

        with these lenses use nothing more
        all that is not goggle is giggle

take this most intricate tide
in your own way knowing the cost
forsaking all others if need be
it at its dangerous crest

mortuary bottom

Gallantly these fine surf horses
(innocently capturing a beach as daylight
finds the old sea at its best cooler
more quiet the dawn strokes
a way to greet heroes   the flat hues
let them rest)
              battle form

we acquiesce

            the purchasable line

promptly renewing our lids/our eyes

to negotiate each splendid day

we do this from wave couch

in shrewdness meditate

the expanse   the artful dare

I Ching

I Ching

Light   strikes   light   father   strike   light   stroke

Light   strike   father stroke   light   strike   stroke

Father light   strike   light   strikes light   stroke

   tubetun   tuntube

   tubulartunnel   tunneltubular

tumescenttumtum   tumtumtumescent

excite   recite

incite   excite

reciterincitingexcitingreciterinciting

wrath   frigate

wombfoamwombfoam

fjord   whelm

quiet   skin   still   top   of

soother   thirdly

silencer   thunderless

sticking   to   burning   glue   to

shiney   glue   two daughter

shining   laughter   sticking   to

joke   lake

joking   lake   joking   lake   joking

lakejokelakejokelakejokelakejoke

Moscow Mansions

Red Lilies

Someone has remembered to dry the dishes;
they have taken the accident out of the stove.
Afterward lilies for supper; there
the lines in front of the window
are rubbed on the table of stone

The paper flies up
then down as the wind
repeats, repeats its birdsong.

Those arms under the pillow
the burrowing arms they cleave
at night as the tug kneads water
calling themselves branches

The tree is you
the blanket is what warms it
snow erupts from thistle;
the snow pours out of you.

A cold hand on the dishes
placing a saucer inside

her who undressed for supper
gliding that hair to the snow

The pilot light
went out on the stove

The paper folded like a napkin
other wings flew into the stone.

Illyria

And I was right as dawn overhead
listening to the buoy as is often done
a bridge while brows float under it yes
it was a way of steeples of construction
of pilings of verbs. I too admire the way
water spells in the hand riding this way and
that and also the moments of green which
like paragraphs point out the stations
we must enter and leaving them count trees
more scarcely; there is much to emulate
not only iron bands but those waves you can
no longer dive into and the seamless rifts
which are noble as you explain omnivorously
having devoured both nail and hammer,
like an isle composed of rhythm and whiteness.
Night is gentle with the promise
of a balanced pear such is it this drop.

Egypt

for Tony Smith

Because nobody knew whether it was Monday or Tuesday
the park that was on Monday began on Tuesday

This water flows either way with exceptions
for blue moments described as loaded when

Never to make a remark about merely a generous lump
leaves no ivy over your tough Pharaoh meter

Either liked to parade in front of mirrors
going underground was a busy strike so that

When examined the bird's tread went which way
and that the pastime was being amazed

And getting out the size of a hump

The storage space it occupied "simple, very
authoritative, very enduring things."

A vigorous antiquity into which the slab was
inserted and either said not enough in spite of

The ribbons of oozes nobody made an oasis
out of it until dissatisfactions

With sizes more confusing than the tomb
where zero unwraps Ouch! you've printed my thumb

You have lost the original which was perhaps
better but the boys did their best lying on the

Mowed grass whispering butter as a matter of fact

Nebraska

Climate succumbing continuously as water gathered
into foam or Nebraska elevated by ships
withholds what is glorious in its climb like
a waiter balancing a waterglass while the tray
slips that was necklace in the arch of bridge
now the island settles linear its paragraph of tree
vibrates the natural cymbal with its other tongue
strikes an attitude we have drawn there on the limb
when icicle against the sail will darken the wind
eftsooning it and the ways lap with spices as
buoyancy once the galloping area where grain
is rinsed and care requires we choose our walk

And the swift nodding becomes delicate
smoke is also a flow the pastoral calm where
each leaf has a shadow fortuitous as word
with its pine and cone its seedling a curl
like smoke when the ashy retrograding slopes
at the station up or down and musically
a notation as when smoke enters sky

The swift nodding becomes delicate
"lifelike" is pastoral an ambrosia where calm
produces a leaf with a shadow fortuitous as word
with its pine and cone its seedling we saw
yesterday with the natural flow in our hand
thought of as sunlight and wisely found rocks
sand that were orisons there a city in
our minds we called silence and bird droppings
where the staircase ended that was only roof

Hallucinated as Nebraska the swift blue
appears formerly hid when approached now it
chides with a tone the prow striking a grim
atmosphere appealing and intimate as if a verse
were to water somewhere and hues emerge
and distance erased a swan concluding bridge
the sky with her neck possibly brightening
the machinery as a leaf arches through its yellow
syllables so Nebraska's throat

On Mt. Snowdon

Existence omitting other details winds up in a cupola
where the committed elegies are difficult like space
transpiring grotesquely to unite the self
with emblems somatic and conscious as elves

Who have leaped too high for domesticity
yet wings do not dominate that sparseness
graphic and elliptical as toes we use
for sonority claimed as grace

This interpreter of shelves is modern
in regard to depth width a despised
alternative such as death
"finds here no echo" the upper leaves

Stay green indigenous to the quartz
as a night station calms with its enduring
light a minute in immensity a fork
raised above the meat when the sweet chewing

Scarcely reaches the plate this realm
this astral occupant is heady as mission
boring as vision with its rock stairs
and mechanical escape emulating elf

Hideboundness of the winter road
it grieves displaced from sea and that
rocky bottom climbing aggravated and solemn
with a scattering of shell and rain

For memory the lattice of its troubles
not even virtuous as house but opportuning
weather ending in the artifice of toad
with that final detail of hair tossed from the window

Rosy Ensconcements

The Spanish bed overlooked by the Chinese courtesan
has a dimension as subtle as the island,
which is not so wild as it would like to be,
although the building that overlooks the estuary
is tall with the homely aspect of an escarpment
overlooking the channel that bathes the island
with a genial parental arm splashing the waves,
although no pines grow or palms, the land
is content with its placement overlooking the buildings,

the channel, and watched sometimes witheringly
by the sky which can be seen in toutes saisons
by the Spanish bed and the Chinese courtesan
especially when the telephone rings and the person
who overlooks the bed wakes up and repeats,
"that must be the temple gong" or "it is vespers in Alemeida."
Once or twice the bureau has been inched
so that it can overlook the rug, although lately
the rug has been removed to another niche,
so that the parquet floor may add a ton French
because like any good salad a bedroom requires
several greens and the amorous couple has tired
of being overlooked by a Chinese courtesan while lying
on a Spanish bed and reasonably enough given

the slice of island in the water, the couple asked
that a window be cut in the door and now with a
certain delicacy, that applied by the knife to a cake,
the icing can be slipped to the couple
in the bed which is Spanish and anemones admired
that have never been published before, overlooked

by the Chinese until eighteen years ago when the courtesan
was painted and added to the collection of the Spanish bed.
Although generally more subdued the island
welcomes the activities of poets in particular those
who overlook the impoverishment from the conservatoire
of the Spanish room with its air enriched by plants.
They transcending purely artistic considerations
crouch seductively under the gauze of nature
clairvoyant and courageous as Spain or Chinese sand.

Even Ovid

The vivid report of your gracious diehardedness
has wounded me, expecting the palm leaf
in a forwarded letter, not realizing
the dismal street was our way of greeting.
Special azure was once our way
and we beneath umbrellas nodded,
so tenderly we born on the cusp and knowing
it when suns struck and the moons
at your fingertips were yellow as that cloud
over the rooftop which today is a pompier
and the burning trees will assemble themselves.
I too am minute as ashes with the fine
grain of my feeling running crisscross into dark
where I sight you enviously at the blurred roots
and the ospreys play there, they have second sight
like sponges, loving both canal and river,
commuting as you on water, fearful of this group
of buildings, even going underground.
You like it because your eyes see further,
even as a rock quarry is graceful
with your initials at the sorrowful poem's end.

The Interruptions

It is a landscape inhabited by Baudelaire
    his *îles*, his *fantômes*, his *sang*
the faithful birds with their quick orgasm
the agility of the wave that attacks and plunders
    bruised bones, pallor and sleeplessness,
the fresh sand the treading skies and Spring
    a murderess in her photographer's gown

Rather it was the way I felt that morning, having
dreamed of a person who drew my blood there
in the shadow of the pier a frantic projection
having been permitted to exclude all care
and taste from its beams
there like a shingled and iron albatross
it lay with faint breathing on the sand
that was on its way to becoming prepared
to be a much larger station; that is the truth
of what lay before us and what we lay on
making telephone calls with air running
over the legs and into the palms which held
the voices with their visions of days this version
partitioned by explanations of why
the letter L had so much strength due to the extra
line attached to the vertical certain persons
becoming famous and even happy after this discovery
then dying over night

This tells you why my impartial sadness
needs you and desires you in this part of the Covenant
because you are a native especially through your shoulders
where all the wild chasms and snow boundaries
have been captivated and subdued
changed from missionaries into ravens
the fanciful hippity hopping being
your way of breaking into me through the pantry's door
on your path to the bible and the snug windows
the storm a little over to the left where the wince
is clouding in on you and on your eyes
of a natural brown like a barn or a spout
where the nest of eggs waits to determine its
eventual size after the gusts and the rain

Your fear of nature—no laughing matter—
like mine and Poe's
if you notice Baudelaire stayed close to the city
although Paris and her environs give us notice of few
lapses in taste where planning is concerned
those acres being confined to plots
and sacred wildernesses where
one can escape to the country at a minute's
notice and read Childe Harold surrounded
by verbena under oaks in a familiar arrondissement
yet that might make you nervous
remind you of home and its haunts—

An apprehension, not stepping in puddles,
and gluing your eyes to the spot beyond the horizon
a fixed stare of multiples and hues yet desperate
all the same like a bird in its covert
or an acorn on a bush or the quatrain soughing
the grass at sunset where we stood
after the toast and the kiss lifting what was lust
to the instant's light before its retreat
into dusk where the evil papers glow

Moscow Mansions 1

Give me your pencil
                    Stanley

While it is necessary
                    we speak
            of Pushkin.

And the outside Gods
            brought in by
                    Joyce

Ohrru those Russian growls

Joyce has turned up the
                    fire

And we are speaking of

Arrogance and poetry
    (no question of it)

As if there were soft flowers

That burned quickly

One left for the Louvre
      not cellophane

Stanley is speaking
      of Dostoevski

He says there are 2 volumes
      for $1.50

And Joyce says, "Baggies are
great for wrapping up art."

And Stanley says, "I am intimidated"
      like Gorky.

Moscow Mansions 2

      "Rightly are you dispossessed virulent blue
who have given so little kasha to the pot"

      Simmering this winter under the cool of river
its rainbow was costly as seaplane its idiom spoke
while the steamboat churned alas as walks in the morning
are disappearing and the attic sounds of Misha who fished
at dawn

      We shall move at Christmas when the elder
families return

      Already the hospital has a curious sad break
where the window is yet gallant for those wings
that were our interns kindly lifting and reflecting

Certainly affectionate with alleyways
discerning as pigeon the tiles with their oil surface
beckoning to set our feet to make a fond gesture
of renewal and continuity we always considered
mare nostrum never forbidding as dark pine
or a wrist in a cast

Now you shout for other roomers mansion
I shall not describe where the boats left your prospect
sailing with ribbons dispatched to stair and tune

Indeed there was a happy whiteness to mix with
the blue and quarter notes we breathed on the ashes
then there were urges there were tubes for the music
and mistakes

It is not delightful to leave my ruins
with a head wrapped in a turban or a kerchief
to carry these pencils or a wrinkle where the sighs
drift away on stone when brick was such a tomb

Knight of the Swan

He left the trees when he left the lake
because he was careless with catacombs and fear

He mounted the swan and rode away

Knight of the Swan

Those feathers you press with a heavy intent and
thoughtfulness gathering speed while the reins slip
loosely the muscular bird neck   on past
The Girl Asleep in the Window   then later
The Farmstead Beneath Trees   he smiles the bird
quivers yet sober as bridges in autumn
there is a haze on these miles and the swan needs
water whose body is heated with mountains

They walk in   tattery   rain

A few quick oaths   long space

More lengthening   a gentian

They fly   he has made

(an escape)   .   the swan is furious

The Knight feeds it some smiles

They lumber on

                                        "shadowy evening"

Makes her escape

                        and a garment falls over the swan
an umbrella poem of pale irons and acrobat tones
a confusing reward for sleep instead of that sweet presence
until morning brought the rainbow in different styles rather
than weather; yet they were relieved and hastened on
more enemies now than beast and knight so it seemed
but it was less so they were stumbling together; hidden
under his feathery pants and the swan's heavy down
were landmarks that were similar despite the knight's
peasant past and the swan's poet future

Things that might have been bullets hit his insides
(he was wary) they were not bullets they were adventures
which sting although not lethal and because they often
flew very high what caused his sensation was hyperion
or a bolt from the sun and it was azure which caused
him to sink onto the swan's down it was that bordered
by snow and flower when a quick look would make you dizzy

and below a tidal swamp was dark and lurking strange
faces were lit by fire the heights on which he perched
made them unordinary there were instant foamings out of
the dew where this knight sought a castle he trembled so
he fought with his damp forehead he clutched the swan
for he with his new agony asked the swan if

                        the swan responded
flights are macaroons it almost said being weblike
often lacking a breeze they have an order like my neck

I would like to make love to you said the knight

The swan with an abrupt gesture of its wings set him down
in the forest (nearby) nearby was a lake from whence
they had originated   it was indeed nearby   the knight
began to relax and to breathe to   suspire   he cast
aside those odious thoughts of his origin   he began

(with dreamy asides) to like wings   there was obviously
too much noise when a wave hit a concave stone   yet here

here in the lightness which repeats itself as darkness
he often returns a wanderer   he stoops for the token

                         the token
            wizened   as an orange tooth
                        becomes an irritant when the wind
            harshens and grass is seamier than old rags
            in the knot of the hurricane   a vase of empty
            rags the healthier shore calls "refuse" thus
            sends them spinning like nutmegs from the shoots
            that bore them

                         we see signals
            as tokens they burden our clothes when light
            buttons down and sheets are shaken in the dust
            of widening rooms

                         we see where asphodels
            we hunt archways where turtles are strewn
            like wreaths of sofas and rugs (the daffodils)
            and draperies (like hands)   tokens
            the statuary and rabbits   the tins   the gasps
            going to the theatre   descending
            he was seized with a fit of tokens they caught him
            pitilessly   joylessly   noblessely an eyeful
            the parent company made the toys (a token)
            the sibling company sold them
            going to your desk in the meadow
            finding a token in the drawer . . .

                         the drawer
            "It seems I can't ever win," he said shaking out the drawer
            "Until she appears" then she did appear she did fanning
            his wrists like an old timer she had croupier spirit
            in every breath she drew like a swimmer who draws the ocean
            or a worm who draws the earth or I who draw
            your heaviness as you draw the drawer as
            daylight draws to its close all have endings
            like berries drawn in snow
            like brownness that once was berries
            drawn in snow

a snow tale

of a foot having a high instep
that was frozen in a storm when somebody
took off its snowshoe

the shoe was only an idea.

Counting 2 lunches and 2 teas we've done rather well.
We haven't lost any snows over it.

the gingerale

was a lesson in how to do nothing if ever he watched one.
The shadowy spot at the top where the shoe used to be
the token   the drawer   the gingerale
could be put in a chimney
and out would pour a shadowy spot or so one thinks
yet a purr glistens

on the rock
where a tall man sits puffing and he lengthens
his shadow by drinking in sips as one would tease
gingerale by spitting or by reading
the spirit goes out of it and presently there is only
a tall glass a bird sings in the tree near it

it

stirs up a little rain
on top of IT
(it) must
go inside of IT

returning the token was more like a landing commenced in a moonsoon
the feathery tides nearly drowned it where the lake's waves

the waves of the lake swelled like mulberries in a damp tin box
whose very grin was icy like particular thoughts of finding
and loss and the difficulties of property on sand

in the autumn

rinsing the token and ridding it of dispiritedness a cold
foam bath and icy smiles the lips permitted and the knight
was refreshed then also the mountains had reviving airs

nesting in the hollows from peak to golden peak and there were
lairs for robbers which altered the loneliness

for always he wished for his swan even its shadow even
a shadow on stones that once were heavy and warm

        and the swan's story

he cherished along with the memory of his ride that as a basin
is filled then emptied yet its curve remains and its depth

he would never forget nor the exact three quarter of his waltz
there on the fringes of clouds and the embrace in the chasm

with snow and down erasing any doubt the act was modern

        as mountain climbing or looking for gentians

any ruin has its surplus   or wrinkle there on the mask

        fed with dishes of rain

the knight was no exception he even wore his hair like a legend
whistling a lot from a need for quaintness he plied himself
back and forth pretending he had an occupation like speech

        of course it was the same

even the military and the religious wherever there was a crowd
especially at the inn the enjoyment was the same either
more or less creating a contemporary scene against the morass
also the skis were the same with their question of advance
or slumber the echoes were like that multiplying the same

avenues

        they were the same as trails
with the heavy youths attacking the scrub the same
as sidewalks in summer like pointed firs the escape
was the same as the cellar door a language of weather

and straw

        much faded while he slept.

The night animals advanced   the tender snow
roofless and perspicacious the way apples mix with cinders
the animals tore at his coat they reminded him of the chance
he took and what it meant in terms of courage
and the tendency to keep his eyes closed in daylight
he wished the oyster snow would go away
or the paws and he quietly atone for those meadows
employing a different voice he woke himself up

the creatures fled through the trees but the brass struck
harder in a persistent rhythm both alarming
and lulling

                    a cantus firmus

          "I must   the most of"
          "I must   to the"
          "I must polish my armor" is what it added up to

the rest is flurry or a forecast of   the terms
were regular owls returning to their pasture spooky too
unlike a crowded barn the slope with its slight condensing
of timber and snow reflected an austere history   the story
of a family that had passed its days dutifully
(rather like the knight before he met his swan)

Now he shook with glee and oaths   violets thrust themselves
up at him and he seized a handful so a tremor of Spring
passed through him not knowing which way it was meant to go

with the tilt of flowers
with the floral tilt

                        with the wilt of snow
like a building surfaced in stucco
or a white machine crossing a bridge
or air with a cloud woven in that space where
a motor threads it a short black lace thickening
the atmosphere the way a weaver does

so a chivalric mood occupied the knight

                    like a hand.

                Occupied by a chivalric mood

the Knight refuses to disturb the hand

it was the hand

                    opened books and doors for him
that fed and soothed when the long train
crossed his brow stirring the cars above his fears

the hand

                    forbidding encounters even excursions

as winter light interpolates sun

                what was shiny or angled

cleared/straightened in a tiny slaughter

> the objects rocking back and forth

unharmed yet like a torrent cut off from
mountain water and somewhat shallow as birds
skimming low were fleshy and bright not so poignant
as the swan in white intentness trial of wings

> the hand

was a substitute

> an arch leading into the proscenium

yet
the aspect was bare

> it shivered in short grass

where
possibly ruins or ornaments lay

> breathless.

The Knight preferred the way his swan
> had kicked up its wings
this limp air and that calm hand
> made a classic life
he realized he could get on better
> the way one progresses through green
on a minimal plain

> without exasperations & doubts

he regretted this loss of impetuousness

only gratitude seeped over the thin stream

and his smile placed by the hand

> was sweet

one or two muscles quivered
reminiscence of his flight

> he wished these books

were thornier

> the doors

noisy
> when he learned their names

> It's raining
> said the Knight
> let's walk.

Carmen

Delicate manufacturess,
it's just that point
in one's career before

On a respectable evening one takes
the ship of delight
having washed all stains
from the fingers

Having prayed to her
of the eyelet embroidery

Tested one's slenderness
as a castanet is balanced
on two fingers

Adios to the solitudes
to the surgeons who have hung
their scalpels from your balcony

To the men of culture
who would have you choose
between good and evil

Your adagio is applauded
by factory workers
to serve is your dedication.

The Ramblas leads to the sea
it is a leaf
rushing to its grinder
it is the smoke
of the friends of Carmen

It is an envelope that withholds
its message until the ship
is far out at sea

The script is one of confusion
to all useful tips
as to how to make one's way
to succeed in a profession

Because of the bitter
mixture of tobaccos.

Who would guess
watching her mantilla
that soon it will fall
on purple snow

Only the invisible courtyards
permitted to sing,
"Whose tears, if not mine,
will turn to rage?"

Museum

I am not distressed by your volunteer work Citadel
nor am I disturbed by the volume of your mourning gloves
insomnia makes us equal as does Euterpe who has a gracious
wrist in the quick dissolving cloud of your areaways
speeding into a gauntlet pearl of the lesser

My antimony my mitre glued to our secular causes are the
little violences of meter tasting better and earthier
and different from moment to moment sound of the walls
falling altarwise vagrants in their coats of paint away
from us also where the obelisk burns there in the park
a synonym for whatever is exact and green within us

Cheering us on is perhaps your avocation Citadel the one
for which you volunteered even while you scorch those
ivory tokens you distribute our embers evenly
and that is "isonomia" when the better people make their
plans among the laces and daisies later there is a clearing
of picnic baskets actually if I didn't appreciate your manner

I wouldn't leave my track on your floor
along with the tickets and the drums or pay you a cent
but your ripe blossom has breathed inside my calm
so Citadel I will not leave you to isotopes
nor will I become a warrior although you have armed
me with poison for the midnight sunset in which you
and I will sup above the plumey underground you have hired
like the heroes we are and the chirp we schemed.

Byron's Signatories

1

His air of the underworld

His air of the underworld . . . the underleaf
of the catalpa together with the ruddiness
of his lisp.

2

Lately he said you've a shocking
amount of premature histories,
your stockings have runs. It is
the Alaska pipeline all over all
over. In the polar morning that
should be dusk does it matter
                        about gloves?

3

Supposedly more religious
to do it in geometrics, without images
with an acoustical sound,
like "ees" that are closer
to a childhood of alphabets

The way that it murmured. And
you were here all the while. Sleeplessly
as a diet counts grams those
valves continuing with you
in the distances

They are asymmetrical. Also mountains
with their dark and quiet.

4

shabby sequences as sorrows repeating

or the soft voice of her who found rest
in the rich cracker not wanting to breathe

      with your buttons and marbles
as the day turned with lateness and monuments
        consumed all that
          now it's not a dream

5

                I admire you
in your Byron green suiting clipping away
at a language. And I liked also the fragments;
the bit of sail, the heel of the island,
even the letter going clop clop on its piece
of thread especially that hint about your
half sister and nearly setting a tone

6

Clarice recounted her summer near Lucca
swings and whispers food
at the fountains and the baths
surrounded by marble (Carrara) near
turnstiles yet it was only a week
I mean the vacation meant longer
but politics put them all to bed
on a train the chesty part was reaching
the Alps in a Rover—alas!

7

Yesterday I saw an etching by Hirschvogel
called "Landscape with Two Buildings
Surrounded by Water," such a derivative
title I considered tearing it up it was
really so literal, yet the drawing was
spooky in the German fashion one
kept peering up at windows conjuring
rigid sleeves and hearts plunged
or purged was the intent of the arrows

8

Having a rough moment and indigestion
the rug clung to you George Gordon
even if its repetitions were termed neglect.
A little went a long way
(like bricks on a Turkish oven)
still . . . the tent didn't hold in the foam.

9

Living solitarily in the garret reading Strindberg in the afternoon
stuffing the window with paper shortening her walks because of
the cold . . . she welcomed his visits. At first they were daily, then
hourly, now only minutes would elapse before she heard his rap at
the door. His arrival was usually preceded by a twinge on her left
retina something like tequila, a rough peppery hotness she called
it the "flavor of eyes." They would talk together as long as they
could. There were various passages he liked to indulge in and she
would follow him there rubbing against the wall, avoiding as best
she could the damp, but liking the shreds of scenery he invited her
into and the hesitations in his vocabulary that were like shrubbery
brown at the squat root and silvery green on the charged outsides.
And so she was isolated no longer and rather thought of him as her
drawbridge similar to the one in the picture by Hirschvogel . . .

10

Up at the "Mansion"
Davy sat on the bed lighting a cheroot.
Peter talked of Agnes in the arcade.
A thing or two "lifted" there.
People whistling in corridors
riffs from "Ecuador."
You could see the mold
from which the jelly was pressed.

But the world changed
leaving us on its lid

       patches, mostly, elsewhere
       a fugue and then the scratch on the arm

More snow floating from Moscow
there on the road; the bandana

       chortling at a few prisoners.

The Poetess

after Miró

A dollop is dolloping
her a scoop is pursuing
flee vain ignots   Ho
coriander darks   thimble blues
red okays adorn her
buzz green circles in flight
or submergence?   Giddy
mishaps of blackness make
stinging clouds what!
a fraught climate
what natural c/o abnormal
loquaciousness   the
Poetess riddled
her asterisk
genial!   as space

Losing People

for Ira Morris

The days when you try to recover
your wits are lost days
yet simple as sandwich
of three layers the crunch
that's easy

Loss
          "pure" loss
you attend its reconstruction
where you are three persons also
a sandwich

Loss
               not hearing a voice
again as threnody

Loss
you begin to rhyme it with walls
or shoeshine

                    Loss
of your presence with a gait
and hues

the surface of persons
in restaurants eating sandwiches
they know there is a car parked outside

O images viscous and daring with the squeeze
of a fork inside your thighs that are delighted
with atmosphere and real weather

                    missions
over the backward curves rather like water
                    that moves this day
          under the bridge:

you decided
               the stone
no longer supports the bridge
                              well.   Ira died.

The Poem Lying Down

Unlike the swiftly lying down and becoming a supine object
nor the thick air circling snow
quite as an adjunct to your proper person lying down
as Venice rests or Guadaljuarto that place of

cathedrals or pictures your restful quarter where temples
too had their place and lost it as quiet relates to an arm
auxiliaries like moths your breathing goes with
a "passage" explained as Cézanne permits the
branch of a forest to melt there a tree later
translated   toughness
                              that permit

Sassafras
for H. B.

                  Today a field of pumpkins
yes.
                  Also the sea imagining granaries
the slight narrow fish tangled in its weed.
Pretending.

Imaginary objects
                  and what isn't
there's Sleughfoot on the rug
attacking his quarry
as if it were alabaster and not a door
                  a cat!

                  Which isn't as imaginative
as your kicking in the glass door of
Metropolitan Telephone and Co.

                  Or rain fancying windows.
You said,
                  Ellington travels so much in his music
everyone bumps into him.

                  Considering the wind
on the plains out middle west;
the strict mountains whose claim
(in our time) never varies. Can
we say they have imagination? We know
they are far out; the plain was an introduction.

There is conjecture.
Fog on the mallows. Bloom of mallow
in the fog. Now you cannot see it,
                    was *it* "invention"

                    Or sassafras
a tonic,
                    whose bark
a digestive

                    to be taken
when wild red harshnesses
range the system
                    causative
of sillabubs; they make
for disorder
                    they lend themselves
to the imagination
                    like Nereids

You are absolutely crazy
racing past their scream

Circassians

I become excited when I am with Circassians
I am almost in despair.
            That cousin with his moustaches
they seem to know what to do
            with sadness and ecstasy
almost like the Irish

and who am I with my mixed feelings?

            I put down my pen
and I have found a pencil
            not any pencil
            but this one fabricated in Germany

I bought it in France.

Caroline has asked me to lunch.
We eat a steak
cucumbers
radishes
we drink vodka. Polish vodka.

       I look at photographs.
They are her grandparents in front of their tent.
       Grandfather
is dressed in his tunic and pants.
       His belt carries a knife.
His blouse and his blossoming pantaloon
       is the way I should describe them.
His wife is shy and she too billows.

       We are in a village
       at the top of the mountain
       look at that drop!

Those are her grandparents.

Caroline too is photographed.
On the beach at Amagansett
       look how it shows
       her face of the Caucasus
       even the sloped eyelids
       the tense skin near the eyes!

How remarkable she is!

       Caroline is many versts
       from Yahni Polyana

       Caroline's apartment is
       in New York City

We are neighbors and we admire each other.

Have some vodka.

Another July

Earth on my foot.
Bhims. Bhams. Hooplas.
Gorgeous morning cakes
Air without stripes.
Under the eyes a new fragrance of shine;
Blossoms and tints at someone's doorstep
(Schuyler eating salami in his kitchen
thinking of the empty ghost of Clare,
extending his hand with a little mayonnaise
toward it)

Downstreet a postbox blue as phlox.
Thus.
Some weeding. Out.
Ouch.
Earth falls on my foot
Warm as death. Or
In memory of it.

Drawing a Blank

There are blank moments
and I feel sorry for them.
Something doesn't make it in the sky
the clouds fall apart what was lithesome
lifting a plane lets that plane down;
the metal nearly breaks in an
horrendous flame blue cannot put out.
What was needed there was water
and that too happened; it rained on
those blank moments and there was
the sodden blanket with its smells
its warmth (we remembered as useful)
a mess of sighs.

Yet blank moments can be kind
as tender as the blanket composed of
tunes with woof and warp running around
the mother who had her uses in her once
upon a time.

Drawing a blank
permits one to sleep for a minute or so
nodding away and waking to find
on the island a shell with a sound.

Stupid Physical Pain

Rumer Godden
I think
a mouse in Australia
leaf

        curves

in radiant painless clear
quoted clouds like bannisters

        now

the sides of leaves
have railings
I slide down them easier

       fresh as a poem

in the morning when nothing is

       "uppermost in your mind"

dew against the page

the scratch the sea makes
not simple dots and dashes

eastern trade syllables
orange juice squeezers
on the sand abandonnés

        cluck cluck

sailing to
Robert Louis Stevenson Samoa
a distinctive invalid
sequestered there

      all that grass matting

      lighting your pipe at dawn

the leaves
hatching stories on the verandah

                    Mynah birds

I wouldn't mind
I wouldn't object to

with this black a streak of cyclamen

Roses

"painting has no air . . ."
    — GERTRUDE STEIN

That there should never be air
in a picture surprises me.
It would seem to be only a picture
of a certain kind, a portrait in paper
or glued, somewhere a stickiness
as opposed to a stick-to-it-ness
of another genre. It might be
quite new to do without
that air, or to find oxygen
on the landscape line
like a boat which is an object
or a shoe which never floats
and is stationary.

           Still there
are certain illnesses that require
air, lots of it. And there are nervous
people who cannot manufacture
enough air and must seek
for it when they don't have plants,
in pictures. There is the mysterious
traveling that one does outside
the cube and this takes place
in air.

        It is why one develops
an attitude toward roses picked
in the morning air, even roses
without sun shining on them.
The roses of Juan Gris from which
we learn the selflessness of roses
existing perpetually without air,
the lid being down, so to speak,
a 1912 fragrance sifting
to the left corner where we read
"La Merveille" and escape.

Lights of My Eyes

Lights of my eyes

        my only

they're turning it off

        while we're asleep on this shore

and the thick daffodils

        are crying

Lights of my eyes

don't be afraid of me

what we saw

rivers and roads

        ruins

the cast of the sculpture in winter

they will return your voice

and I'll go on singing "adieu"

Passage

for John Coltrane

Words
    after all
are syllables *just*
and you put them
    in their place
    notes
    sounds
a painter using his stroke
    so the spot
where the article
    an umbrella
    a knife
we could find
    in its most intricate
    hiding
slashed as it was with color
    called "being"
    or even "it"

Expressions

For the moment *just*
    when the syllables
    out of their webs float

We were *just*
    beginning to hear
like a crane hoisted into
    the fine thin air
that had a little ache (or soft crackle)

    golden staffed edge of
    quick Mercury
    the scale runner

Envoi

    C'est *juste*
    your umbrella colorings

dense as telephone
     voice
     humming down the line
     polyphonic

Red plumaged birds
     not so natural
     complicated wings
                    French!

Sweet difficult passages
                         on your throats
there *just* there
                    caterpillar edging
                    to moth
Midnight
                    in the chrome attic

Hohenzollern

Asphodel isn't in the
          Gardening by the Sea
               but
Perdita is:
          "For you there's rosemary and rue; these keep
          seeming and savor all the winter long:"
The moon is there
          "shinin' through the trees"
Arrogance; savagery; loneliness   the moon
half sharpened   a day later
          like asphodel first introduced
the same time or a day later than *The Winter's Tale*
          daffodil moon
                    "seeming"

Hohenzollern bloomed at me
today on Wickapogue Road
the princely banner high masted
over the dunes
potato dust settling
on the homestead sign

      Hohenzollern

formerly a tenant farmer cabin
outside the Henry Ford compound

      Hohenzollern

What glee! What ghoulish joyousness!

The Stragglers

If you lift your arms
against the white door
    "not to fall"

Or if autumn or climate
or the pencil with its skill
    "almost germanic"

a contest where the white will
    that shrinks
in weather . . . under the moon

    they assemble
the portative number
    the bridge with its figures
the blossoming twelve
    treading ice

those closets of doves. also figurative.
and walking home. on rugs.

Olivetti Ode

How difficult it is   to recall you
are not Polychrome Limestone
Building received from the administrators
this day of coil and honeycomb

I must trace your steps
here on the keyboard
I must assign you to space

                        Proof of your history
                        will be this route
                        I am hitting
                        this siren note
                        I strike

on a ribbon your archaeology

The first cry of awe
that tear mixed with cement and glass

Your brow
lifted above the numerals

As now I quote
                        "Auguries of steep romance
                        highland blend of bracken and rock"

The rituals have been observed

Vanish   Vanish   *Building*

Except here on my calendar

a last iridescent bite

On the Verge of the Path

What inspires me?
                Picasso!
He's there on the right in the photo
Where are we?
                In Mougins, Cannes
tributary states and rivers. Yes!

Here I am in Penthouse A rue Ninety Fourth
thinking about Picasso.
I detest this pencil. I wish I had a "crayon"
or a cactus or my life were being consumed
by villas called Jacqueline.
It was a summer evening
in the 1950's when I attended a performance
it was something like "people and animals
in their habitats in Montparnasse"
by Picasso
The dog was played by Frank and John
I had not yet made their acquaintance
but I lived on a nearby rue
Picasso!
Yourselves consider me in profile
when I am awakened from a dream of pottery
rattling like candlesticks in the factory
of Apollinaire and Eluard a century
looking up at me from the shelves of O'Hara and Ashbery
those odd tables where we mixed our cement

Gravel

"Gravel sounds like snow when a car
rides over it crunching like snow,
yet it has a stick in it meant for leaping
if there were any leaps here in winter."

Gravel
is grim although. A rasp. A burr,
not even a cough like veined jasper
  or careless cornmeal or the dandy
   surface of porphyry, or an ivory forehead
      with lace curls; somewhat like
        Portuguese.

Certainly not a stone floor
or the obscure taste of moss.

Gravel is a habit that keeps repeating itself
and I dislike the gravelly attitudes of
    myself like natives in winter or early
    summer before the orange light has begun
    to dim me and others; then our arms will not
    flail so entirely like gravel
When we fall there's no skin off our knees,
we'll tumble in grass on the moistness of fetters;
roads serene in moonlight will pass shrub
and doorstep with a little hoot
at what was hurtful before.

                  He wrote
he was waiting for that orangeness
stronger than rain's grey egoism;
"there's no refuge under the rectory umbrella
they're sending emissaries from the gravel
landladies
                baskets of Art Brut:
what's Art Brut
                but gravel?

                Gravel bursts the pane of
my ear," he added. A lover throws gravel
up to her window. She runs to meet him
under the window with its wound of gravel
She also will be subject to its aim

                There's no comfort
in gravel.

Bicycling

That child

Doesn't want to go home to supper

Thinks:

I'd rather see a pantalooned goblin

      The sea is at a vertical
      The hedge is horizontical

Hanging over the hedge in a vertical elongiacal

                    position

        is the goblin

Sea runs by hastily

                 road crunches along

Everything has a mathematical proportionate

               in space

        Exact and relativinal

              physical

       except

The trapezodiacal pepsicotial

             spheeriod

                  of

Merry Times

Shifting the Iris

Collapsing so this is not what I expected
the vision had more altitude and escapes,
a broader seam, certainly more current laced
with green, altogether outstanding not
this sash of door or mantel or knob or lintel
or stair swindle certainly not a curb it was a street
not a bottle cap, a volume rather than envelope or paste,
it was scissors and meat, not hive but swarm.
The ladder slipping away from the roof
to where one landed in a disguising sort of way
on one's side, a pause in the day's
precariousness fitting ill, but regularly
into the wild snow.

Peanuts. A throb of peanuts.
The next time
"crab meat" across your eyes

If you keep falling off that ladder
there won't

And what with the buckshot
you'll
this wintry afternoon of walnuts

Shift the iris!

I can't   enormous
Aphid-Sonnet's feeding on my toe

Green Revolutions

Being drunk upstairs and listening
to voices downstairs. The roll of the sea
sounding calm
                    after the voices
and the machinery
                    Tibet with Monaco
thrown in for measure

                    Distant greens
they appear on walls when one is tired
the dark background greens then the light ones
bringing us closer. As landscape appears
with its fresh basket approaching the car
then relinquishing, going away, telling us
something that is secret, not even whispering,
but indicating as if an ear of corn might be over there
choice and ripe, but neglected.

                    The cars go away. The voices
go away. For lunch. At noon.
It's harsh with old Donne in his steeple.
I'm upstairs "looking at a picture"
like a Bostonian in Florence, "looking at a picture."
Now it's green. Now it isn't.

Poem

Disturbing to have a person
So negative beside you
I dreamed last night
The Mississippi Belle rolled over
We were all drowned.

I promise to do better.
Look I have a net here
Filled with trout.

Ain't nothin' like river trout.

Evening

See why it is this way
and after that what goes and
when and each
I will call you properly toward
inasmuch as quiet goes the hour
so it slows
neither requires which
and I am softly going either way
the leaves are bowing toward that
                    their path is not always
sincerely and softly spoken as
                    an axiom its north
toward your south victorious
as calm gloves
                    the white apron dawn bowing
in the kitchen area   ah wholesomeness
beside the coal bin
                    we never said it was so

The Old Silk Road

When beauty that's arranged — a choir — a desk

        mocks and beckons

    the quiet groceries
the task, even autumn; not very strong
their arm lift —

      when the self-dividing verb

pushes

      The Old Silk Road
puts down a foot;
we like to hear that noise of grapefruit
being young and shy

          T'ang

        T'ang seeds

     T'ang

Now

           It's Autumn
        It's Fall. A red cloth with
        Yellow leaves is chosen. And the
        Sophisticated color of mauve
        Burnt orange for the couch. To affect
        A change. Where the ripe dawn
        Hurries a red is.

          Dieu soit en cette maison

That building's going up before a poem is finished; it
won't be autumn anymore. A definition is all that
shall exist. The thing planned like a girder's iron
presently we shall not be permitted to see. Autumn!
you're rushing off in that freighter you are
ecclesiastical and safe trying on the hat with fur captured
in winter and its rhythm strikes back at you like snow.

Let me plead for your brownness to remain, your shoulder
of leaves and your poignant tongue that writes so many
songs about yourself and your melancholy character
singing these songs shuffling the dead vines.

Dieu soit en cette maison

In autumn to sing of oneself like Guillaume
with his riddle riding South where
those buildings were adding in advance of the cold years
but his song came first!

Are not buildings completed
before works of art break off an if
in the middle region where
whereness commences a reign

We have a right
to Autumn. Like stairs
going up. Also closets
furniture, a bathroom
on the first floor, a household
toughness that defends us
going into autumn
fewer shadows

Dieu soit en cette maison

(Autumn's departure)

Ecce Ecce air! an airplane climbs into it
blinks, shakes, natural now the ice air and immediate
but we're accustomed to change   making war   ending it
going to sleep with a shawl   waking up in snow

The weather at your eyelid   say it's Spring
I mean Summer   flowing is air borrowed of course
when I breathe   from you hot air!   Yet

critically despite our behaviour it is winter

Quick   the strangeness catches up

Dieu soit en cette maison

The Countess from Minneapolis

1

water wheels river turns river asides over and under falls
splice rapid brown slow turn fist thrust signal ahead
winter autumn water barge season thrice water bank
bridge system barge deep search over falls rush edge
search nearly there river bottoms watersurge bridgespread

2

Believe you Madam yon building of ice was built
for thy pleasure?

I do.

Yu're right.

3

50 Floors

The glass stops midway skyways.
We look up.
The Indians look up.
My hood's up.
Their hood's down.
The glass gets stuck in my blue eye.

The glass rattles past their black eyes.
Crystal Court. King Flour's crystal court.
Blue eyes. Black eyes.
Gracefully King Flour floats down
on his quilt of white.
This quilt distributes free sifted flour over our
shoulders and when he lands near us he sticks
out his foot. I kiss it.
(The Indians spit on his toes.)

4

Thinking of You Prokofief

The steam settled into the atmosphere
        steam in atmosphere
it was cold; so the steam did not move
        it became lonely as a field of daffodils
on the earth we kept looking up
on the horizon there was admiration
                those waltzes.

And the ivory of our lids felt vaporous
as if crevices were gained in the shell
where our eyes kept their hoods

        Thinking of you Prokofief
that tricky snow outside makes a steam indoors
and the china tea we brew keeps us quick
        as Prokofief
whose doors slam.

        Steam never lessens its latitude
in the sky
        like Prokofief
while many cars creep over the bridge sweating
finally equipped
        with their Mahler treads.

5

River Road Studio

Separations begin with placement
that black organizes the ochre
        both earth colors,

Quietly the blanket assumes its shapes
as the grey day loops along leaving
an edge (turned like leaves into something else),

Absolutes simmer as primary colors
and everyone gropes toward black
where it is believed the strength lingers.

I make a sketch from your window
the rain so prominent earlier
now hesitates and retreats,

We find bicycles natural
under this sky composed of notes,

Then ribbons, they make noises
rushing up and down the depots
at the blur exchanging
its web for a highway.

Quartets the quartets
are really bricks and we are
careful to replace them
until they are truly quartets.

6

Portrait of Mary Rood

After we left the building
We avoided the wire fencing
Being dressed in suede,

Like Spring more pliable than fur,
As a jar of oil allows the vinegar
To settle and the beans to quiver there
In new dressings of garlic and things.

Now in the garden with a black dog
Who shouts, "the snow's gone!" we
Celebrate weather and profiles and
The reliability of telephones that bring
Us together in the days of brightly lit
Stones, something like olives, or
As I said, beans, or as I say each
Time the door closes, Mary.
The Mary of R's and Crosses
Named for gestures with rains.

.

7

Eating Lake Superior Cisco Smoked Fish

When the flageolets verts are finally cooked I shall be high on Mississippi rock water. The water flows over the rock leaving rich traces, unlike Alpine water that is so pure and sprightly like Fauntleroy Alpine deer, never touching rock or pebble. Pure. Yet feeble. Weak because the minerals are lacking. They only follow the tough arm of water that likes to mingle with the crowd and pick up its bitters in a dirty old smokey fist. Like Dickens.

.

8

Musings on the Mississippi

Although Paris has only one river, the Seine, this river behaves perfectly reasonably within the city limits, or arrondissements, approaching the isles with a courtliness and depositing its burdens with a verve one used to associate with the beret. A manner thus is maintained by the Seine which we define as raison d'être or Steak Diane or the French way of looking at things, sometimes it is true through a pigeonhole. Let's say neither New Yorkers or Parisians are inclined to "river worship." Certainly they are appreciative of the uses commercial and aesthetic of a river, yet neither is inclined to "go overboard" on the subject. Nothing at all here Oriental or Indian in that respect, or Hungarian either.

When I come to the subject of Minneapolis and its posture on the Mississippi, a confusion like a drought descends upon me. Minneapolis persistently nagged by the unreasonable river that both gladdens and disturbs her heart. I may become convinced that the only way to survive a long, unsettling, barren Minnesota winter is to sit in a hut by the log fire and looking past the tears of confusion and loneliness falling down my pinched and overheated cheeks study, chew, harry a map of Minneapolis. Thus one might survive until spring.

The following winter I would exact from my tree chopping, whiskey thawing, sullen recounting of woes active and mystical, the labor of studying the Mississippi River. Her windings, divagations, idiosyncracies, bridges, dredgings, falls, destructions which yearly drive a mortal to the furthest limits of that angst called despair triumphed over by a northern people only through the spiritual suicide of its artists.

9

Legends

Little Withergield was talking to his pal, Freotheric, as they walked in the woods near the Minnehaha Falls.

"I don't like skeletons, do you Freddy?"

"Nope. They scare me."

"It's the way their backs curve and sort of turn up into their skulls," said Withergield.

"When did you ever see a skeleton?" asked Freotheric.

"Last night."

"Where?"

"Here."

"That was no skeleton, silly. It was Hiawatha."

"Hiawatha's no skeleton."

"How do you know?"

"I seen him a lot. He's real strong. Strong enough to hold Minnehaha in his arms."

"That ain't Minnehaha."

"Who is it then, smarty?"

"A skeleton."

Just then a boulder went crashing over the Falls and plunging like a feathery plume it tickled the sandy bottom of the river, tickled so hard that up sprang Hiawatha with Minnehaha in his arms, two tawny brooms sprung from an opened closet.

.

10

I adjudge with rugged counseling I might cross that footbridge without jumping over the rail.

The unappetizing swell of the muddied water could appeal only to the truly desperate, the men with garters where stars were elsewhere strewn, or someone who got mixed up in his laces, or a shoe with a will of its own. Otherwise it was trudge trudge protected from the winter blast, but nudged along by cold, all the same. One remembered fireflies on the riverbanks and mosquitoes, the snow falling onto vanished wings, despair's equivalents of winter crossings.

Old Chinese men with shoulders bent under their thin kimonos passing over bamboo bridges. Mountain paths going ever upward into fog swirls.

.

11

Despising the heavy food that was going to give them all gout, as Arnholt always reminded Pedersen when they sat down at the long wooden tables in the University cafeteria expensively built to resemble a Swiss chalet (not a Chateau en Suède). There was such an anachronism lurking in the snakelike room that

Pedersen frequently mistook the potatoes in his soup for boulders and searched beneath them for the hidden reptiles.

The Art Classes above the basement cafeteria clumped about and dragged things across the floor. "Picasso's heavy easel," murmured Arnholt. "With Las Meninas on it," shouted Pedersen.

.

12

Prairie Houses

Unreasonable lenses refract the
sensitive rabbit holes, mole dwellings and snake
climes where twist burrow and sneeze
a native species

into houses

corresponding to hemispheric requests
of flatness

euphemistically, sentimentally
termed prairie.

On the earth exerting a wilful pressure

something like a stethoscope against the breast

only permanent.

Selective engineering architectural submissiveness
and rendering of necessity in regard to height,
eschewment of climate exposure, elemental
        understandings,
constructive adjustments to vale and storm

historical reconstruction of early earthworks

and admiration

for later even oriental modelling

for a glimpse of baronial burdening
we see it in the rafters and the staircase heaviness
a surprise yet acting as ballast surely

the heavens strike hard on prairies.

Regard its hard-mouthed houses with their
robust nipples the gossamer hair.

13

The problem proposed to the lemon tree. When
will your green fruit turn yellow? When shall I
understand Minneapolis?

If not grain by grain, at least loaf by loaf.

If not the river flow, at least its turn and tributary.

Still there are permissions to approach through that immigrant air.

14

"The refinement of what's special takes place between the meat and the
bun. N'est-ce-pas?" Signor Reboneri who was paying a visit to Minneapolis
(well recompensed) insisted on this point in his lecture.

He had been somewhat influenced locally by a visit to the "1½," a bar fre-
quented by Viking heroes, and his correspondences to the mythology of so-
called "cruder" peoples, or bluntly "sauvages," was somewhat tempered by his
excursions to the saloon. In fact, when dealing with the late Romans he was
hard put to call one of their conquerors "a barbarian." The myth of the blond

was gently settling over his own toga. He liked what he saw. The beer joint. The athletes still of medium weight, in their Attila hiatus, i.e. the hefty maidens and the food as junky as that served in a mead hall.

Those slides with pillars and capitals soon to fall, accommodating his lectures, trod under by these self-same mythic hosts, required apologies. Never had he lamented more the Roman Empire's Fall. Never in his own bed had he envied more those thighs so decadent, delicious and declining as now when confronting these tribes! These god-like men! These Vikings! These hairy arms, blond, not swarthy. And these limbs any Caesar should welcome, if only the brutal club were hid. As now it was.

Signor Reboneri lent his curvaceous smile to the peanut strewn floor and ordered another brew.

.

15

At the Guthrie Theater

The lengthy slow cooking of the Children's Opera "Lentils" caused some consternation among the paying members who constituted at least a tenth of the Theater's subsidy. The rest, naturally, came from a State grant which to everyone's surprise turned out to be as unlimited as the grain supply. Yet here one must give due respect to the administrative abilities of its director, a native son, who unlike transplants was not prone to the cultural shock suffered by administrators shifted from New York or Washington or an Ivy League campus to these local art enclaves from whence they viewed the unmistakable disaster areas of Minneapolis.

Au contraire, as the Countess would humbly say, Helm Wulfings and his assistants: Hnaef Hocings, Wald Woings, Wod Thurings, Seaferth Seggs, "Swede" Ogentheow, Shafthere Ymbers, Shaefa Longbeards, Hun Hetwards, Holen Wrosns, Ringweald Raider, are true Deors, heroes *vraiment*. "Their enthusiasm," she would add, "is catching." She used some other word than that, possibly, "*Ils prennent la couverture,*" but she meant their swordsmanship served us all.

.

16

"Amaryllis, favorite daughter,
I miss those long ago hours we shared, our mutual whisperings and field and
town delights. I pray soon you will answer my letter so that this separation may
find its fixity in the space dividing us, or rather, may enrich the space that sep-
arates us."

"Like cat's moans, draughts soughing under
wooden doors. Whistles on the river.
The plunge of a floe when the wild
garbage flew past,

> *yellow hair frost pinned . . .*
> *embers with their brilliant grins . . .*

The sickening passages from Longfellow
stinking up the night, carapaces,
nerve castles strewn with aches and crunches
where the roof bone began to sag and thin.

I am writing this to you Father to give a true description of what the
winter has been like:

> *not without pleasures altogether,*
> *disguised toes, heavy boots on the floor,*
> *the erotics of root cellars . . ."*

17

Persians in Minneapolis

They are lithe, slim, dark. They
travel up and down the elevators all
the way to the thirtieth floor like slim
geniis emerging from their bottles.

No one knows why they are in Minneapolis.

The spring leaves which are thin and small
like Persians are closer to them
than anything else in this vast
brokenness of upset structures.

These Persians have a continuity which they
have left somewhere else and
this makes for surprise and
puzzlement. Not only for the
Persians, but for us who stand so
tall and thick beside them in
the elevator admiring Persian
determination and finally not finding
it reasonable without rugs beneath its feet.

.

18

The sunroom in the house on the river bank with the heavy rolltop desk, the desk evoking Ford Madox Ford. He wrote: "We used before 1914 to have the simple old view . . .

> *Que toutes les joies et tous honneurs*
> *viennent d'armes et d'amour.*

But upon these lines one could scarcely now conduct a life . . ."

The desk in the Minnesota twilight that edged in through each window a light the color of the lemony moustache of Ford Madox Ford. From here "a simple old view."

In the galaxy of apprehensions present tonight restraining oneself from adding to what should remain simple . . . leaving Madox with its single "d."

.

19

(Scop—A Poet) *Widsith*

Scoping along the Mississippi. I a Scop. Coasting the Myth-West, musing the margins, earth yearned river wracked, grieving and groping, I a Scop making my weird. I saw many fellows, lithesome liquor hoarders, drawers of the dream, also riven by the river, daughter of the Rood. All have heard of the musicians ravishing, the museum-walker's mirth morsels, the lake Scops inland, inward impressing the bairns words, his ribbon of runes. Gusts from the Guthrie's stage spoken ear oaths, alas of an afternoon the wind sprung word tokens, host hoardings, sharers of sheaths, the frames of finished fine arts like jovial jousts surmounting the silence where prairie plumes cuddle and clash.

.

20

JOHN GRAHAM riding in his coach to meet the Countess stopped at the mansion of Larisnov on Summit Avenue for a sudden glass of tea. The two men strolled in the garden that overlooked the city of St. Paul commenting on the various fixtures and incompletions, the domes, the central plazas and that avid air of chance hanging, as always, over a capitol.

It was in that garden the laws of Minimalism as opposed to Baroque were formed and the great Futuristic statements came about, climaxing in "less is Mores" which led to a general razing of the remnants of the late nineteenth century that in their generous furry way were suffocating the capitol.

"Remember deterioration is embarrassing," added John Graham, (Ivan Dabrosky) and jumped into his carriage to continue on to his rendezvous with the Countess.

.

21

"This street reminds me of scarceness, even loss like searching for hen's teeth in the rain," murmured the Countess to herself as she picked her way slowly down Hennepin Avenue. "I feel frightfully sad somehow and truly lost. I wish I had a glass of sherry right now, only that would never do. I mean I couldn't drink it here on the corner. Look at that gutter. So muddy. The wind's from the Southeast which should mean . . . I never know what it means. The prairies confuse me so. Perhaps Liv will have a hot bath ready when I finally reach home. That and the new frock from New York with the twin reveres. I wonder how reveres shall look on top of mutton sleeves. There's venison for supper. And the St. Louis Dispatch with luck should have arrived." The Countess hesitated for a moment as the sidewalk drifted into dirt and her grey eyes filled with dust.

22

Seated at the mirror rolling up her hair, feeling the thin papers curling around her fingers, the air in contrast thick from the low glaucous clouds, the color of flour, her fingers twisting the papers into shapes like grain bins — cylindrical . . . exactly the shape . . . remembering those one passed driving out over the rutted roads. The same routes she often dreamed of as passages to better things. Such as a lime laden or elm heavy driveway poised within a privacy, a refinement, a collection of tested images with their fragrances not here in the grain struck air, the summits of flour rising like pillows over the landscape. And her imagination hastened to where all was still, aged, and quartered.

The curl papers were shredded, dropped onto the floor, parquet as she had wished, yet so disturbed by its removal here to Minneapolis, broken in spots and mended that the surface reflected a suffering which she shared and thus its beauty still in shine (like hers) did little to comfort her. She tore into the curl papers as she would attack a silo, knowing she had rendered them useless as the silo wrestled from its usefulness would in turn relinquish the fortune that yet sustained her.

23

   She waited. Within her limited mathematics she comprehended space. She understood the Dutch room in the paintings. The face behind the mirror. The walker in the dark. The captive tree. Not difficult. It was only within the picture she could breathe. A simple woman sat there wearing a cap, holding a pot. Another woman peered from a hall. You could sense how close the house was next door. The Countess worshipped that confinement, the enclosure of the scoured space. The eye never wandered far. The little mirror to tell you who walked in the street.

   From where she sat there was the lake and she looked out on it. The further shore was now ripening. After that the flats. After that the river.

   Her skin was growing rough. The wind placed a skull upon her face. Her face where it fell sideways had begun to toughen. It might grow to accommodate this life.

                                                                        .

24

   "What you need is a sophisticated cat."

   The Countess reread the letter. Then opening her escritoire she took pen in hand and answered:

   "Contact nearest available feline breeding — kennel — was it kennel — was it shed? Whatever. The sooner the better." And she would watch over it. It mustn't run wild, think itself a dog and have problems so difficult and different . . . especially those aristocrats. "Preferable non-pedigree," she wrote.

                                                                        .

25

The further exoticism of reading a British novel while visiting Duluth. The Countess usually "tucked one into her dressing case" when preparing for a visit to one of Theodoric's relations. The excitement of the Lake precipitated an unconscious association with former boating parties when she had been younger and, alas, inhabited a narrower world.

"Rather like reading of the River Niger while dining alone in New York," sympathized her cousin, Glanville.

.

26

When the scandal about Eofirth broke out the Countess vanished into her bedroom giving orders that no one should be admitted, especially Theodoric who would take it upon himself to bring her all the newspapers with the interviews, etc. One could hear, as if emerging from a shelf under old newspapers, the music, "Songs From The Auvergne," which the countess perversely kept listening to.

"Of course," she repeated as she paced the room, "Eofirth could not be guilty of any higgledypiggledy. He was always totally honest and with everyone with whom he had associated.

"Tax fraud! How absurd."

No one with his talents, a real artist, could ever be absolutely above board. Seduction, yes, and domination. But as for cheating! And money! He hid his money under those gilded coaches and in the rooms of those spidery summerhouses. Also in caves, she suspected, where the water might tease it a bit. He was capable of depositing sums with the captain who took the boat back and forth to Eofirth's island.

Eofirth. She remembered his first chess game. His first circus. His tears when age began to beckon those close to him. His first marriage and the scenes from his last one.

His was the only icy hand with any warmth concealed in it. It was he who had called her "my light in winter." Who had led her in a northern country to the first wild strawberry.

She hid under the quilt refusing to hear his impassioned, "I'll immigrate! I'll immigrate!" savaging the room.

Don't Eofirth, she cried, abandon me to these nerveless plains. This forgetful river. You who have made Christ swing from a tree. Who have commanded dwarfs. Never forget the loneliness of Strindberg in Paris. And never, like that other well-known exile, film the politics of loss.

.

27

Reality's tramline intruded.

"Köttbullar med gräddsky!" shouted Liv from the first landing.

The Countess arose. Dabbed her temples with Cologne 711 and seizing a small ripe cherry cane on which to rest the remnants of her grief, descended. The soothing aroma of cream, meat, and onion overpowered her remorse.

If only Eofirth were here to share the cranberry jelly and pickled cucumber.

.

28

"Everything I've told you is true," said Lars.

"But I want to see our son." When the Countess said "son" one almost heard a faint Baltic accent. Possibly. Language intensifies.

"I would never cheat you in the photographs. My lens are accurate. I only use the fog swirls when necessary. Lately I'm ashamed of those early pictures of him I sent you. They were too romantic. I even shot them in rooms with red walls. I've learned much. I can call his face and he responds. See how real, how much truth there is in this photograph of our son?"

"I wanted something more than the definition of a shoulder."

"I gave you his clarity."

"Yet in these pictures he is so quiet. I want to see him move."

"A photograph can only indicate. If this stillness broke, the picture would blur."

"I would love that blur."

"I cannot go against my craft."

"Then I can only guess how his head turns when it escapes his shoulder?"

"Yes. My camera gives you that permission."

•

29

Driving away from the logging camp, despite the severity, the opinions, the formalism which surrounded Lars, the Countess felt again that something heavier than air escaping her lungs. Later lying quietly on the pine needles while he arranged his camera, admiring, as always, his adroitness, the rapidity with which his preparations took place as just before the shutter fell his lens sheltered her face.

•

30

Outside through the window she believed she could see the prophet Elijah, his sunken face pressed against the glass, peering past the angular whisper of the blue flower petals.

.

31

It is here those lives with their difficult parts, their sidelines of disaster. My lot, even if I cannot reach them, yet I sympathize. My isolation is cushioned. From the prairie, the wind teasing the dogs. Someday within my fingers this skein will untangle. Then the region becomes a fairy tale with steeples and castles. Now there are sod huts. My broken slipper leaves few splinters on this path. Perhaps the moccasins . . .

.

32

      There was a poem with
A Moon in it travelling across the bridge in one
Of those fragile trains carrying very small loads
Like moons that one could never locate anywhere else.
The Mississippi was bright under the bridge like a
Sun, because the poem called itself the Sun also;
Two boxcars on the bridge crossing the river.

.

33

Countess:

Correspondences Peking-Tokyo their
comparisons and differences in her character

or the Shanghai-Peking axis

consult oriental arbiter

34

And still she said,
walking toward Crocus Hill Market,
one desires to live. I wish there
were wishes and not lists.
I wish vegetables were grown
by heart and artichokes would heal,
I wish this rhythm
of my approaching the butcher
were more than a knuckle
attaching itself to me
perhaps a crocus, a
root of limited possibilities,
yet promising a livelihood.

35

Crocus Hill

I had dreamed the night before I awakened that morning I would be on Crocus Hill. First we lost our way then entered the Freeway then left that for Summit Hill. Whereupon the towers of St. Paul stared up at us. It was interesting architecturally; geographically speaking, where was Crocus Hill? I was thinking about tomatoes, Apollinaire water, kidneys, sweetbreads, truffles, limes, Crocus Hill the finest grocery store in St. Paul. Finally after crossing, recrossing, submerging, indigent technical encounters of bumps — discovered. On the long polished counter expressive items breathed expressively and even husks luxuriated, cross pollinations from Eastern sources experimenting in historical fineries. From the counter the telephone rang.

     Madam! Immediately!
Choice! Prime! Tender! Aged! Fresh!

     Madam!

The Countess was ordering.

                                 •

36

Heliogobalus, Heliograph, Heliology, Helium, Heliotrope, Haiti . . .

The Countess scanned the map for Caribbean Kingdoms. Borrowing a piece of burlap she had been intrigued by its aroma of palms and her day began to be replaced by exotic blossoms and sea airs. That Chantey her uncle had taught her began to echo and she tried a limited sailor's hornpipe on the rug Theodoric had purchased in Constantinople.

She supposed after swabbing down the deck one might dance a hornpipe. If one were a Scottish sailor becalmed on the morning Sargasso Sea.

Idly, because she was often idle, she traced with her nail the mountain path up from the port, sheltering under one of those tropical trees as the rain blew up and birds fled past, their brilliancy lighting her face. Her skin's sallow inwardness turned outwards as unexpectedly the sun struck.

A toning like a tuning began to strum her nerves. Like an excellent massage this journey she was making. A purr sounded throughout the motor system. Sun piercingly yellow. Her face changed color and once more a tiny parade crossed her temples.

                                                                              •

37

Activities

Grain Belt Beer, He Who Gets Slapped, Vikings vs Dolphins, ice skating, fishing, Japanese food, meat, square dancing, collage, Rimbaud, New York Painting, Showboats, Baskin-Robbins ice cream, La Strada, Basement Studios, renting a house, visiting lecturers, tourist flights to Scandinavia, Crystal Court lunches, Dayton's cotton undies, leather shops, Indian crafts, jazz, blizzards, mosquitoes, Betty Crocker recipes, Lake Superior Poetry, silos, covered bridges, Artichoke Hall, brawls, aftermaths, forecasts, illegal turns, incontinent highways, building, building, building, razing, razing, razing, Milwaukee complexes, abandonment, lost frontiers, height, girth, pride, prejudice, toughness, agoraphobia, agoraphilia, alewifehood, navigations, symphonies, tornadoes, sauna construction . . .

nostalgia for the days when one searched for furniture those pre-Saarinen days. For some the pre-Aalto decade.

                                                                              •

38

The hints of ruggedness, such as the
window's slipshod, the twist where
the sash should have fallen true. Dark
objects falling. They were permitted to fall
because their characters at first were not
dark, merely fringes, one guessed. Later

when the axes appeared like meanings, we
understood but it was too late. "I have
explained this to you before, Countess, and
there were those wrenches at the end, whenever
Ingmar came to the conclusion of his story."
"Only a warning," he said, rising from where
he was sitting. "I cherish you."
She nodded, as was her custom. "I only bring
warnings like lesions, so you may know the true
nature of this weather." He kissed her.
And that, also, was his custom.

39

June

dust dust dust dust dust dust
only small rain small rain small
thin thin rain starved rain rin

40

She waited on the terrace for him to arrive, a small nut in its shell on the ter-
race. The little wife in a tale sitting in her rocker in her shell house. She read
stories and told them back again to herself, rehearsing, memorizing what she
was doing while she waited. The sun ripened, fell. The water receptive reflected
the illusions the sky was trying out; those illusions flitted away. The sky became
exhausted with its innumerable positions, its plans. And she, she curled up in
her shell and went to sleep, because somewhere else in the Village he had made
other arrangements.

41

Originally the Walker Art Museum was formed from the nucleus of the Walker Chinese Collection. Even now there is a minor space relegated to the once sacred and exotic collection. There are disturbing moments when one comes upon cities carved in jade, oarsmen, mountaineers, flocks of bird and cattle, tribes far from the palatial coastal cities. There is activity and there is repose and especially magical the jade mountain where:

> "In the beginning of the late spring, a gathering was held at Lan T'ing for the purpose of repairing the graves. All the celebrities came. At this place there were steep mountains and magnificent mountain ranges, heavy frosts and graceful bamboo plants. There was also a clear rapid running brook. One cup of wine and one poem were enough to bring out the hidden emotions."
>
> CHING DYNASTY
> 1784 A.D.
> (The Emperor Ch'ien Lung)

From here it is only necessary to mount the staircase thus transcending one hundred and ninety-two years to the sculpture roof garden where Tony Smith has bestowed his *Amaryllis*.

.

42

Amaryllis

The orange metal plant spread its tendrils aloof over the museum's roof. With all its fragrant captivity asserting the immigrant rites of sculpture.

Restrained by metal from whispering, from complaint, even from homesickness, Amaryllis with its antique name, its distant origins, held a regal stance.

Between its position and the blockades of the city, between it and the nearest reliquary there would remain no communion. Amaryllis would never yield its superior stance. Its moods, glances, were those of an observer less restless as time passed, yet one who possessed the claim to restrict its grace.

There could be detected something of the borrower here, rather than the lender, an attitude the Museum's curator recognized would never change. He questioned the effect of those regal metal blooms upon the visitors. He worried if the city were aware of the undisturbed and selfish enchantment Amaryllis cast. A piece of art that through a collector's whim had come to dwell in Minneapolis.

The Türler Losses

Türler patterns
        distinct as
        Palmyra ruins

Nighthawk

Peen   t   Pee n t
the shriek tenses when that shadow passes
"and midnight all a glimmer"

The crossed panes keep the shadow
peent is heard
in scraps   against   dawn
listen
               wind scraps
grass ashiver
       field   tree   profile
               Peen   t
take oath upon't
               Nighthawk gothic

The sun dropped its leaf like a sun diary
turning a page to shadow where the body lay
in the shrubbery. The body moved, but with a stilly
motion the way a wave curls over a birthday
where nothing remains except the foam streamers,
like giggles after deep laughter, like death closing in.
It should be falling, no tears. It isn't. Mournful?
Yes, the sand's ribbon overturning the shell. The mollusc
pause. Such prettiness the shell and drip of water,
later dryness lent to a shelf.

The body no longer moved. That body is a bird
without rhythm or tied to decanters.
making informal wind notations, then love.

Wristwatches surround themselves with danger.
Signs. Worn clasps. Their time flies, stops.
Gallops. On a street. Dropped like an egg from a tree.
Expensive signals flashed in moonlight. Semi serious
stones wearing themselves out on wrists reaching
for decanters.

I like innocuous rhythms, don't you?
Less isn't so important.
When nothing lies there wearing a ring,
even the Türler loses time.

Water's blue day in the pool
the lake beyond its rim, even that temple
quoting distance an hypothesis,
tricked by fog, three columns reduced to two.
Water's depth and splash
thought margins.

Today the children lived in syllables pushing rafts
pushing themselves, the clime of heads on them the sun —
balconies, a summer stroll to odalisques. Later
a strewn room, the actors gone, disappeared
the pottery flowers. Méchant.

I miss the sparrow heads. Heads dip into the pool
as that smaller mark of time the arrow on the Türler face.
Tone values important when pointing out the
landscape.

I'll take you back to the station. Later
there'll be time.

Butterflies are silly, "planes of illumination"

Substantial contents alert in tombs. Presences.
As loss is absence.

> "skipping along the Roman road eating
> a tomato . . ."

Encountering the marble exactitude of things.
The precise pared from the round, the nubile.
Dawn after nightfall fog . . . heavy semblance
sheltering like that chair. Waiting for balance.

> Moving into elsewhere music moves us
> to boulders.
> These columns. Shadows secure in thunder.
> As boats move thick against water, forests
> contained by sky.
> These are contents.
> Loss gropes toward its vase. Etching the way.
> Driving horses around the Etruscan rim.

After the second Türler loss
a lessening perhaps of fastidiousness
            the Timex phase
and who says the wind blows to hurricane
escaped virtue . . . or that indeed
Timex is ripeness
the scent of potato field

Time calls hoarsely for sorbets and gestures
of sparrow; when locked in rhyme the door
sways and whines like a thief,
"the thief of time" was the original fellow
pushed out there on the street, caught beneath a wave,
leaves brushing past and weed tumbled.
The wintry awful noises of sleep with empty
harkening, lids crossing cheeks like pines
swept outside the sun, glitter of parakeet
tickles the eve, an awakening from warmth,
breeze on the lamp and the ridge, something cold
like an ice counts the chimes.

Out of this the Türler face
throat against darkness, we say a nose
examines with dignity, gives thrust
the painter uses the nose like a trowel.
See there René Charl
Differs from the Goya nose Don Carlos
with a filigree of disaster.

The apparatus on knees, yes supplicating
behind the crystal, the olive light dims
as the ambulance beam brightens and the highway
sombre while time passes
like death on certain stars moments on the stairs
or twilight when sand darkens
the wave shaped like time at its lamppost
all shades drawn, the intact crystal

Pauses between apparatus and crystal.
Pauses examined like sand those areas
we examine while waiting.

"Time's fool."

Vases! Throats! Lactations!
The milk of time in the reservoir moon
                    Stones with cloud current as sylphs
in nightclothes swim, moon on thicket
stems climb vases, wastrels.

.

(I wondered if he had taken my poems away with him.
I could find no smell of it, the poem. I understood
the need to explore. Departure imminent. Landings made
every day. Fragile marks made firmer as the eyes adjust
to horizons. Perhaps even now the poems lay in his valise,
unpacked. Perhaps they were unwritten. The poems were
huddled somewhere. They might be picked over by now.
Tossed from bed to bed or hand to hand. Greasy, losing
the glossy surface. I still refused to believe they
would disappear like the Türler watches. He could not
be so careless as to drop a poem on the street, let it slip
from its black strap like a watch struggling, embittered,
neglected, slipped off the broken stem of a watchband.
I read the letter from a firm called "White Walls," the
revered immaculate surface on which words pleaded me to
place a photograph of my poem about a photograph or
leniently, if I wished, to send a poem pasted to a white
wall. I thought of the white poem I had written whose face
might even now be speckled with dust, and the white pen
used to which I attached the poem's name, "The White Pen."
Surely among the belongings in the kit where the shoe polish
was kept there might be my "White Pen" with cream in its
nostrils.)

More and more memory began to circumambulate the
Türler losses. It began with the arrival in Zurich.

Strained hotel morning. Enjoyment of balcony,
clouds. Descend to garden. Decision to take
trolley to grave of Joyce. Return by trolley.
Downhill trip by taxi to Zurich. Lengthy promenade
of Strasse. Decision to make first Türler timepiece
purchase.

(Will enact same motions for purchase of second watch,
deleting trip to graveyard. Insert instead taxi ride
to gallery. Lack money to pay taxi. Search for bank
which is located immediately thanks to monetary geography
of Zurich.)

Passage to hotel made difficult by rain, yet spot the
Nervenklinik.

A year later visit Strasse and buy second Türler
timepiece with further trip to railway station where
someone takes a train to a mountain. There is the
added vertigo enhanced by the Swiss currency exchange.

Little did I expect the following year to lose the
second watch at Lexington Avenue and Eighty-sixth
in Manhattan.

Nor did I foresee I would read the Zurich Journal by . . .

Hatching away in her nuttery, she came to a sign saying
FLING. Actually she was too troubled by heights to
throw herself over, but she did observe that tokens were
necessary, so she took off her old watch and FLUNG.
Immediately upon descending from the tower she ran into
difficulties in the person of Markie who asked her what
was missing from her wrist.

That evening when Junie brought in the shepherd's pie
there was more contretemps all agreeing that anyone
without a watch was unreliable, but that to lose a
watch was even more UNRELIABLE.

It was she who suffered the most. Alone on her ledge
there was no familiar tick-tock to comfort her. When
morning finally announced itself in the shape of over-
head spinning and clumping she resolved to go into
Zurich even if it meant encountering slipshod vowels all
the way.

The first part of the journey was free of hazard. Just
outside the city she met a kindly Zwinglian curate who,
taking his arm out of its sling, pointed in the direction
of his own watch and told her to bear slightly to the right.

The road branched and ricocheted. The noise of pebbles
pinched her ears. A small bird fell from its roost.
She could scarcely believe that these were the perils
of a city to whom exiles turned in despair and disgust.

Faithfully she pursued the curate's instruction and
in less time than it takes to read ENGLISCH SPOKEN
she had entered a shop where the second Türler watch
was purchased.

At home she recorded this event in her DIARY, JOURNAL,
LETTERS, and the Sundry Shopping Lists later discovered
nestling in the shrubbery outside her workroom.

Your loss softened by that golden
museum. By tales when sudden air pours
through the still castle. Birds sing difficult
songs no other birds can sing. The spindle
whirls and gossamer appears. Faces stare
in dark corners as from trundle beds we
converse in rhyme. Wishes newly pasted.

Soon the regular hours would be let in.

*Though nothing can bring back the hour**

What was the other look you brought?
Houses with gardens, laughter like
the necessary wreath?

*Wordsworth.

Wearing your Timex you gathered the October harvest.

Every inch dowsed by rain
pumpkins rotting and corn,
no tassel there, no sheaves
coves windswept. That summery wristband
blue and yellow faded like folded skin
voices overheard pacing acres
in the archery mud.

"We've all got to take our lumps."

You made the autumn ginger cookies

Sniggered like mules, kind of a dumb show.

Let that embrace last on the rim of the inkstand.
Wearing a white collar and the weight of it
holds you down like glare, like Zurich.

You are creating two watches.

You enter the laboratory. Look out for the watch
called "Never Loses."

(Later they embrace as winter slides over the sill.
outdoors we would wear snowcaps on our skulls.)

Don't interrupt.

Continued in the kitchen under the Seth Thomas.

Seemingly realistic codes have pointed to other
levels of images beyond their limits, ice
permitting time to decorate a block.

Likely rivers graduating into lakes the desolate curve
my image against your shoulder, the homespun
logic of our twosomeness, a fabric time
will displace the threads, a shrivel here,
there a stain, the rotting commences like lanes
of traffic hurtling into air as the sun comes down.

Subterfuge

When the tribal months
come trooping over the clocks

I'll have mine plain
or I'll wear the brown.

Another old magazine while something
darts into the shallows

Tensions as the clock strikes
muttering envelopes, envelopes
"clouds surround their faces."

Seeking the chute or drifting
these rafts hourless in the breathing
admire the quarter hour
brave sofas surround

Breathing test while we waltz
a curious toe pointed toward hours

Eyes with negative irises shutting
as the minutes fly
birds crossing the deep chambers

Shoes at the fireplace or homogeneity
decided while the drops
elaborated before our envious vision

A child entered the room
wearing a clock costume
A child of pigmy size
unmodified by time's blisters

And time's throat burrs and time's screens
across which time's numerals

Flash ruptures

.

*Look now forwards and let the backwards be**

1

Frost villages on the slope
that's the bell peal
icy mountain time!

Scampering to the inn carrying our pumpkins
best not to be late in this region
rites are observed
habits called "old as time itself"
women go coiffed.

.

2

Arriving at sea level he hands her a Valentine
named "Coast,"
the sky is white and grey like February

*Ouspensky.

the waves whiter while reflecting the sky
in patches of thickness that beat
on the coast with timely strikes
preparing sand exits.
She holds this landscape
the wet snow falls over it.

3

There were movements
in the garden with leaves and bicycles

Torpors suffered under cellophane
ripening and grasping

4

A bride and groom wait
beneath a canvas, cellophane
separates them from elements,
the groom steals a look at his watch
he would like to ride off
into the far bicycle spring.

Autre temps, autre moeurs

Yes I'd like to reorganize
the way it was in the October scheme.

A wrist for every watch
releasing doves

In the blown haze
a search for crystal

Broken glass

Biography

One

The people inside

> how to transfigure
> the way night transfers its stars

As heat nets this room

> where are we
> caught in the ruts
> where are they
> defused   withering?

The difficult stabbings
required by detection

> introspection arraigned
> a warning
> waves from the honied vaults.

A gliding outside getting out
beyond the old feathers

into the courtyard

postillions lay wait

Ready for racing the years
there were: transfers, excursions,
analyses clocked by their tears,

Irregular vines covering
the cottages
concealing the entrance ways

Pockets filled with words
mice sliver the curtains and wings
                beat.

Two

Did you locate the forms in the vests,
the particular bride's visit to the magistrate,
the divorces, were they hidden under twine?

Delving into the lime, unscrewing
taking out the corks at last discovering
the white shawl; not so much climate with
the exception of rain; a few good days
for bathing, the usual fog, however later
a wonderful isolation surrounded by plants
with doctors securing the ice lanes.

(When we foundered in the labyrinth of word
puns set like traps, and when the first Angel . . .)

The day it snowed on the statues and the light
whispered of coming to grips with the problem, of a thaw
when the sun lit the mounds, the sky grew blue as its
burden fell in drops and over my shoulder a new atmosphere
of comprehension, of desire, of yearning . . .

Three

An itch
           the width of an elbow
an urge
           really to "know"
when the flea entered the garment
anemonies
where were they picked?

Icy shadows
           grapes in the "goblets"
           the fabric ripped

An excellent "e" for evening
when the spicy shrieks sent out alarms,

           then a word like Egypt.

Four

> The reason for caterwauling
> on the stair was simple
> it went up and I went on
> of course the chamber was empty.
>
> But the view
> made up for the journeying
> although I don't enjoy real lakes,
>
> There's something there on the bottom
> like Galuppi with his music
> a kind of dead stick,
> it frightens me
> here on the fringe
> just beginning to discover the swans.

Idiosyncracies set out on the terraces — hers and mine.
A need to escape so we breathed separately, the air spun
into a pact, as wistfully the figures disappeared into —
Geneva — as the chairs reassembled themselves, hers
and mine.

Five

Yet another day
among the boxes

> what was the year of the prune
> whose telephone rang in the flat?

Dizziness shared
a hint of disgrace amid the pines,

The card said, "William Blake,"
yet the notes were from another clime.

Birthdates absconding
I read the stars.

This one of mid-morning
weaving its plume from the sky,

Again the Angel descends.

Tomorrows begin to wither
the ashes form their ring
and voices whisper,

There's sobbing too
behind the arras

And nuttiness hits me
a sting like rivers
you forget in the rain
their flash.

     Then you see from the window
     the physical features —
     the bangs, the brow, the frown
     where it lingers on its arithmetic
     of cities, trading symbols

     The archer, the Virgin, the Twins.

     Mutinies of celebrations
     like birds in aviaries
     or spies at the diaries,

               I read all that.

Six

To make it look so simple. Finding the bee in a cup, stone on sand, flowers flushed. Rhythms established with chants; shards decorated into vases where you looked for a winged foot. Using the same initials, repetitions of black, pitying the frock on the doornail and the clutter of letters that never came back, not even after you called, throwing out your plums, the uniform was attacked. It vanished with the lover and musical tree. Well there are the songs under the gorse.

     Still with the fresh heat
     of the child's body standing there
     in the sun without need of arrows
     or marble, the smell from
     a child's warm body.

Seven

This town I've bored into
while kidnapping the rooms
and being crude about it,
yet admiring the orange linoleum
the black chair.

I was proud of the snow
the way it struck at the statues,

Later the daffodil
found in the bronze buttonhole.

Seasons honoring the dead
and I among them honoring,

Avoiding their eyes
their thumbs,

A pretense at Roger de Coverley.

Eight

Biography a dubious route

    curate's disease
    the offhand way they plunge
    into the locker room

    subsidies for living,
    raven's wings shadowing the wall.

Deadly moon-struck

    weed-stuck
    gardens

the too calm sea.

Nine

A single seeming blinded object
   a sentence   a voice
        the throat
then the rushing. Sound rushing dramatic
away from its disability
there's a note selective.

Passage without a pen
through the hurricane
   whorl   shell   Shade

Fictions dressed like water.

Quilts

"Couch of space"

Thought nest where secrets bubble
through the tucking, knowing what it's like outside,
drafts and preying beasts, midnight plunderers
testing your camp site and the aery demons, too,
waiting to plunge their icy fingers into your craw
and you crawl under, pull the quilt on top
making progress to the interior, soul's cell.

Following the channel through shallows
where footsteps tremble on quicksand squiggly
penmanship of old ladies, worms with cottony
spears, the light pillared the way trees crowd
with swallows and then a murmur in the ear
as deeper flows the water. The moon comes out
in old man dress thoughtfully casts an oar.

You float now tideless, secure in the rhythm
of stuffing and tying, edging and interlining,
bordered and hemmed; no longer unacquainted
you inhabit the house with its smooth tasks
sorted in scrap bags like kitchen nooks
the smelly cookery of cave where apples
ripen and vats flow domestic yet with schemes
of poetry sewed to educate the apron dawn.

Not exactly a hovel, not exactly a hearth;
"I think a taxi's like a little home," said
Marianne Moore,

this quilt's virago.

2.

Initially glimpsing
an ivory Pharoah figure
First Dynasty 3400

> quilted for warmth
> papyrus for words

stitchery sophisticated after A.D.

　tribesmanship

> later religious jaws went boning
after Renaissance windows, the straw
harshness strikes hangings rebut

> then

up went those quilts soft with their clout
I'd like a little cloud here to nestle over the straw
I'd appreciate less straw　　more feathers
opposite types — straw and feathers
like the moon nestling on thorns

> words you see through windows
threstled words tousled "La Lai del Desire"

> Clouet of silks

3.

Egotistical minutiae of STITCH

> Gambeson
> Habeton　　　　MEDIEVAL
> Pourpoint
> Habergon

Worn simultaneously for protection
quilted medieval circuits

useless against fire
but charming and tender
as the wispy fingers
that stitched them

I like your hearth fire
it warms my fingers on
your useless currents

weaving obsolete war garments

    .

        •

4.

ON THE BRINK

IT WAS DISCOVERED THAT HERETOFORE UNCLASSIFIED
(WORN) ATTIRE MIGHT BE USED WITH MERIT, GRACE
WITH THE HOUSEHOLD ACCOMODATING

                    THUS USHERED IN
A NEW ERA FOR   PETTICOATS

cold in their flimsy   put them on the wall!

          WALL QUILTS

not so gaudy as Eyetalian velvet, but nevertheless . . .

          NOW A BIG SECRET

Sicily invented the first BED QUILTS!

          From then on
          it was into our beds

India   China   British Isles

Calico ancestors
snuggling under quilts

          "lozened over with silver twiste"

Calico ancestors
Calico Appalachians
Sniggled like Barney Google
Like Louisey

"Mutts Sneeze"

take 3 across   4 under   5 over   6 down
multiply
once use blue
twice red
third time white like autumn squash

5.

"Tomorrow is another day"
let the lawnmower grab those threads

"A porch is a place for sitting"
do this in cauliflower colors, not too elaborate

"My heart's in the Highlands"
let yourself go with calico

"The darkest hour precedes the dawn"
use father's overalls

"Will O" the Wisp
use your own gears

      (None of that Paisley
      spooking with gaudy thread)

6.

Old time seas of quilts

               coverings

in the gull dawn

            like picking up a sardine
on the beach   I see those tickling threads

minnows on muslin

7.

         QUILT NIGHTS

September equinox . . . people walking home
from the Pisan prisons . . . a luxurious shadow
quenching the star I wished on . . . "looney in me
loneliness," James Joyce. Goldenrod is bad for
hay fever. Is that all? Take the single
hollyhock. Kilt mosquitoes. "Green, abhorrent
slippery city," D.H. Lawrence. Socialist
creatures inhabiting moth skins. Insectophobia.
Pulling up to Reality's little northern curb.
Where reading — illustrated by — deposits one.

So sleepy.

8.

Fisherman's glove filed in a cornfield. Seen on
the way to Aunt Dinah's quilting bee:

Aunt Dinah

Phebe's visitor   Rebekah
from Chattanooga Falls

        Phebe   Nellie
            Liza   Sarah
            Emily Jane

        Quilting the Log Cabin Pattern: 1850

And there was moonlight on the road and Nellie gave
me her arm when I was seeing her home
he used to sing it at home after supper when we
were full of home cooking and I was reading Longfellow
in the near dark's gristle, before he left the farm
and settled in Fayatteville with a girl whose name
want Nellie. She had a dark embrace was what Ma said
after she had travelled twice to see them. But Ma
admitted the girl was mighty fair at stitching:

        THE AUTOGRAPH CRAZY QUILT

9.

Only consider, said my author, contemporary painters
who bear a resemblance to quilts:

                    Rauschenberg
                    Johns
                    Rivers

Reality could be their tassel
and Reality is there, that's what I think about a quilt
it's Reality, and it satisfied Rauschenberg.

Mushrooms on the village green
some white, some black,
some high, some short,
they gave a dimension to a pattern
weaving in and out in streams

that's Reality.

Once you start looking at real
mushrooms
you see art everywhere

            THE MUSHROOM QUILT FROM WATER MILL

10.

                THE TOOTH QUILT

Say farewell o tooth like the Isle
of Lump no longer will you be connected
to the mainland.

Remember the Gandy Bridge going to St. Petersburg;
I remember canals and other indecent crossings over
the mud-struck crocodile river where the inlets
produced their flowers and the quiet, poisonous
links discourse with roots.

So shall you be severed. No stamp will be saved
in your name. No equipages gallop up to the post,
as in Guernsey when Hugo was in exile and Julie
lay under a quilt.

It will be silent as a residence for those
recovering from the Indian sun, or others in seek
of doctors. Remembering, as one says in the twilight,
the banyan quilt with its twisted ropes, recalled
the throat like the senior building, all
was struck, the Occident, the East, a brightness
nervous when the tongue left its theatre,
there where the first quilted words crept out:
"like dying the definite loss."

11.

REVERED QUILTS

Yesterday Andreas came here and I showed him my quilt
of Lord Byron in Albanian costume.
"Ah! His was an unnecessary loss," said Andreas.
"I don't think so, not nearly so much as the untimely
decease of Shelley. There was a real loss. And just
think of all the unfinished quilts — I mean — poems
he left. I consider them ideal losses." I couldn't
resist setting Andreas straight.
He then surprised me by mentioning the grave of Gramsci
in the Protestant Cemetery in Rome. "Gramsci was a
great loss," he whispered.
I then nearly shouted, "Only to the Quilt Party!
And you didn't even mention the grave of Keats in
that same cemetery. I consider him a supreme loss
to romantic quilts."
"Well we would have lost him anyway, considering
what century he was attempting to live in," said
Andreas. Kindly he added, "I too consider Keats cut
off in his prime, dropped like silk into calico scraps,
one of the losses of all time."

12.

SUNFLOWER QUILTS

Sunflower quilts so golden
and so commonplace,
this makes their egos violent.

They are Scythian
and would nod you
gleefully off to troubles.

A row of sunflowers
covers me.

Blackbirds don't disturb them,
they have black eyes,
large like the birds who
rustle against their shields.

At dawn I like
their raggedy yellow ears
in my mouth

Like waking in
a field
after a dark sleep,
not calm but bright.

13.

FISH QUILTS

The fish arrives
with his eskimo quilt

Staircases
narrated by fins

14.

OTHER QUILTS

Commenced in February
finished in August.

Musicality

The wave of building murmur
               fetid   slough from outside
a brown mouse   a tree mouse.

                  two trees leaning forward
the thick new-made emptiness

                Naturalism.

           Hanging apples   half notes
in the rhythmic   ceiling   red flagged
rag clefs

               notational margins

              the unfinished

                    cloudburst

a barrel cloud fallen from the cyclone truck
they hid under a table the cloud

           with menacing disc

Leafs ripple in the dry cyclonic

levelled crusts —

for four hands   of chambered
breeze & cloud   design

her imposing composition of cloud weight

upon the sketched-in roof   small jumps over
the roofs

a sonatina
edges in like sand grains under the orchard trees

pitching marbled stripes
of dusk like casino awnings near a vast pool
or contrasting mountain elevation

light retires in gradations
flick and flutter

"a favorite view"

Gieseking's troll marks
follow gauze undeterred by erroneous
dew the piano reminds us

the wayside is littered altering
"try" into fog cast

      the suite of "remembering"

         in forest guise the "theme"
shy of Niebelung thunder requests the artist
who is shy driving her motor
watching big mountain thunder fall on shy trees

            the composition is shy

the example of cyclonic creativity equally devastates.

to sketch "A Favorite View" ethnically positions
      two strangers who join hands in a movie
            without sound

one leaps on the other's lap
        a cloud

or Purcell muslin intimidating in
anxious-less moments when thoughts provoke

drained hands
      lightning held to a border of trees

patient exercise of drawing a visible number
chromatically the structure unfolds
      a formal delicacy

when she hitches up her notebook and sits under
the Steinway the blue trees vanish.
         "the Willies"

cobbled breeze
a pearl snatched from its shell

in that moment

as the sky slowly

Musicalities

orchards in most of their
depth the stubbed mountain
a chain of miniature birds

you understand the euphemisms of nature
how the figure appears in still life

and you understand the creation of orchards

your hesitation is not forgetfulness
something else hides the view

Evanescence

the bather in the pool

Fair Realism

Wild Gardens Overlooked by Night Lights

Wild gardens overlooked by night lights. Parking
lot trucks overlooked by night lights. Buildings
with their escapes overlooked by lights

They urge me to seek here on the heights
amid the electrical lighting that self who exists,
who witnesses light and fears its expunging

I take from my wall the landscape with its water
of blue color, its gentle expression of rose,
pink, the sunset reaches outward in strokes as the west wind
rises, the sun sinks and color flees into the delicate
skies it inherited,
I place there a scene from "The Tale of the Genji."

An episode where Genji recognizes his son.
Each turns his face away from so much emotion,
so that the picture is one of profiles floating
elsewhere from their permanence,
a line of green displaces these relatives,
black also intervenes at correct distances,
the shapes of the hair are black.

Black describes the feeling,
is recognized as remorse, sadness,
black is a headdress while lines slant swiftly,
the space is slanted vertically with its graduating
need for movement,

Thus the grip of realism has found
a picture chosen to cover the space
occupied by another picture
establishing a flexibility so we are not immobile
like a car that spends its night
outside a window, but mobile like a spirit.

I float over this dwelling, and when I choose
enter it. I have an ethnological interest
in this building, because I inhabit it
and upon me has been bestowed the decision of changing
an abstract picture of light into a ghost-like story
of a prince whose principality I now share,
into whose confidence I have wandered.

Screens were selected to prevent this intrusion
of enacting light and add a chiaroscuro,
so that Genji may turn his face from his son,
from recognition which here is painful,
and he allows himself to be positioned on a screen,
this prince as noble as ever,
songs from the haunted distance
presenting themselves in silks.

The light of fiction and light of surface
sink into vision whose illumination
exacts its shades,

The Genji when they arose
strolled outside reality
their screen dismantled,
upon that modern wondering space
flash lights from the wild gardens.

La Noche Entra en Calor

Like a highway
it leads to the plaza

where this shadow rests
on a bench eyes closed
to the feral heat
or the smell of a nearby candle
dust forming
on its shoes like mice
who have entered their own
cathedral, of a neutral color
where it is not necessary
to repeat the liturgy
in either tongue.

Already activists
have set up their canvas
and a merchant within his store
starts his nap with a dream
of red, orange, he feels
color scratching his tongue.

And a cloud has appeared
like a wind, but of hotter
apparel because of the
concentration
Its heat burns the skin
of those dogs who take
shelter under it,
unwisely as they pant,
their tongues hanging out
like lemon trees
in the vague and growing
more vague distances.

These stretching and halting
measures remind us of trains
advertising "La noche entra
en calor," the trains
were the color
of the heat they disturbed.
Color or calor repeating
words that were also bird-like
stranded on legs against the stove
of many colors charming
the landscape.

The message of this
night was distributed
wrongly within the spectrum
of your eyes, its multi-
colors flashing.

You provoked the
night so that its
behaviour was that of
buildings whose color
which should be dark, black
in the night was not,
was lit up with an electric
substance that
was burning gruel
on your tongue that
could no longer speak in
any of the voices or the nuance of languages
distracting a stranger,
because the night was indecisive
about its color and
the heat translated incorrectly
so it burned too brightly and far too
long a time.

The mice became crisper,
crisper as their organic
eyes burned the shoe leather,
coals finally, even as

Stones fell from
the cathedral
when dawn began
to shift its body
against the glow
in which ceases
the idle color of night.

The View from Kandinsky's Window

An over-large pot of geraniums on the ledge
the curtains part
a view from Kandinsky's window.

The park shows little concern with Kandinsky's history
these buildings are brief about his early life,
reflections of him seen from the window
busy with preparations for exile
the relevance of the geranium color.

Partings, future projects
exceptional changes are meant to occur,
he will rearrange spatial decisions
the geranium disappears, so shall a person.

His apartment looking down on a Square
the last peek of Russia
an intimate one knowing equipment vanishes.

At Union Square the curtains are drawn
diagonals greet us, those curves and sharp city
verticals he taught us their residual movements.

The stroke of difficult white finds an exit
the canvas is clean, pure and violent
a rhythm of exile in its vein,

We have similar balconies, scale
degrees of ingress, door knobs, daffodils
like Kandinsky's view from his window
distance at the street end.

The Thread

Welcome brutal possessor
of the memory cards,
on the wall under wainscoting
a nail holds the thread.

Allegories ranged invisibly
variances of touch
lapses in speech
the urn burial containing ashes
of belonging to lightning.

We have not taken heroines
to snow, thrust hair under waterfalls,
we sent them to museums
they own splendid eyelashes,
giantesses who wear no clothes.

Sharing mineral fasts
to extend our eyes vertically
we advance beyond
an expectation of number
in bodies that swim at the last moment.

This concern for time
exists in memory cold
it is innocent of earth that suggested you.

Ilex

From the doorway we watched. Alexander
at the basin washing   his face shone
              in bottled water from the green doorway.

                       ~

Qu'ad Ashir besieged   the iris in bud
blue water with blood   camel shackles
then a comet fell said the astrologer
        castle emptied   yellow bonneted meadow and bone.

The mountain covered with sharp ilex
locally a spiky plant called holm

Iran heresy like manna
on the giant winged eagle rock

damascened

    oasis lily of silk knives   Babylonia.

~

His passion for abstraction is gripping —
the phalanx in bird leather —
when you parted the copper-eyed leaves the armor
squeaked   sparrows in   modern setting —

    looking out from the invisible
    into the past without heads —

    gifted with "living" —

~

    White daphne   Thrace silvered
ghost trained hares in the young snow patches —
    lit by fir-cloud   risible Danube
where it widens   blaze of hunted water at horse teeth

    ode grouping
    Illyrian sequence —

apprentice oars.

Alexander's "greatness" — a linnet

~

                    from a floating rock.
three bathing maids   ilex tangled
mauve bassarids —
cavorting   thump
across jealous   sands   the warriors

            Olympias rakes the mirror.

      (the noisiness of maternal fame)

            boisterous geographically
                married in tumbled red
            and appropriating mythic comfort
                endlessly Hellenizing
            in a jeweled casket his guarded Iliad
                    hero wooing.

                    ~

            He wears pleasure trousers
                olive bird —

nomadic filter — the harsh bridals —
            sand eclipse Oxus . . . .

        "Beyond the limit of our world"

        we beg for lustered sleep — Argival —

                    ~

    psychogenic   they live as if alone
    with a shadow thief   Macedonians move in innocent

oil lamp   "esthenia"

now he is called the God of the East —
        ilex forgeries — elegiac

                    ~

He comes to a Babylonian garden feverish
beside the pool — "thirty-two years old and
six months" —

            over-stepping Aegean wideness —

We inquire of the night God if we should move
him to the temple . . . . the answer is "no" —

                    ~

white palms . . . . molded lattice —
Sirius — are his watchers —

        we wait in bronze liquid air
with the pull of soft knots

                    ~

            we lost him. he disappeared.

rinds of gold   stitched to his aura —
at the entrance armed with blocks —
the stylus blunt —

            mood of helmeted star light

Spring Vine

Fresh I thought a bird
lighted and fell downward
so bending the vine,
climbing it reaches the windowsill
direct, obsessed, insouciant.

A paragraph written to instill
in you the objective lent
to a corrected mind,
a man whose name
may be Carruthers takes his umbrella home.

The eye reaches more or less
evasive solutions,
iodine passing for a cloud
a pair of sheets afloat in the aimless sun

Medieval Columbine
amid dove-like petals
married girls water her.

Dora Maar

1

A woman weeping about an imaginary fall from a bicycle
"the bicycle has been stolen," he knows
it waits outside her door, asleep
a piece of *tailleur* on the brake: —

"*her hair was all disheveled and her clothes were torn*"
enemies had grabbed the wheel, they upset her and threw
her to the ground, she said
she had a knob on her forehead from the fall —
when he places his hand there he finds nothing
only the shift of veins he once painted.

This girlishness should feed on mirrors,
if there had been a fairy tale . . . to influence
her noise about damnation and enemies,
mystical exhortations he dislikes —
she moved about the room so nervously,

She tells him to repent:
"you are a cactus of stars."

2

In a cafe he watched her throw the knife
between the fingers of a gloved hand —
her character pasted with drama,
lights of rhinestone green . . . .

he is the collagist who admires the gloves and green . . . .

3

At Antibes they stroll the narrow streets
watch the night fishing —
her noble forehead is a sand cap water deftly clears,
one of her eyes is red, the other blue like a portrait
of Marie-Thérèse though bolder
with brunette make-up similar to *a poem by Eluard*
where black runs out of color . . . .

He sees her as *the woman who weeps,*
her tears benefit his painting —
when he made the bull
or a woman flinging her hand from a window
she was that woman holding a light

She was the woman who fell from the house
in the daylight bombing —
She photographed the hysterical success
stage by stage with her alphabet of sighs
without liveliness —
her tears damage the heirloom.

4

once he had drawn her torso with wings
afterwards she saw the river
with a translucent depth
when her arm was a wing . . . .

she changed into the oryx he shadows.

5

Her appearance is meddled with like *Io*
the tears are mother-of-pearl —

Eclectic and careless like Jove when changed
into a bull he finds the classical
screams of maidens exciting . . . .

He raids her hallucinatory bicycle for an object
he calls "found" as the handles and bicycle seat
are transformed —

Jovian in dispensation of property —

6

She was given a farmhouse filled with spiders
in a land of dried raisins —

The invisible occult is her halo and hangs over her
when she washes linen — as she tends the smudge pots
she is guarded —

Sweetness returns to her scorched tongue . . . .

Once she had known people who enjoyed verbal pleasure
and employed long sentences to restore their grandeur,
or stanzas to refine the lyricism of their meandering —

These artisans are valued by the medieval stone in
the holy village where even a dove is made of stone

The old weights — sand, a limpid ceiling,
blunt charcoal lift

Grief is banished from her coveted roost.

An Emphasis Falls on Reality

Cloud fields change into furniture
furniture metamorphizes into fields
an emphasis falls on reality.

"It snowed toward morning," a barcarole
the words stretched severely

silhouettes they arrived in trenchant cut
the face of lilies . . . .

I was envious of fair realism.

I desired sunrise to revise itself
as apparition, majestic in evocativeness,
two fountains traced nearby on a lawn . . . .

you recall treatments
of "being" and "nothingness"
illuminations apt
to appear from variable directions —
they are orderly as motors
floating on the waterway,

so silence is pictorial
when silence is real.

The wall is more real than shadow
or that letter composed of calligraphy
each vowel replaces a wall

a costume taken from space
donated by walls . . . .

These metaphors may be apprehended after
they have brought their dogs and cats
born on roads near willows,

willows are not real trees
they entangle us in looseness,
the natural world spins in green.

A column chosen from distance
mounts into the sky while the font
is classical,

they will destroy the disturbed font
as it enters modernity and is rare . . . .

The necessary idealizing of your reality
is part of the search, the journey
where two figures embrace

This house was drawn for them
it looks like a real house
perhaps they will move in today

into ephemeral dusk and
move out of that into night
selective night with trees,

The darkened copies of all trees.

Valuable Mörike

Mozart's journey to Prague
the value of Mörike his long gaze
words leading to escapades
piled against the carriage window
substantives ingratiating so dogmas
in the marigold basket droop,
visual wishes keep us waking
the wire basket deposited near home
immortality in the spun sugar
fragments littering grass moons,
the syllabub dark lifts a slow aster
unfolded a letter begins, "Palomar."

    Palomar searches for Mozart
    in the garden behind the sprinkling system
    where Mozart impishly drinks his wine,
    reads an old alphabet of signs
    and makes notations with the dried
    ink of a quill his dutiful wife
    placed in his portmanteau, hiding
    while the brightness of inspired sips
    touches his mind. Mozart likes
    the caress of genius it feels
    like moccasin skin, the soft patina
    belongs to musica dell'arte,
    Palomar to the fictive stars.

    "Valley ghillies laced by sponsors
    more sheep's ears to be shaved
    in the rural squiredom pastoral quirks
    lay intimate decoys, voices without lumps"
    an accent not unkindly Palomar's
    tonal glimpse of mountain trees
    like umbrellas fading, verse crowding
    their spinet, the stanzas
    piquant gait of rhyme and toasts.
    Palomar on the memorial stone smiling
    at distant Mozart the plum of Mozart
    in his hand and Mörike holding a small wren.

German (Swabian) lyric poet and reluctant pastor, Eduard Mörike (1804–1875), was devoted to the music of Mozart. In 1855 he published a prose homage, *Mozart's Journey to Prague.*

The Rose Marble Table

Adoptive day replenished by shadow
chooses octagonals such as chatter
and swimsuits at an angle
where smiles become orange.

Sea whose translucence disturbs inferior atoms,
that passage from ice to shallow removes familiars
as glass changes to foam, the parallel lake diminished,
combs drop into fur.

Between sea and lake a shape manneristic residence
of blue, pool waits the diver shock. Sylphs
luxuriate in ripples seasonal branches they tease
the spread of trained water, their silks reply yes then no
their dive provokes,

Gentle disruptions on certain days ruminating in
clear water, thoughts trailing the slap integrating
there with east of lake the westerly sea at heel
pool repeats an omen in sky dip,

Emotive waters possessed by bodies their octaves
glide on marginal air, light weighing its touch
here and thither to an arc of shapes and drips
from wings. Couperin wades to his rock,

Branches graze and sink, an unsettled stress
pleads antic decline, let the dead limb fall
imminence remains arms flung into dirt alarms.

Creative soul you hesitate, I with my hand
on the rose marble table, like you a difficult creature
ignoring the universe, igniting shadows. Gulls
over porches, bamboo familiars mine.

Ultramarine is cold it shivers
until the scumbled white of foam distributes
wilfully from sea to lake to pond we watch
heads revel in occasional dips
while background thoughtful water frames sestinas
they repeat a sobriety like a rose marble table.

Supple nature declares texture lends
formality to words a flight of marble
can rearrange the speed of waters,
we pass hands upon its surface and embrace
the creative object, throbbing waves fly over.

Shuffling Light

Dawn has other obligations
and is preparing them for us.

That I can see, shifting in bed.
There are ignoble thoughts running
over to that corner and that.

Ideas of much simplicity,
like threads in the sheet which
tie it all together, obeying
commands other than beauty.

The clock tick and the cat meow,
a wrist above the coverlet.
A book slides off a table,
pages marking no page,
unfavored literature.

Light shuffling across the ceiling
with a careful tread, making mush
of history. It reminds us a name

changes several times when it crosses
those borders that bring barriers
to speech, voices would enjoy
profiles on which to rest

In figurative space engaged by others,
the spoken wish for a violin.

The Screen of Distance

1

On a wall shadowed by lights from the distance
is the screen. Icons come to it dressed in capes
and their eyes reflect the journeys their nomadic
eyes reach from level earth. Narratives are in
the room where the screen waits suspended like
the frame of a girder the worker will place upon
an axis and thus make a frame which he fills with
a plot or a quarter inch of poetry to encourage
nature into his building and the tree leaning
against it, the tree casting language upon the screen.

2

The telephone is Flaubert's parrot and it flitters
from perch to perch across the city. Or someone
is holding the dead thing in her hand in a remote
hotel. A sensitive person with a disability who
speaks to the inanimate. She may even resemble
Louise Colet or the helpful niece. She hasn't sent
her meaning and I am absent in these reminiscences
of her. The telephone is the guignol of
messages.

It may have been cold moving down from roofs,
a continental wind caught between buildings.
Leaves and pollen blowing onto fire escapes.
Windstruck hambones lying in a gutter. Equinoc-
tial changes the body knows, the hand feels, the
truck passes without notice and buildings con-
tinue their nervous commitments. The earth may
have been moaning underneath this junk. I am
caught in the wind's draft.

3

At night viewing the screen of distance
with shadowy icons framed by light
I understood the rasping interior
was rearing other icons,

No longer gentle they flashed ripened clauses,
or images raised formidable projections of ice,
the wall was placed in a temporary position
where words glittered from a dark cover,

Narcissism lived in a silver hut.

4

In the lighter time of year words arrived
concealed in branches. Flaubert exchanged
himself for words, night became a night of
words and a journey a journey of words, and
so on.

Words became "a superior joke," I trembled
under a revolutionary weight, a coward fleeing
from a cloud. The ego of words stretched to
the room's borders assuming the sonorous
movement of a poem.

5

I entice this novice poem with a mineral, *Beryl*.
The dictionary bestows on Beryl a skittish description,

    like a sequence in which a car
    moves over ruptured roads and slices
    into ghost veins of color —
    a camera follows each turn,
    examines the exits where rock protects
    a visionary tool that prods it: —

    "A light greenish blue that is bluer
    and deeper than average aqua,
    greener than robin's eggs blue,
    bluer and paler than turquoise
    blue and greener and deeper than beryl
    blue—a light greenish blue that is bluer
    and paler than beryl or average turquoise blue —
    bluer and slightly paler than aqua."

The speculative use of mineral prevents an
attachment to words from overflowing, inserts
a vein of jazz, emblems of color and overcomes
the persecuting stretch of racetrack where words
race their mounts . . . .

6

Beryl became a distraction as one speaks of color
field or someone as a colorist or of color pre-
dominant, so the paper on which the poem would
rest was grainy with color flashing lights
and the depth, the deepness of the country lane
on which shadows found repose was a wilderness of
color, ditches and trees lost their contours. I
created a planned randomness in which color
behaved like a star.

.

7

To introduce color to form
I must darken the window where shrubs
grazed the delicate words
the room would behave
like everything else in nature,

Experience and emotion performed
as they did within the zone of distance
words ending in fluid passages
created a phenomenal blush
dispersing illusion . . . .

.

8

A difficult poem intrudes like hardware
decorating a quiet building, a tic taking
over the façade, a shrug exaggerated by a
column —

Shelley sailing into the loose wind,
the storm of neurosis hindering the formal plan,
a suggested dwelling left on the drawing board
with clumps of shrubs indicating hysteria or,

Daylight gleams on the rough street where a
blameless career sighs, the poet beak dips
in air, his little wings cause a mild stir,
as someone comes down the stair
he pleads with infancy,

A woman speaks to a dish, old forks, amid her
preparations she smiles touched by history.
Chipped, sundry evidences of temporal life
hiding in a bush. In formal dress domestic
remarks reel into a corpus known as stanzas.

9

The Bride raised the cloud settled on her
aspen head and stepping away from her bachelors
she seized like wands the poem I handed her:

       "A life glitters under leaves
       piled for anonymity . . ."

She would lead us through glass to view the
enigmatic hill where a castle slung a shadow.

10

There was a dream within a dream and inside
the outer dream lay a rounded piece of white
marble of perfect circular dimension.
The dreamer called this marble that resembled
a grain of grecian marble, "Eva Knachte,"

who was blown into the dream by the considerate
rage of night.

Her name evoking night became a marble pebble,
the land on which she rested was the shore
of the sea that washed over her and changed
her lineaments into classic marble, a miniature
being, yet perfect in this dream, her size
determined by the summer storm with which
I struggled and seized the marble.

The marble was a relic, as were the movements
of nature on the poem. The sea had lent
a frieze, waves a shoulder when the investitures
of a symbolic life feuded. In that dimness
with bristles, straw, armor plate, grotty
Alexandrines there appeared a mobile fiction . . . .

•

11

A man who calls himself a Baron yet strays from
his estate into the cadmium yellow
of a bewildering sunset rendered by apprehension
where a broad approach to a narrow tunnel
is fanned by leaves is faced with a decision ——
at the stylized ominous entrance he wonders
if reality will maintain him or empathic snow
subdue his quest . . . .

•

12

I sifted through these fictive ambiguities
until there was a plain moment
something like a black table where

Dialogue set in motion urged a search
in memory for that tonal light
illuminating the screen,

The Baron faded as distance gleamed
a clear jar multiplied by frost.

Heavy Violets

Heavy violets there is no way
if the door clicks the cushion
makes murmur noise and the woman
on the sofa turns half in half out
a tooth slipping from velvet.

The world makes this division
copied by words each with a leaf
attached to images it makes of this
half in air and half out
like haloes or wrists

That separate while they spin
airs or shadows if you wish,
once or twice half in half out
a real twirl jostles there
lips creased with violets you wish.

The Farewell Stairway

after Balla

The women without hesitancy began to descend
leaving flowers —

Ceres harried — bragged of cultivated grain —

I saw Hecate. the gray-wrapped woman.
in lumpy dark.

farewell eyes revolve —
the frontier oscillating —

pleated moments.
Hades at the bottom —

~

they laughed like twins their arms around each other
the women descending —

birds dropping south out of wind.

I thought there were many. good-byes twisted
upwards from the neck —

tiny Arachne donating a web —

~

a common cloudy scene. no furniture.
a polished stairwell —

women magnetized. moving. chatting.

responding to the pull —
the vortex —

~

curves rapidly oscillating —

undulating to rapid pencil lines.

or water —

the look of stewed water.
sensuously.

and gnarled Charon —

~

their clothes — volumes —

folded over. blowing.
dresses approach the wide pencilling —

Hecate was present
and that other woman looking backward —

tearful. holding onto the rail.

I saw it futurally —

stoppered cotton slowly expanding. released.
sliding from the bottle —

~

I was outside the vortex. close to the wall.
            Hecate managed me —

                        at the curve. the magic.
                        floated up — spiralled —

                    ~

they were fully dressed. their volume.
the modish descent —

            antiqueness —

                    ~

a roman *scala.*

            in the neighborhood of the *stazione.*

                        gli addii — gli addii —
                        velocity —

            whipped the waves.

the vortex centered. reverent.

                    ~

you who are outside. over there.
can't feel the pull. it makes you wonder —

the oscillation. the whirling. urgent.
indicating air revolving in a circuit —

without interruption. free movement
in *cielo puro* — spider-less —

       scatters everything.

something overheard — beyond Lethe.
whispered — and the corollary —

       ~

       diminuendo on the stair.
       the slowed *salutando* —
       flagrant barking from the shore —

keeping a stylish grip on themselves. serapes.

       futurally extended.

       ~

       south dusk and fire balls —

the same at Nauplia. mythic potency —

       winding down the tower —

       farewell. farewells.

Words

The simple contact with a wooden spoon and the word
recovered itself, began to spread as grass, forced
as it lay sprawling to consider the monument where
patience looked at grief, where warfare ceased
eyes curled outside themes to search the paper
now gleaming and potent, wise and resilient, word
entered its continent eager to find another as
capable as a thorn. The nearest possession would
house them both, they being then two might glide
into this house and presently create a rather larger
mansion filled with spoons and condiments, gracious
as a newly laid table where related objects might gather
to enjoy the interplay of gravity upon facetious hints,
the chocolate dish presuming an endowment, the ladle
of galactic rhythm primed as a relish dish, curved
knives, finger bowls, morsel carriages words might
choose and savor before swallowing so much was the
sumptuousness and substance of a rented house where words
placed dressing gowns as rosemary entered their scent
percipient as elder branches in the night where words
gathered, warped, then straightened, marking new wands.

Twilight Polka Dots

The lake was filled with distinguished fish purchased
at much expense in their prime. It was a curious lake, half salt,
wishing to set a tone of solitude edged with poetry.
This was a conscious body aware of shelves and wandering
rootlings, duty suggested it provide a scenic atmosphere
of content, a solicitude for the brooding emotions.

It despised the fish who enriched the waters. Fish with
their lithesome bodies, and their disagreeable concern
with feeding. They disturbed the water which preferred
the cultivated echoes of a hunting horn. Inside a
mercantile heart the lake dwelt on boning and deboning,
skin and sharpened eyes, a ritual search through
dependable deposits for slimier luxuries. The surface
presented an appeal to meditation and surcease.

Situated below the mountain, surrounded by aged trees,
the lake offered a picture appealing both to young and
mature romance. At last it was the visual choice of two
figures who in the fixity of their shared glance were
admired by the lake. Tactfully they ignored the lacustrine
fish, their gaze faltered lightly on the lapping
margins, their thoughts flew elsewhere, even beyond the
loop of her twisted hair and the accent of his poised tie-pin.

The scene supplied them with theatre, it was an evening
performance and the water understood and strained its
source for bugling echoes and silvered laments. The
couple referred to the lake without speech, by the turn
of a head, a hand waved, they placed a dignity upon the lake
brow causing an undercurrent of physical pleasure to
shake the water.

Until the letter fell. Torn into fragments the man tossed
it on the water, and the wind spilled the paper forward,
the cypress bent, the mountain sent a glacial flake.
Fish leapt. Polka dots now stippled the
twilight water and a superannuated gleam like a browned
autumnal stalk followed the couple where they shied in
the lake marsh grass like two eels who were caught.

The Nude

Studios are stations of reminiscence
in the nimble wind they are shadows

The artist attaches himself to the shadow
he attempts to revive it after the wind ceases,

This mixture of dark and light
is mysterious and adds depth

To the position of his model
who rephrases the shadow.

She reminds him of attitudes
beyond the mere appraisal of subject,

A peace without clothes
with its bestowal of light and volume

Where nudism is born.

The behavior of the landscape of nudism
varies as mirrors reflect

Curves, syllables of grace,
drops of water or trees elastic,

A native body beneath its plumes.

Is a weight become effervescent
when attacked by knowledge

Of shells and other remainders
of sexual consciousness tossed from sand,

They live in a contradiction of time.

The narcissism of the artist escapes into a body
that defines his emotions,

An interior where his own contour is less misty.

The figure is a nominal reminder that existence
is not pantomime as relieved by the artist,

The body of the model, the lift of her torso
the extension of limbs, fold of skin

Express reality beyond tenure of the brush,
shell or escapist sail,

A severe distance is established between her realism
and his anxious attempt to define it.

The painter desires the image he has selected
to be clothed in the absolute silk of his touch,

Lonely himself he has admired the glance
of kimonos, mirrors, fans and bestowed them on her

Who for many minutes of this day
borrows from art to cover her nudity.

The artist chose these objects to enrich space
around his model's hair or even her breathing

Which you notice as it shifts the atmosphere
in which you keep watch with a calm become necessary,

You are the viewer and without you
the picture cannot exist, the model shall cease to breathe.

The artist will sorrow even as darkness
replaces his brilliance of color.

The viewer inherits this nude
as a reminder of his own weightlessness

In a natural world
made winsome, or tense or aggravated

By the requests of an unclad body
with its announcement of dimension and clarity.

The need of the artist to draw the body
is like the love for three oranges,

He searches the world to find those spheres
that will confine the fluid nude,

There is with him a desire elemental
in its urgency to savor the skin of the body

The hues of geranium before they exit
his allotment of reality.

As the swan entered Leda
so the actual timing of an artist's abrupt gesture

Is supernatural despite interferences
of local ornamental mundaneity,

The supernatural contacts ecstasy hidden
in a guise of nudism.

The artist borrows mannerisms and technique,
he is free to copy, the other world is ambitionless.

An aura once restless now subsists
through residual favors on reverence,

Eve stands by her cypress,
a quiet nude studied by Cranach,

The solid body is led through crocuses.

You are with an artist who notices everything
which concerns color and shape.

In the restaurant the artist says a blouse
you are wearing goes with the decor.

The blouse is a watery blue like somewhere
off the coast of Greece, like these walls

The colors you wear tumble into mild earth tones
again like a country, nothing literary

Where the rough body reaches out
a wave rushes over the sand denuding it

You share the classical nude landscape of sand.

At times a silence overcomes the artist,
a fog at the base of columns,

He explains he is thinking of the body.

Its behavior is strange, hiding behind leaves
he can never trap or bribe it.

So deep is the body's memory of self.

Each day there is a different voice,
today while wearing no clothes

It spoke of the essentials of life which were evident,
but the body took an invisible position,

It is arguable whether he shall ever see the face,
her back was turned from him like a goddess

She was either admiring herself or bathing.

Morning traverses her breasts
where she sits under the window of white curtains,

Trees are outside, their branches fix the sky,
she is thinking of nudism,

He draws an odalisque,
it is love they are asking for.

She looks at a canvas,
nature covets it,

Where a fever blots the muslin
clouds start to rise.

There is no figure.

This is landscape,
portrait of nude melancholy

Or its glow which is austere,
she asks, where am I?

He has not drawn her,
the sheen of her body only survives.

She turns herself into a star
above the unattended foliage,

He views her as she glistens,
silver enters the picture.

He confides,
"Each day I define myself."

He notices a coarseness of flesh,
he thickens his paint,

"It is a glimpse into the future,
fields light up," she sighs.

To replenish the sallow on her throat
he adds sunset tint

She reaches for ombre, noir
"It is the narrowness of time."

Respectful moonlight inhabits them.

Western Additives

More goatlike than the other
this seen as rock
the other stair.

The radiant usefulness of these terms
remain in the fiddle hidden by a cane
the tune unplayed the hall unlit,

As a canyon strip where stairs
welter in subtle growths of raggedness,

A bureaucracy of seamed myth
having horns not names but mental
widths of triassic bottoms,

The nearness whips solos into shape
an ignored valve whistles as it listens.

In Medieval Hollow

                      Smother
floating in air headgear lit
                  "Light,
splendour, beauty, form, rule of the world"
                        Alan of Lille.

Dwarfs assemble with hook and thong,
tracing rivulets, plane trees, tidying rooks,
passing papers, muddling Thomistic drafts
while monks shift their garments and a thud
says fallen dwarf "ach" cries the priest
over the ink blot he has ruined November and
the plowing . . .

Aflutter with pagan tales the Mong Chieftain
spreads his rug the acrobat turns milk weeps,

From turf and dugget
hospice in a wafer
evensong alone in swaddled clothes she holds

No more trees
building on top of building
the archbishop fetched by a donkey.

Medieval surrenders by tallow light
labbed and lobbled into cellars
strew garters tightening the gyre

Simples sail in light hosen
their glides make a run for the moat
before it closes for the bridge crowd
in dank and fuses,

Plunging into a hollow
a hoard limits profits on sibilant limbs
and gaited throbbers braiding hair
look at the vision sitting on mud.

Under the bowed blue
in rhythmic joust pattern shadewise
gauntlets toss lances the moon
rises edging green Mundis,
gentle equerry the plague killed him.

Shut off that inner sound,
a fierce place needed douce
more than amethyst
dealt a rat lust,

Living in a medieval hollow
went into tatters

Mute tambour mute viol
thrown out of the welkin.

Bleat

drawn on the burden of light
the pottery throw
in bleat turning

ballast makes fingers twitch
shutters close
"going to pour"

wet to root and pavement
tent sagging like an oyster

"the city has another soul"

gnat passes someone swallows
"another soul"

figurines

"the city also"
stole the bench and echoes

blight and shuttered bleat
soul chews a wilted corner

Ropeo Sway

And chevettes like geese. The rumors. More
porridge says Sinful opening the case of twilight
soup, onions and small grains with an oysterish hue,
memos.

I have promised a greater catch, something off
the tide in yellow enveloped with whisper discs
rolling between lobster shrills,

This brings click clack into the morning,
the planets Jove and Juno cross the Tiber bridge
arranging larger waves while

We sit in the air as if Italian crossings spun
sugar ropes in air blistered with cornice storms
chipped into recognition,

Ropes sway molluscs.

These endeavors in their immense whir pass one
another police filled with spit for the smell
of audacious miniatures,

Chevettes like geese.

Country Cousins

Country cousins possess different rhythms joined
in irascible lightning. Madam is stung by a cloud,
the nomad bee drowned in it. You are in the parlor,
the buttermilk curdles properly, my share grips its
haunches becoming violet, evening purl where Ceres
seeks the Persephone dark it has been mannered
they toss shells
tales you recount.

Winter month you are a mouthful, the first course,
seas tumble, tides raise values then a serial
of watches and generator of rulers who twitch
on thrones as dignified frost, or russet root carriers
there is much destination in your marrow, hidden
in a godlike silhouette that glows, a Roman
beginning, the two faced lullaby dog.

Laura and Phillip, Robert and Lucia
all they can think about Athina and Paul,
Victor and Ida pine for chemises,
cloth of white, ribbons towelly,
Recca and Richard, Claire and Noel recollect
spring in their larking, struts commence
windfass, rabbits surrender dustbinned
with minor fledgling bulb
these singular aches a promise of jumbo
stitches in rain.

Goose girl leads chevettes to the pond
where she reds down the rumor of hiss
in the dry season of quack, the shorn sink
at her pout the distance runner and the holder
of metal tires, the white
saluting mellowed feathers.

Savannahs

1.   Congress of the value of you
make the situation
of active platters

     mutable when offered
on time

     grazing the nubiles.

     Grateful before the hammers converse
that consciousness still arrives
with its timely art

     grasping an old spoon
the declensions
where with bottoms failing
arches begin their wonder

     at the grip where it widens
roses appear opulent whiter

     if only hourly.

     There at the beginning

     the song shoots forth

     a frailty
gifted
on the edge of burned.

2.   Now that I ride
whitener there was on the ice
thumbed

Faintness of molasses
dark and molecular
rippled under

The stress being opposite the strain
an ouch wintering there.

3.   One eye opening
      and unopening

      a mixture of envy
      where the cement refused to rattle
      reasons neatly anchored
      rasps fitted
      where ice once held
      sleds and light
      struck the sides,

      hurting the eyes
      less amorous of winches
      and apron sauces dashed
      out the window

      splaying the shadows
      hanging in ripeness
      vines where the old
      wall trembled and shed,

      at your back
      solids thoughtful of you
      will o the wisps.

The Cradle of Culture

Is this a short story?

Is there a script attached like a new tail
the one the dog grew? Use the flamingo.
You have already focused on cats.

Like a day you encountered an intruder
by the pool's cracked basin
considering the use of tiles,
he said they were the pool's eyes
they endure abandonment
they exist in reminiscence.

This stranger wearing a hat
kept drawing, he placed his sight outward
the sea returned it to the pool,
the sea sent him its metals,
"Down with the Mediterranean," he said.

He took a piece of crayon from his pocket
he began to draw stars, starfish, pebbles
a woman: "The Poetess" you saw him write
above the triangles, circles, jingles of color.

Recall: the brilliant window
recall leaf
brushing stone, vertigo
looking down the gutter
of hillside, straw hat.

"The Mediterranean was the cradle
of the whole Greco-Roman culture." And

"Surrealism detested culture." Then Miró
laughed and shouted:
"But I am no longer a Surrealist!"

You believed you saw a hand
rising from the water,
when dark soaked hair thrust
from the water
when she turned her face

You called, "Come back Mediterranean!"
that word learned from Miró
with its heavy foot and watery
whiplash tickling your ankle where it bled.

Lawn Bumps

The horseshoe print on the lawn
that started
on hooves
the carriage trade
a smart two wheeler running up the drive and Andrew
there at the wheel. No one had thought the horseshoes
would dig so at the turf. And no one dreamed
I would return years later and uncover the leaves to
find those same prints, the ones the horses made when
Andrew took them up the drive in midsummer.

        "You seem such a stranger," she said,
        "when you look out on the lawn, why
        don't you turn out the light? I'm sorry
        I was cross today at the shower. It was
        all those wild things under my feet with
        a sort of U shape and I kept stumbling over
        them. I think the shower should be put
        somewhere inside the house, even if we do
        bring the sand indoors with us, it's better
        than that funny smell out there and something
        running under your feet."

Because so much was said about being alive and
it was talked about boats and islands and
keeping cruisers drifting the way they were supposed to

A brick is replaced here and what is left
of the curtains. As the wind folds other things.
Where that is disturbed and the stumbling toward it.

The maritime use of quiet exits when it was carried
down the grass, a kind of free booting as opposed to
looting. A series of inverted Us where the plaster
had fallen, and there appeared an ivory circumference
of ears. Drips and dabs until margins are released.

A complex denuding of place once occupied
by house sitting on bumps. They were photographed,
afterwards the dance to the phonograph.

He arrived with the negatives, rather like greasy stills.
We looked them over and remarked how much had changed.
It proved our instincts to restore were correct.

Just possibly and with luck the house. The attic
might remain on top. Where the letter had said
ma chère and a different order was imposed like
wisdom settling accounts, although an opposing
effect might be gained from the wind arriving off shore.
Someone might challenge saddles laid out to dry.

Units. The measure the cup takes to the handle,
nearly full. While birds in cry on the veranda. The
sound of hurdles. Jumps. A neighing as of wedding.
Bells near the grass. Visible prints showed under
the shifts of ice where the key was thrown. A winter court.

> Usually the most stormy of us respond
> Sometimes shipping in the harbor
> Where the portrait hides
> Often waiting.
>
> Wilfully as clouds whimper near bridges
> Desiring to settle somewhere
> Cause trouble
> Bits and pieces fall apart

Generations in disguise remove
A few we like the least
Housewifery, certain tricks with knives
What resembled those hooves

Our apartness from that grasp
The mazes and the greenery
The permissiveness of growing
Into variousness

Further explanations covering up moss
Even a form of intermarriage
Lending strength to the lawn
Heavy ways firmer tread

Brightness like calico was only piecework
Yet with remembrance the ruddiness
Meant a lot of cutting corners

Losing the trail was more trouble than finding the
beginning, the tale of the hooves went beyond all
that, faster, with more rhythm to slices. Lopping
off branches and unsmoking the parental tree there in
the wind sloughing about bringing tears to the eye
and the need for further equipment to handle the seamy
adventures sewn into cloth, scent in the upstairs drawer.

Obdurate blue, a thin casein
as warm draughts fell sideways on
elbow and hand, like writing where
there is order of a kind. Lawn bumps leading to —

the river in the dark,
people eating beside it under lights or lanterns,
fishing at twilight,
canoes setting northward with strangers
interned in the futurist cabins,
"Excessive disappointment after the premiere"
and "Animal behaviour the Balkans never knew"

the hooves bestowed their print

Tessera

1

Sadness and felicity
you're coming back
ghosts in your striped Greek dress.

Tears go into the urn
Philomène brings the brazier
things heat up
water, wine, thistles in the jug.

2

Hot turns.

More.

I said to her, "Go away Inertia,
beautiful, fragrant, violet as you are
go away."

She kept talking about letters, diaries,
quotations, explanations,
words linking me to sleep.

I said, "Go away Inertia,
even if you bear a Latin name."

3

Then it was dark on the quarries.
I had to hire a truck to load up.
My boxes. My images. My materia medica.

The driver arrived.
The truck was loaded.

I'm here in the land of sunbeams and
silk oak.

Very easy. But heavy
on the initials.

                                                                         •

4

Ghosts in stripes.
Thistles.
"I wish I were quieter," she said
at Thebes.

What echoes from legends,

Or armadillos or bees.

Defensive Rapture

Paulownia

i

ravenous the still dark a fishnet —
   robber walk near formidable plaits
   a glaze — the domino overcast —

seized by capes — budding splash
whitened — with strokes —
     silvertone gravure.
     knifed tree.

straw beneficence —
        ambient cloud. riderless.

ii

vowels inclement — tossed off figure
  lisping blot —
     running figure.
     bowled ripe.
stood in the wind sheet. a femur axis.
  virginal wail. as grain. storm motif.

iii

pierced the risen sea.
   coxcomb.
slides around.

      day and night.

      "remedy of darkness"
      lit body.

iv

etched in powder

sequence — a solace

     the monument,
   width of grape — is praised.

v

     adherence to sand
the loam division — the quagmire

     foot sink the rind —
    or   rindswift heel
astonished acre
      chewed wire.

vi

   as instrument

     threaded sky
     burnt.
torn from the corner.
     on your knees

vii

plinth in sour bloom.

the idiot cone. rummage.

•

viii

held   in mortar air.

"weight of stone"

     fragment.

ix

their whole selves —
   or were they?

burden of face
   from one to the other

   quaking sun.

     abstract arm.

Dove

        experienced in rounded

dove form

   belly up the child toy

anointed.

other codes —

like granite where the toy

the ground submissive —

splays

lightness under curled vapor.

"we wear open clothes.

and we are

broken up into time intervals."

one day bridges.

neophytes passing over. three vans.

flight of open sticks.

waving.

repeated —

as idiom —

"their fear of absorption —

a common scale."

what is printed —

determinant lion

as music —;

                   ordinary leaves

estranged — proportionate wind —

         felled.

and plots of sandust.

"the thing that was dear" —

                 scenes with table.

                 an intense

idolizing.   frame with multiple rose.

                  sunɔet

                  venom in rust

                     the small breathing.

of cowhide.

                  employed

a chalk wing.

               the globular

solitude

                  invisible swell

"touching the beyond"

has no body without another.

walless.

at the nib — dove shunted downward;

survives — in buoyant leap

admits the crater lump — the advance

performs more violently as violent solution

picks up speed

outside of character

outside the dovecote —

a rascallion soar   multi-layered emotional

suffix.

"he may never know why"

The scribbling

dynamic — skewed

meter shift   the merging

print and tense

range of cardboard

dominant

papier peint

flat ink transcribes:

"the patterned brilliance

through open doors"

on foraged studio cloud

the painted raven

feeds the hermit bread.

the whinnied pupil scratch   anxious

from the stalk ear the eye reached up and the

sublimated eye reroutes the gaze

world of trout   a neutralized shape

the portal earth threw   toad gaze

                on

            mottled dove

            water outside the spoon.

Expectation

(*Erwartung· Schœnberg*)

                more liquid
than eyes adulterous surface —

the bruised arch — a sting
severely clothed — rich in dynamite —
                cord to shallows —;

            a fluid haze divides —
the rhythm vault —

— single movement — topped with purple hills —
                contralto shift —.

            _____

            variations

masked throat —

            gradual broken ascent
            — means intensify

through an aperture — the tilt

grave —
ropings.

— they flutter — pick on straw

tinted bird
band around the slender hollow —
tight noise — rolled

— of itself
smoke white regal   chromatic rise
of itself
unattached.

----

pieces laid
placement vital to
disguise.

the basilic   arrangement
in view

unaffected

leaning on elbows

----

tumescent — whitened girders — the spatial breath —

delicate mouthing — a pain hesitancy —

the tread of corn husk — aural sky —

between inheritances —;

brevity emphasized — an unnatural heartbeat —

without the nominative curve —

to be grasped — the wooden handle

        diminished —;

    a gravelly endless pact —

littered octave — disrupted —

knee bound — mutinied — spells the translucent.

Geese Blood

            height of trees

      the papered chamber —

a breathy click — low volumed —

        the stalking men —

        outer motions

leading to holes — unstable lacing —

      an elevation —

        controlled surface —

seizures — the fallow lining —

        a bird interrupts —

groping for layers —

        lip fold —

loosed on the hillside —   dun panorama

continues a secondary

reliance on ledge — the nearest forest — reversed

kilometres — a brusque rim — the outer motion —

as figurative —

                extension of features —

leading to holes — an elevated fissure;

                these intervals control —

in bold gaps — marked by flaking — The empty lining —

The bird in fallow sky — the motion

                exits into forest shelter —

the lighter than expected — height of trees —

                aware the figure

now withdrawn in commotive patterns — agitates

low volume — men stalking — the open visor —

                ruffled leaves

held with cotton — gloves — in pursuit of sunlight —

the raw bloom — polarized —

                tunneling.

the ace spring —   an inch into —

            mosaic.

         eye bell —

a mirror dice —   an opening.

        sand bowls in —

cotton gloves —

        two hunting knives —

the dried-up glint —

        spirit guide ▬

under three arches — green hand.   sunken bowls.

        "red geese blood."

Fleet of White

      i

    coming into the park

through the white magnolias —

only those eyes "veiled" —

        saw Syracuse.

"*Scipio's tomb*

        contains no ashes now."

ii

piece of cloth in evening storm

sideways into air

mullion glow

"hugging" the shore

flute-like barque

wash of quarter-tones.

•

iii

arranged

on the same level

figures

on a dusty shoulder

move to another level.

"stuff of   dream"

mistakes for   shift in place

return and fade.

Fleet of White.

Atmospheres

faster — than the stare

         — salutary — ornamental bruising;

the ellipsis — a thin ring —

precedes thunder — triggered — heathery

discipline — lining up — unshakeable granite —

the normal morass — green and white mix —

above the sea crop

settled   and retrieved the skin — vocable

dust-skeined — rim —

fence proof — firm date — the uprising —

the quartered horse — from tree to dowser —

torrent clad — in night pathetic.

dog quickness — in the burned-out tertiary —

the grimace — a nerve fault —;

             combined ochreous —

   hesitancy — tumbling — the marsh period —

      sod — mounted antlers the common

dark — murmurs — — unheated — stoic ground

        — burst with the imaginary shadowless

crawls —;

domination by modal

alliance of moves — sculptured

weighing — the tube circuits slicked —

out of sky.

in widow — field — to establish multiple erasures —

a plain mobility — diatonic — released cloud cuttings —

a simplex — within the marginal

— giant originals.

squeezed — from memory the ash zones — collective ritual —

astronomic mood power — into memory pushed —

a piping reservoir — elemental softening — subliminal

as through the stations — in astral grip —

intravenous search through structured — visible —

faulting — the loud test — a slowed metabolic —

release — chaff filters

the disease pattern — mirror particle —;

under the skin — a loss of time —

under the heroic — memory cap — retains the wall —

the thickness mined —

levitation — passage.

to the stick road — to the track —

hurt — in the narrow — shoulder

passed — the threshold — lightning giblets — after the

burning — the crossfire

                tied — thrust outside

primitive method — conjured —

diamonds into the hand.

The Surface as Object

        the visible

as in the past

            subsisting in layered zone

                    refuses to dangle

                oaths on marsh field

            whitened or planned

                    memorial distance

                rather than vine

        that which proliferates

the bittersweet grapple

                    initiates

          a mysterious mesh

forbids   the instant disclosure

          delays a humid course

or creates a patina

          jungleware.

or she moving forward into

the line of sticks

          circled by sticks

her hand flies up

          in the direct line of sticks

odor of lines.

    knowing the difficulty

    annexation of Egypt

        oaths on marsh fields etc.

        a possible intimacy with

the tomblike fragrance of stone

        the cult-like

expressiveness.

    (the perpendicular

millimeter stone

    less raw

  or, gangling

as the artful

lessening surprised.)

   tree grown guava

    oaths on marsh field

the hungry minstrel and the forager

gold on the guava lick of rosin

and the chill latched thicket

marsh weed

regardez-là

the untamed ibis.

II

Defensive Rapture

Width of a cube spans defensive rapture
cube from blocks of liquid theme
phantom of lily stark
in running rooms.

adoration of hut performs a clear function
illusive column extending dust
protective screen the red
objects pavilion.

deep layered in tradition moonlight
folkloric pleads the rakish
sooted idiom
supernatural diadem.

stilled grain of equinox
turbulence the domicile
host robed arm white
crackled motives.

sensitive timbre with complex
astral sign open tent hermetic
toss of sand swan reeds
torrents of uneveness.

surround a lusted fabric
hut sequence modal shy
as verdigris hallow force
massive intimacy.

slant fuse the wived
mosaic a chamber astrakhan
amorous welding
the sober descant.

turns in the mind bathes
the rapture bone a guardian
ploy indolent lighted
strew of doubt.

commends internal habitude
bush the roof
day stare gliding
double measures.

qualms the weights of night
medusæ raft clothed sky
radiant strike the oars
skim cirrus.

evolve a fable husk
aged silkiness the roan
planet mowed like ears
beaded grip.

suppose the hooded grass
numb moat alum trench a solemn
glaze the sexual estuary
floats an edge.

Beautiful/Evil

fifteen diamonds in a row

and one red

      "ruby"

brought down the gravel — in lumps.

out of the fire orphanage —

      with a carpet bag.

      "celestial essence"

all-gifted.   *Pandora.*

owlish — the lifted eyebrows —

      Minerva-like.

wrapped in a bird coat

      geworfen

      "hurled into existence"

        breathed into.

beautiful/evil.

Borrowed Mirror, Filmic Rise

Arriving speeds the chromatic
we stay with fire

arrows jasper pontifex declare
an imaginative risk.

fermented moss a
bulge in amaranth

motley filmic rise
that welds a natural

shield refreshed in hutch
of oak.

from borrowed mirror
rain a seized and

crystal pruner the limned
and eyed cowl

eyedusk.

Restlessness

1

      oh conscript not the forest
a stone and laughter

      it sports a halo
filled with drops one after the other

in the efficacious zone they fall like minerals

and the courtesans move to a narrow spot
where their lids are tinted and the slight
huskiness of

a cat's mouth enters.

2

it was when I stayed with her that I first heard the sound of
violin and piano and orchestra . . .

in that part of the forest these instruments were unknown
. . . the first "scent" of the West.

3

he swims holding the wood handle
eyes smudged below the iris
burned leaves thrown from her fingers

wildlife running from the edge
four persons inside a hut
a passage from the shared bowl
throwing the rind outside the bowl.

grown ups working in the forest
tidying hair at the car window
noodles, plasticity.

4

now they move through indigo
the shape of their shoulder
armpit
even the bag of garnets
they rave about steals from
dark blue and they

---

*italics above: Hasegawa Shigure

wish to copulate
in that medium
hands in the noodles

wayfare in shadow city.

                    5

        a lantern
among the grasses
        smoke from white lanterns;

yonder the corpse
wrapped in straw.

insect voices
        filtering through the woodcut

upon the tombstone the last
poem of *Takahashi O-den*

        oh the straw hunchedness.

                    6

even the willow
vanished from Tama River

the shivering flavor
disappeared.

naphtha on her skin.

when he stays with her
"the violins the piano and orchestra"

the western "scent."

Chalk

i

you await assumptions induced by temperament —

ecclesiastic in wing power —

narrow abridgement   yellow slanders the island
lavable breeze work.

the catalogue within the visor —
reticule of mannerists.   employable objects.

minor tenses born in the scrubs —

irregular

flame —

exiled   grass.

ii

voiceless Etruria
the mythic quarry —

fireball tunneled.

jovial stone cipherless —

hijacked.   lively.

iii

with eyecatch —

on rocks off Scylla

silvered goats entering.   leaving.

Memory plunge.   tossed.   refined.

post-attic rhythms juggled.

in beggar garb Odysseus

— the Cyclops pinched like rose plums.

"steals   memory"

brittle nosed.

shuttle loom.

iv

1.

unfashionable —

bent at the waist.   professional at descendant hour —

vase galop

unarmored amid

glued piecework   impotent   vessel —

Thracian meld.

skidded root power.

2.

a fairly simple footwork

the body painted white —

an air of decay   in the toothless pattern

light in controlled areas — lavender extensions —

the chambers tied into bundles

says the body.

an oiled leap

embracing the skin   minimal in shyness

circling — crumpling — rising

the six scenes.

cricket music for the robing.

v

the Orphic rite film releases

bathybius

miniature displacement.   mountain   dialect partial.

(ph formally silent)

indices proper to songster.

zephyrstorm and flute —

heroic spin beneath subsoil —

regal smiles.   conversation shaded —

black currant tin.

vi

a half root elasticized

the upright valve a harpsichord

in steel diminuendo   *historicism* —

alabaster hooded —

reduces complex Medea — the narrow unbridled hand —:

"mere   antique queen"

aisle of lopped off heads

vii

little is missing even plumped shadow —

a knight observes his dress —

under the rough mountain

tree growth out of rock.

a natural tone in the poems.

lid pried open   volumes fall out —

lightning sinks into soft thunder and

weights of earth balance.

viii

a slice paradisical

flickers into melted *jaune*

astrew the careless Arcadian —

red-tiled slumber.   dowerless.

the waxed emptiness — moulting stone —

agrarian fable.

III

Borderlands*

The return was like a snowbird like the cutoff

    before the orchard we remembered;

they came to us as rustlers

        the steeds wore foam.

The girl in the bonnet the man with shoulder pads

were familiar the rustic was anyone's choice

he chortled; there was mutual glee

      it clamored.

    Welcome in a new fashion a century had passed

    bones tucked away even wreaths

        headbands

    where orchards joined an isthmus was winter.

    Our preoccupation began with grass hoeing when

      it starts to roam, folding down corners

    watching the tubular form;

desiring no money we were

serene like a nation.

We shifted our feet, tribal

at desolate speech or,

canoeing a worn river,

fought separately when they held us up;

why is this remembered, how is it explained?

"Escape with me!"

we hear them say and look at the drivelling

margin at the inch where stone refused to burn

light on rural habitation.

You cannot tell them what glass resembles they

skid on the track;

reindeer eat moss

the subject is not the assassin.

---

*Lands incorporated by the Treaty of Versailles in 1919 to form Czechoslovakia: Bohemia, Moravia, Silesia, Slovakia, Ruthenia.

Dissonance Royal Traveller

sound opens sound

shank of globe   strings floating out

something like images are here

opening up avenues to view a dome

a distant clang reaches the edifice.

understanding what it means
to understand music

cloudless movement   beyond the neck's reach

an hypnotic lull in porcelain   water break   mimics

tonality   crunch of sand under waddling

a small seizure
from monumentality

does not come or go   with understanding

the path will end

birdhouse   of trembling cotton

or dream   expelled it

parcel   on the landlocked moor.

explaining music

and their clothes entangled

who walk into a puddle of minnows;

minnows in a bowl

consonant with water.

the drifted footpad

ambushed by reeds signals the listening

oars.

music disappears into oars.

in the middle the world is brown;

on the opposite side of the earth

an aroma of scarlet.

this accompanies our hearing music;

the sleeve of heaven

and the hoof of earth

loosed from their garrison.

dissonance may abandon *miserere*

on bruised knee hasten to the idol.

and what is consonance — the recluse —

entering and exiting

as often as a monarch butterfly

touches a season;

by accident grips the burning flowers.

in the stops between terror

the moon aflame on its plaza.

autumn of rippling wind

and the noise of baskets

smell of tin fists.

and harsh fists

on the waterfall changing the season;

the horse romps in flax

a cardboard feature

creating a cycle of flax.

    music imagines this cardboard

the horse in cardboard jacket

flagrant the ragged grove

red summit red.

dissonance royal traveller

altered the red saddle.

The Advance of the Grizzly

go from the must-laden room

move to the interior

the remarkable bird in the case;

    wing

(like a pillow).

bird out of cloud — dissembling of trees; locks;

the icicle; out of the margin

falling from the grim margin the axle of skin;

enamoured with the fell wing.

I will move in my skin with the hollow

the neck and the brimming over the latitude

over the latitude onto the brink.

frame of snow "within

squares of diminishing size"

ink hushed the snow; a blank sky rolled to the verge

parable heaved through drift

and the moon weighted

with this the coil

evoked our willing to believe in a sudden pull

of the immense frame at the heel:

spilled exactly

to destroy a circular return

from the ragged prose clump

clump on the cold landscape

white grown fatter . . . place of sharpened skin.

romantic fever and snow

fresh from the gorgon bed

dendrophagous "feeding on trees"

to sustain the romantic vision route over snow

the sudden drop into pines:

"feeding on trees"

new mouths red of Okeechobee.

(and ate the alligator and spat out the part

wedded to the green clavicle.)

loss of the sun

blight of the sun the looney forest

who will walk out of the plush interior into

the excited atmosphere?

an outlet for prose the advance of the grizzly.

The Glass Mountain
in memory of J.S.

        i

    king as wanderer

  replied   we do and always

the least recounting

pelting dew

bird in the sunrise room;

once or twice the landscape burns

what we are after tires

clouds mohair.

rhododendron bring

       pods to the mountain;

a tremulous position

harp on a mountain of glass.

       ii

       is it a power

you pass in the night

taking water from the tap,

fog or phantom

the king stares at.

       you are not the snake lady

gold filament above

the snake limbs

nor does she tell

who taught the dance.

iii

    the king watched

in flat country the

caravan at ewe season

a density

sand and thyme

    near the threshold

where they milk

have bitten the nut-

like substance

                                                  •

iv

bauble of sound

mahogany the king

travelling the length

overhead a climate

of twang the rushed snow

unstoppable space in the bold

different in the next imagined

movement the breach

is inimitable

a phrase others believe

there is no escape

the towed rock dims.

v

why not live

      image strewn

and goes pitter pat

next to the resolute corridor

and a diadem would hang on the fringe

actual pieces of tame fibre shut off.

on the steeple with the watercan

and thunder in the earring she

caught the speech of the termagant

the roll

was seen the plummage and owl

a raft on the cold river; skin

on the raft a king

picked up boards and sunk them.

              vi

the shades lavished

in the ideal

climate of planets fear

steam rolling up;

holding hands in a ring

wet to their waists

              hair

a slippery blossom.

exposure beneath the May apse

              doggerel;

chunks of filched

              objects not

lapidary; a king.

vii

attent on detail

    the hullabaloo over

rule half water half worn

    running the notion of land;

tells us where light comes from

    white curtains in its beak;

closer closer to the splintered mountain

O king endlessly

scattering.

Otranto

    At sunset from the top of the stair watching

the castle mallets wrenched from their socket

fell from ambush into flame flew into hiding;

above the stoneware a latch like muscle hid

the green; he stood waist high under the rapt

ceiling and hanged the sparrow; where the kitchen

had been a mirror of eggs served in a tumbler he

saw the ring when a lancet pierced and threw it.

In a basket and lowered it where sails enter

the harbor over a parchment like dominoes;

the petrel-like eyelash.

To the sun and its rites were pulled the dried

banners; they flew past the ruins the tower

and window where ivory guided the mist on his back;

he rubbed his eyes and counted them kneeling

wrinkled as grass.

A ghost in their nostrils put a heel at their

forehead; they saw only the moon as it

fasted.

ii

If the ship meant anything if he heard a world

view in the midst of his rhythm or the spell

lustrous like hair on his arm; that groaned as

it struck near the tumble down or

combing hair; words burnt as they quickened.

The bitter they share crept into forage and

muster is in their skin; the grey

worked like a vise they brushed this

to turn arrows; they shut off the vast

cellar and the turret leaped to a pattern;

the mosaic blended was untouched.

iii

The frankish hills and hummocks metered

the greed over sun and cloud; voluptuous

in the straits turbanned held scarves to the

water each sail embroidered;

who washed in their music a lattice.

A major or borrowed sky this aspect provides

the lily stalk inside the frame; a gesture the lily

pointing north as if the wrench from sky decides

cold rain or change of tide; the lily

she chooses.

iv

Waking in must the high pierced window dew on

the furnaced bar the poaching hour the cup

takes smoke from the tower; they drink

in the smoke the print cradled; cut in dark.

The siege made cloth a transfer

learned from invaders who craved it;

spindle thieves.

She sang high notes and pebbles went into her

work where it changed into marks; in that room

the armor-like wrens:

rites turned with thread a dower

begs lapis; eglantine on a spoon; the castle

breeds tallow.

v

A change of tide might delay the run

they watched as if by simple water

read magisterially whatever the book decided;

night outside covered with filmic screen

ghosts they store; then bring an experimental

wheel out of hiding.

Even the Nile wind; fortune cards

jugglers a remedy from old clothes;

to appease the fable — pearls

rolling in straw.

The way a cowslip bends

they remember or Troilus as he stared;

they agree on brighter covers; looser

shifts fluent tower to tower.

More ephemeral than roundness or

the grown pear tree connected

with vision a rose briar.

vi

There was only a rugged footpath

above the indifferent straits and a shelf where the

castle lay perhaps it was sphered like Otranto;

there the traveller stood naked and talked

aloud or found a lily and thought a sword;

or dragged a carcass upon blunt stone like a

corded animal. In weeds in spiritual

seclusion a felt hand lifted.

Winter Horses

placed two sticks upon a dazzling plate

unlike feudal wars you remember

their saying she is stalking

and the fortifications are blocked

abruptly they held their breath until it froze.

carpeting the greensward a foil of sunset

"idyll of the kings" and shut the moat;

did not forget the promised tawny

situation of splendor.

again twists in the passage

or is it rhythm overturned;

to regard moodily a cask something

borrowed or fable stuck the snow.

.

ii

sea grey cold a door one boulder

slams another.

instantly footprints

in the sand corner.

grief spell was thought something else

records what was cried out.

the shrived warm

     turns into serpent

    are

no kingdoms

    is grass.

.

    iii

    winter

you know how it is *la gloire!*

    they bring you a fig dish.

the dead in white cotton.

fleece on the platter.

    wind crept

the white shoat and buried;

the cramped space ran

    out of breathing.

iv

bars of snow lanced the brightness

crippled windows flung

lute with two notes unevenly.

ice breaking and noise

envelops sobriety.

slice of boot on the frayed sylph

came out of dazzlement into

fisheries was intended.

IV

The Altos

. . . the warbler

    where did he locate the bell

    . . . has crossed the river

      field plane

  table of   syllabic   water

        out of rock

  moved backward

    in floated matinal

chimera

    rests his eyes.

      circle   lavender

       of

    in the tide region

modular lope.

"located harbors"

rice in autumn

emplastos over the signet

"papered halo"

to walk somewhere

an image falls

out of the figurative sky

offers what bell it is.

from the walk   voice asks   whose

covered walk from

the past   a white satchel

the embonpoint

is sacred   mortar

on the threshold

beside the ragged dome

dust lips

running it cannot stop

it falls into segmentary rushes

narrow gauntlet

a slipper untied it.

with staff   the bony road

came toward us

pallor of grey harbor

bird eye of the Altos

from open green to take the purest juice

it strengthens the turbans

the braided helmet said "mine mine"

heir to evening arches

oh the ace of evening

butterfly   on the night drop

across the pavement

viols

call to mates

balloon smell

with the tiger

an invisible weight

swam in the

night   into thunder

cannot find

the platinum

bird coat

dreamed the stalk image

a gestural branch

lily powdered

distance

in baking dew

with full hands

with many branches

coldest butter

alive in the coal meadow

tipped the grief-scale

an antic of wild

deposition — raincoats dripping —

romantic barriers —

they believe the staged cloud —

even the fountain of Altos

their soft meats cross the border.

Stripped Tales

Stripped Tales was originally published as a collaboration between Barbara Guest and the artist Anne Dunn.

structured

In hollows dim-witted rabbits running out of the barn the storm might
have killed them "don't think much of the girl guess she left the country."

immediacy

. . . handbag with parasol over her head feet pointed in front, strips of
celery, taught to hold her head "high like the Spanish," ripe olives,
a walk on stripped sand cloud over the boat, a sliver, changes her look.

lottery can guess

the moment

a noun

from porridge to velvet dubious
oh disasters   factories   memory and actors   dossiers

a name   piloting balls of speech   worm balls and grape kites

      literature   single-mindedness

       settles into space

Fast-pacing it down the street at a clip forcing legs to move mastering it
lively stepping legs in trim soup of mussels grilled shin and fragrant little
walk terrace he sat with broken leg in a splint.

       germination   *begins*

      undermining

On the coast groups of cars try to reach the city the coast
road is narrow the coastal range of mountains dry spotted on
the hillside a few miles apart piglet-size huts for the forest rangers
and the coastal pattern runs up and down over ridges always a midday
sun or moon cairns in sight of the bruised city.

opposing ides

literature   phantom

Here is the whole story for a living oats in the barn
the hovering cottage who rowed Mad River rain pouring down
Alouette's sandals Berenice the orchard ladder the Parabola
his trouble with sleep . . . who scampers out of the green.

which-away

philosophy

It was our intent to read all the books we gathered not at once but
over a settled sum of months we would know if linguistics or a pattern
of stars ruled the logico if x͟y or a similar construction slightly altered
was the essence it is my intuitive understanding that poetry is the essence
if I were not cautioned to believe *intuitionism* is a fraud.

in Norway

moody

·Once they stalked the *blue moon* where it lit up the clay
cobbled into brew flowing over old joints and bent leather,
a framboise shawl and a knuckle in the lucid bleached zone
grass flattened and white.

adjectivalness

need

In the hotel certain rooms were closed to the guests. They
discussed what went on in these rooms, who watered the plants,
made the beds, etc. The children liked to beat their fists
against the doors and sometimes would awaken in the night to
ask why the rooms were locked.

to identify

odd

lines from favorite books words marched in unison in her head,
but when she wrote them down they did not read consecutively
or crisscross: verbs remained solitary with no subjects
on certain vowels a color like calico was pasted.

pagination   ˎ

property

He changes the scene with its unique nobility into something quite
different he draws around the story a circle and then breaks up that circle
into angles so that the narrative line is abolished. The linear lines of a
narrative are obtrusive and when he breaks it up there will be more energy,
instead of lines he is free to deal with planes. The planes join each other
to become cubes the entire outline of his life fits into a cube.

mix-up

Entering the hallway he stopped before the mirror: "Most
gracious host," and he bowed to his favorite image he picked up the glass

that rested on the table and repeated: "*wszystkiego dobrego wa dniu imienin,*" and to his reflection in the mirror he translated "whiskey drowned with new meaning."

selfdom

a venetian

When the mouth of the pitcher opened we saw thin pieces
of glass beginning to melt a gilt domino shaded the water
the glass moved with a mercurial mothiness alive and yet its wings
closed

pallor

ice

A lamb moves into the pasture; the one-eyed goat pointed left.
A look at coldness thoughts of quality: "her petticoat is an
armored vehicle."

buttons

history

Night confounded hollering at architecture Our Lady
of Fatima thick coffee the fat goose a youth called
Expireus . . . nothing to improve his intellect no buttercup
on the fields of the Ovidian School . . .

ambushed

klebnikov   *lootage*

Velimir they broke into thy *Baku* house and drank from thy cup of
numbers and Destiny improved their zero.

useful

    we remember the jumping frail iambs
upside down hat
fish moving backward.

   techniques

         loose grams

Continent with shelves engages the Queen and her Knight,
men in the boat, the movement of laps as pebbles recede,
shoe attached to the shore, and the body is lonely. The sky
whether it runs or stops . . . cosseted in the mimic field she
under water looking out from his stare.

       of nutmeg

typestry

Apparently   TIGRIS   *your vile husband* Two Rivers
Aspect   *in normal times*   Research Tells Us   *difficulty with MESOPOTAMIA*
breathing   *[an entire section missing]*   Research Tells Us
In Round Number *mild calcification somedays I would* BABYLONIA
gladly   TO ARMENIA   *yours as well as mein*   Refrigeration
lovely lilies   Blossom Neither Sow   *sidewalk Dispense Vendors*
EUPHRATES CAVIAR   *indigenous to   to to* Nightmare
like OLD TIMES.

ghost

Is this an eidolon?
Given the rough pagination lottery can settle the moment
infallibility is afloat permanently real a goatskin the dark-mouthed
exposition sideways.

aboard

the French woman

And you connect the runner with the orchid have brought your music to
the Fair without dropping a stitch or hurling the wheel presented the
featherless goose who sang to the white underground *Claire La Belle.*

beckoned

moment

She put the pail on her head then moving through wire she called to the
Master of Sculpture "make way for *Softness* I'm pouring it over the torso"
then the bronze rain fell.

of ingenuity

antiquity

the fortress in a net and he climbing the worn

stair   hoot   Athena's owl

that clouded

net   round thy head   maketh it plainer

"night dust"

what we say

think you by dredging

out of memory slide

may wish it   the secret divides   coo

empathetic

. . . and then the Alpine pasture oppositionally peaks brassy cows
monumental drifts of snow — here comes the *ski boy* ripe berries in
his basket bulbs at his wrist — Nature's thrust of ruddiness on
our cheek . . .

> *three days out from Lac Leman on their*
> *way to Italy in moonless snow Mary and Shelley*
> *cling to the carriage as it tips and swerves on*
> *the narrow iced-over pass — Lucifer below.*

chimes

law

The lady protests she reserves the right to select her
own ghost should you from the parlor call "mine" and where
were thee when grief doubled over the lithe figure running
said "mine."

       of the ether

      Bergson's Law

       So there is truly a mileage between
      vita activa and *vita contemplativa*
in the middle of thought in the golden cloak *contemplating*
         the schemer
      begs to enter the *stream of life*
        not a moment too soon:
   umbrella briefcase pencil pen glasses pills
hearing-aid thermometer map cane purgative plaster
      plunges into erupting *vita activa*

      magicked

were given the privilege of dreaming told to have meaningful dreams:
might draw the darkened lines of a cobweb to catch a dream or throw
out a planet dish to lure the stuff of dreams or a net made of curled
lines like Leonardo or hurl a figure into the sky to catch
the dream's silver ball; a rocket to frighten a dream into their bed;
could place thin-shelled eggs on the path so in careless
walk the dream slides from its dreamer; there were many schemes to lure
meaningful dreams to the dreamers, windows decorated with silver, a
sparkling eagle; dreams of powerful cities Nimes, Narbonne,
Orange; powerful warriors Guillaume, Tibaut, Yonec; and to dream of the
Lays of Marie de France.

the position

whenever Benjamin entered the room as today after his trip to the
toy fair bringing her the Christmas tree ornament in the shape of a
samovar he found Asja crouched in a corner her position like that of
Moscow itself crouched in the snow or under an artillery blast or even
in pedlar clothes beneath an invisible arch crouched like the arch of
heaven that travels from town to town on only two wheels dragging a
broken lock the priests speak of this arch of heaven as that of Moscow
itself crouched in their empty church waiting God's final blast.

anarchial

photo

beauty of the arm how it rises   w-

                                    a-

                        ve

    waterless Bosweto

                        mirage

Quill, Solitary APPARITION

Finally, to the Italian Girl

"O foemina delicata"   (Baudelaire)

touched naught

        herself the coronet

    being gleamy

     bodie of water and uxorious

a bodie

    not luxury

      a bodie

      not imperial

a guise

(if flat noise intrudes)

evanescence

.

protects (and)

•

(may come to adore her)

the white heaven

uxorious;

(with) a slow delicacy

lente delicata —;

(thereafter).

•

Garment

•

Broderie;

the rolled

garment;

window   (ed)   tress (of)

and moonlit

•

not in mourning

and caparisoned.

Garment   *(itself)*

interior of

and even the exterior plane trees.

Or melodious/ly

at a gallop (in full dress)

or,   the context

dusk/

And night's buckling.

Like the thumbed aster

(one   two, or so

the produce of   "having"

entwined)

"*lodged in the sparse soil of his mind*"

Whatever the lantern
                    ripped open

and its *wound*.

flushed with vocal soothing

and with touch

tenderly, between the lines,

bled,   the lines.

(a homespun artifice — once!)

without disgrace in the notation

or scorn for discarding
even
the twelve-tones.

RED SAND AND ITS NARRATION, TRIBAL

            (and appeals
to)

                        the outer vest.

                Arriving at the desired caesura —.

                                                        •

fabric: laid on the table

            and slowly,   a parallel

              (wordsize)   resemblance

            to the plane trees.

                                                        •

Model stranger

           this *hiding*

of "hiding"

        (a necessary evocation

and thee),   *intuition,*

      Armor surrounds his lips

a mesh of wideness and length,

    increases with winter weight —

and fortified by the miniature

(aping of his shadow).

the door open, or
upon return attached to   those difficulties, or
disabilities hinted: "mesh
and its platitudes"

and (this disruptiveness).

in an unreliable tense — difficult the word
backwards

or confirmation

in what casket the thimble:
suggests a frail misdemeanor —
on the outer garment

(one never knows).

spinning   turns it lightens as gleamless — changes into dull
green an idea of *quietism*   dark puddle —

(sleeve of the mind)   *honied in retrospect.*

Scissoring, and

cedilla to improve

the furred whistle
of this garment, if it scampers . . . will pardon
the unknowing site and plane trees where they may belong,
                                        or pretend.

                                                                        .

Fell, Darkly

                                                                        .

            what then will happen . . . if she finally
            withdraws her regard from the lightning-lit
            *revery of her clairvoyance . . . **

                    To you   even following

    disclosure;   made rumor

———————
*James Joyce

(nothing)   and I who was:

            the verbal   indentured

              (even then)

                   breathing

        and separation.

           Figure   (so monumental) indirect

often   (faded)

                 handwriting   with divigation:

        genial, even in that period.

        No matter!

         possibly desire

this hooded figure —;

        (olive branch)

ended usurpation . . . ;

        band of twigs

(their banding)

      in other kingdom!

      marked : the logic (of no other place);   if

    in the game ——————— (a wild king is drawn)

out of many colors

      de facto

           in the presence of
        an arm (perhaps

— of his speech)

.

bred in the same room as,

(in the same room as he)

pretended to shelter

" . . . . . the merciful maiden"

(indicated) and

amid difficulty

formed a separation ——;

(her)   *clairvoyance*

fell, darkly.

.

This face —— *not her face*

as   (after) — the feebleness

(her grasp) —

and the counterpoint/

profile releasing the same profile —

backwards in the mirror

if she lose   her own face

—— *not yet*   examination (of)

the future;

             •

(the past folding backwardly:

        she,   *Christine de Pisan*

perhaps

    under an arch

      shutter   of daisies)

          and she made in other clef;

witness of trial   and bemoanment —

            (of robing)

                    •

outside credibility of surface

(the past

    folding backwardly —)

              her face —

    in other clef.

Pallor

        Withdrawal from the conceptual line — joined
that other surface — afloat —

    (water is missing the fourth chord

    the boatman's shout

"another wave!")

"And slowly. And somewhere other than observable water."*

    : figure on roadside

                who fasts waiting for the brown toad

      the *azure* delicately blotted

    where the planter drops a knife   he excises

            the blocked harbor:

(miscellany of clouds —)

      perhaps their voyage,
        causes this weight on the difficulties they

        cannot be excised even

----

*Marjorie Welish

by *azure* — if a comb should ripple through its pallor —

           (slowly,

on *pillows pillows cloistered (as if alive urged to obedience)*

               an abrupt dispersion: somewhere other than here,
— mercurial flight into absence —;

            (earth's hold), slowly

and the separation may possess its own corrective

yellowed by the broken tide —

                 (a mask and fever)

            the night lamp is out on the verandah

          they took themselves elsewhere

to review her embarkation and destination?

        what she was "mixed up in"

what . . . the silt built up —;

and they are more gentle; she is a portion
of the view —

a (mere) portion —
leaned forward and smiling

observed with the floral usurping

within the palm of her hand the
Venus and errata:

and to find on the book's cover, on its *aisle*

the river's synonymous curve.

drawing on remarks the material of her dress avoided the

ugliness

evoked by their presence evidence of a peculiar
displacement (of which)

the rose or eagle-leaf *appeared*

> *part of the telling . . .*

> *an observer of omens in other life.*

> *slowly, from the drawn-off fountain*

made declaration to the body's stumble   given the
legality of time and its execution

(an opening of courtyards
crossed at full noon)

bone-like structure for the waist length hair —
a fourth chord in the waist length hair —
the bone-like structure   dissonant —.

A fountain returns this dissonant chord —

wetting her skirt with plashed water
and raises its volume (pity) lavishes

another persona *the raggedness* —

pallor crept in
what is rouged in its   made-up history

flown into a storm: torments clear color

reaches into the numb structure sleeve mud color
    (pygmy fountain eelings are young)   *INSTITUTES*

THE FOURTH CHORD.

Leaving MODERNITY

Leaving MODERNITY

as if the encircled doe

Medievality and in her hand, also dusted

apparition no less

dust on thy eyelash

leaving

and the narrowing eyes

"a vanished equipment"

and the idea of *departure*   (simmered between brackets)

and its fountain

equidistant

and near

when soft water gathers
and dispenses

(without)   (without)   intervention

of (eros)

leaving (without ending)

without the streak evening yellows

each day.   each day.

still consummates

that perpendicular

restive procedure of stone

(and the buttress)

the mouthing   *mouthing*

(not apparition)

Not Apparition

larger and further away.

the dark rhyming.

What Has the World Done?

White Border, White Shapes, Black Square

. . . .

.

"a disorder between space and form"

interrupts Modernity

with an aptitude unties

the dissolving string

.

rose of thy lip

(as once believed)

held tight to the beatific ozone:

(without INTERROGATION) .

took form from thy lip!

once thee was ribald

and thought of your vanishment, *Modernity*
on the roadway

through needles:

permanently.

Cold and Its Demeanour

Night or the curtain —

hesitation and even divorce

twilight in the Azores

a skein of wool in the nostril —

and on bent knee

to lightness in hyperbolic splendor!

naturalness the field   as scene

the vicuña acts in what is

filmic, slow

(and idle gold daisies) —

the vicuña's light step and breath

a pretense of grass

were held open doors

and red fur —;

and cold's existence —

inside this zone

a significant warfare

moves to the shutter and
aurora

a step on thin snow
(the fingernail trace)

memory protrudes
and falls on;

and refused the tin sibilancy

perilous — oval shelf

of ancestry —;

.

yes, it is.　　The vagrant

eye of the maiden roving

(she) in harmony with
self and its demeanour

(whilst fear of

gold daisies)

.

if in other clime or more idly

choice!

a cloak of vicuña might cause the invisible

— as here on a windy platform

to appear   (and that)

with many colors   would transform.

.

Should independence

edify

then the archness of fate   *wilfully*

and also, selectivity of fur,   modify —

                        the incorrigible decision
desire, attribution —   *cold and its Self.*

.

Quill, Solitary *APPARITION*

·

Practiced formality   as to a monument
                    (with circumspection)
                OH CHARMER

        peculiar movements circled

            the supposed lightness —

enters so near to Indigo —
                    hastening the solitary movements

                cloth and short rivers, spectrally.

·

    and meditating on self,
        (if) expressive to command
    in habit or writ   perceives what exists

                — possibly fountain, grape, masthead
    (or other) will seize intuition;

HAUNTED REFRAIN

wherever this scalloping permits /in whatever location
   able to repeat
                     or, even

         an excess of *MAKE BELIEVE*

               a masked

tenure responsive to location/
                     embraces the *unmasking*

          on emptied field BRUSHES AGAINST

                     the *feathering substitute!*

               (if) there be NOBILITY

      the self engaged
                     ghost-like presence,
         guards its heraldry.

      (lilac if quill should blur lilac
               with brown —;

with brown   tamed
mossiness,

an *intuitive* atmosphere
joins hands, rock-a-by exclusion —:

GROPING, SUBSTANTIAL, IDEAL)

WHISPER, or

*perhaps a mere tale (the hair combing) placed
on a smooth surface*

contrasts with her

griefless OWLERY

"throughout time and its dungeon" . . .

latitudes provisionally

barmy, and other surrenders:

nightingale, coral.

Palm tree
as subject — moonlight arranges
and branch, within the courtyard
        a bronze capitalization
dares to remember —.

    gift of oneself to this order;
        for the sake of virtuosity, its primrose
    need of defining,

        Beyond hauteur a wandering mind
        desires the latitudes . . .

will it yield
            to the bronze cast —
        (aired in profile)

    "far off face lit by fire"

attached to skull
and secret coordination —;

a solitary cry
and embrace —
masks an embrace of
rosier blandishment

and these recoveries:

the clean

interstices of *composition   and brings*
the tenure or holding   within the quill's
HALT   and miscellany.

A CLOUDED HAND
                closed   over the pasturing

and femur

(a minute dust).

Blow-out

and symptom

White, squall.

If So, Tell Me

Valorous Vine

Lifts a spare shadow
encircling vine,
does not tarnish   bauble
from overseas   and out of silver mine,
drop in clamor and volume.

Along the footpath
returned to mourning a lost stem,

gauzy the stem-like saving, or ruled
over stone to develop muscular difficulty.

In the wind
and overhead, held back lightning. Did
not surrender or refuse visibility and pliancy obtained.

Or confuse VIOLETRY with stone
or dissipate the land   land unshackled,
budding in another country
while dark here.

.

ii

It can be seen she encouraged the separation of flower from the page, that she
wished an absence to be encouraged. She drew from herself a technique that
offered life to the flower, but demanded the flower remain absent. The flower,
as a subject, is not permitted to shadow the page. Its perfume is strong and that
perfume may overwhelm the sensibility that strengthens the page and desires
to initiate the absence of the flower. It may be that absence is the plot of the
poem. A scent remains of the poem. It is the flower's apparition that desires to
remain on the page, even to haunt the room in which the poem was created.

Storytelling

(introduce pavement)
Old-fashioned people in clothes.

Passage to friendship   *(details,momentum.firefly)*
  wave "bye bye,"

idly unfolds.

(dark,light,etc.)

(separately, form,)

indifferent combinations.   *(jest,tears.)*

(Rhythm upswing) (collision with serpent),

repeat and repeat moonlight
*as suspense,*moonlight.

Outside of This, That Is

An oyster, the fragrance,
floating dog   outside and shuffle through hunger,
once again nothing so difficult when it passes in front

December goes before the new year. A battalion
of festival   largely in place by the region's devotion,
a flannel embrace, as if over, the green flavor.

A feathery existential bower shall block
the rude flagon.   A grape
centennial passed
                then passed as taught,
crowded by hope in a corral   or anonymous
by the grape barrel,   by the Ancients and
            mixed the Novella with grievous
        destiny.

        A frame lets in elsewhere, a fairie
flies through Bretagne,   or guessed she flew,
Romance let her in. Others walk outside,
plants that wait their copying into the future,
                                that is.

In Slow Motion

Melting, the melt of snow into midnight,
preoccupied, half alive, an activity in slow motion
        still attached.

        Moves outside the text   into the dark *under text*

        with closed eyes, detached, unmodified.

                        A starry adultness
        took other means

                    to lengthen the text,
                    by emotion,

                    and arguably noise

        wooed in this chapter and

                each page of,
                    O real life.

Doubleness

Robins' egg blue   passes into darker color placed its head,
    fluid blue ascends,   Distance unrolling.

   Continuous reel, as in allegory.

   Another landscape,
                darkly hinted,

              rupture of distance.

   Body in the field — beyond uneven brick,

     meaning in advance of itself.

Tree   bronze birds — sitting in it.

   Imagined brick,
          landscape toy.

       Doubleness.

  This elaborate structure around the text.

a n n u n z i a r e !

Dora Films (1913)
Elvira Notari in Naples
* * * * *

Virgil's body in a grove above Naples
and nearby a camera:

toothpick beside a platter of teeth.

The camera prepares an *explanation* into the sky and to climb.

The mind wanders inside.   The camera is nimble,

touched by fearfulness

becomes more pragmatic.   It needs chiarascuro (light-dark)

should peril approach.

.

Elvira Notari uses the camera hood when il destino enters

in knit cap:

the visual depends on the visible.

Virgil at Naples' harbor leaning on his stick,

the power to see

what is invisible
the stick in a position of power.

A slap of oars   leads to the visual,

gyrating where it ends.

       A likeness   to what is believed

is the poem.   The camera takes us, momentarily.

Lily

reaches the locked door and inside the scalloping
      remnants of leafing enlarged.

Truancy of will where she let it fall   where I found
you after the disaster   the place under the lattice
is a hollow place   did not   remove pollen   let you alone.

   Door, and outside leafing,

      corrects what is random.

      Moss on the lily pond
and not worried. "Thinking is not worrying."

Wish it were set to music.
A carriage ride through a wood
to visit the swan (Ladou, Ladou)

       Moussorgsky!

The Poetry Meter

Miner
of miniscapes, Selector,

bend your knee
to this handwriting.

A special timing
of hand-held meter,
risky when used by buffoon.
Earth-flavored
experience says so.

Phidias

Futurism

Hand-Held Meter

"Nothing but a fine Nerve-Meter" (Artaud)

The Lull

*The lull in rain
is green   where came
this dispute   the lull*

is flat when it rests on a hill.
When a comma falls,

or crown rolled.

When a legend
passed through rain,

lull of rock and shatter.

Part of surrendered air,
the goat-like view,

"The Residenz of Goethe,"

and four or five liters of rain.

.

Russet Flame

"If one goes beyond reality . . . ,"
began the woman at the window,
clothed in russet drapery.

Winter blows under her door.
The Serenade Tchaikovsky composes is made of russet,
streaked with bolder flame.

Russet russet   bandage of hair
indeterminate russet,   redandbrown
Snowrusset window,

russetflame.

.

Unusual Figures

A person stands in the doorway. Someone
else goes to greet him.

They establish a calendar of meetings,
apricot color.

Once they arrived together
in a cab
of electricity,

cool heat, desert air.

The author attaches herself
   to those figures.
peculiar to her asking.

They are needed by the pageant of creativity!

The unusual height and
   dots of activeness.

   Is it from the basket shrub?

         Lightness of feet,
circle of grey, of green overlap.
                    What language
      do they speak?

.

If So, Tell Me

            I give you the unhinged sleeve
dropped the seam   it went onto our back
was fodderless.

         Wilted, say, by the gravel road
who ran a mile with legs apart
            neck hanging and groupless.

Bird shadow crossing the room   leave the outdoors!
Earns a pittance of food on the ledge   mother
of ten eggs   the real bird   feeds on ices
      the shadow is ten eggs.

Do you wonder if a run on sand is better than inside
does this strike you as shallow does it tease aloud
    the action
        is part of a wing.

The building was added it grew from an arm   protruded out of
a thigh   the upper terrace is fighting   is divided.

        To think of you turned inside
your garment rent you are appointed   apart from the rites
        lessened, as in a daring scheme.

        You are beheaded
much cast out that rolls on the ground, toss out thread
    of what worked
            to use or unlearn.   If so, tell me.

The Luminous

Patches of it

        on the lettuce a geography
        on trucks brilliant noise

        on the figure a disrobing
        radiance sweaters dumped

on water,

weightlifting there in the forest clump
striking at the underbrush, digging
past the clumsy curve

skipping certain passages, taking off
the sweater.

That fir cone found its voice on the path
in light after the sun came out

the postcard illuminates certain features in the face
the notebook lying on the windowsill,
the spindle back, the broken stem, all richer,

niceties tend to drop, also words like "many
loves" come forward the surprise of white stars

and the boots step by amazingly on the dried rich clay.

He swings his racket after it the luminous
the ball nearly swerves into it

those ancient people learning to count
surrounded by it, every day,

and navigators noting it there on the waves

the animus containing bits there on its subject
perched like sails,

bright rewards for preparing to strut forth
like the diver there on the board forced
by his greed into it.

Many loves changes to many times falling into
the day's lucid marshes

a tap on the shoulder or a first grasping that
object full of sparks

the wilderness untangled by it.

The fierceness with which it forged its memory,
its daylight, its absence.

Yes to the point of damages,
yes to the stunning infrequency,
yes to encourage with repetition its repetiton,
yes to sober knowledge of its parsimony.

A few fir cones, sails, the stain removed,
blazes from the paper without lifting your hands.

.

Strings

                Wing of glass in high up floating

stave of time, or weight,   ceilingless and

                     of crystal time
                measured, measure of,

                pulls own weight, and dainty

                    protest,

     plucked instrument, voiceless hum.

.

Deception

                              In the long ago days   he might

          take her cloak
and place it upon
                    a hidden arm,   and things

                    before our eyes   work out. She would
     find the cloak
                         near her cloak,
          and walk
                    as if supernatural.

               This Art   and the long ago Art,

     become a comparison with Reality.

                    Remain only themselves,

     if she does not reveal the cloak.

          She shall disclose herself (herself still pointing)
               essential to the hidden

     possessiveness in back of a throat,

                    the double S of the word.

          In the twilight a blue-throated bird
          finishes his song, and Nature is hushed.

repercussions, *soundings*   turn a corner
      meaning the poem may despise, and conflict begin.

By what *soundings* does one arrive at the interior?   *Deception's* use of
deception, a scale suited to its size. *Soundings relevant,*
    yet unpredictable, in depth of poem.

       practices of deception existing: to encounter   arm, and sun,
   cloak   did not have its own ambition until they *vanish and*
return.
     Meaning, also.

An original intention, if lost in its bindery   eclipsed there and not sung

  instinct develops   coveted and heard,   allowed to develop, even
    to deploy or wander   if *glitter* is not abolished

              the horizon

       in back of her throat/

Athletic Writing

  Athletic writing
      jumps hurdles I put
into rain   over the next State   odd forward colors
  become bearers of fact whenever   written with verbs
  I put softening on the rim.   forestry housing.

Faery Land

A cloud opens a ruin of cloud
     piece of grey
   lifted out and patched.

In faery land clouds behave and wands.

  They seek
when I am turbulent have lost the knack,
  beasts and autre pays   tapered claw
they bury
    my skin   go folk
            with my toys

    take a barge and go.

Winter showed   it locked the pheasant
in a yard around it went   I took no notice,

*so long a race I have run in Faery Land.**

---

*Spenser

The Paris Lectures

"What was said, what is meant?"

The Paris Lectures

"Elegies within."
Fog-banked shell,
rotunda writing describes.

White of Oaru.   *The Husserl Lectures.*

"What was said, what was meant?"

The Green Fly

Orphaned caught in a web
the green fly.

No entertainment no grief

where they pick clover

the monument the soldier

goslings into new clover.

More
room   more
fur   more
desire

to cross the winter day, a new magnet.

An excited misapprehension of *la Gloire,*

cheek of

brass.

Fought to the finish   stars

orchids, perhaps,

at dusk severely.

Multiple tunes   sunrise   gloaming

auditorium light.

Naked in thy boat.

.

Confession of My Images

The sliding window

left agape, and
the neck does not swell

an octave with ardor

is destablilized.

Of query and cultivation, of vases not known,
even as the known voice so is the alarm —.

.

Eros freed of the wooden seat

the crowd similarly, as

an elbow

fits into the ancient arm

                   touch
              of sweet vest
  creating furor.

          to create sweet furor.

    the page
           floats on knobbled water,

debris in the atrium,   "to visit Leopardi in Naples"

  supportive
          to breathe the same idiom.

Effervescence

        Spill of ink, not enough
             lather.

           Ink spill
       lather on the Rock.
      Andromeda
        long hair   nude body

NOISE
surrounds the painting   on the right side it is
cracked   the hair color changed dried paint altered the hand.
Wire is inserted into the gold frame.

Figures wait in anxious groups   distance takes away their height.
there is a furious
helicopter wind.

They lower a rope onto the Rock.
The painting is cracked,   her neck is chipped,
pieces of gilt curl fall off. She grows more naked.

Bone is exposed. The canvas mouth torn.

AIR IS PHOTOGRAPHED!

The wings of Perseus flap wildly,
his arm reaches under her.
He wants to lift her   A WING IS ABOUT TO FALL OFF
Strange to watch him holding onto his wing!

HE IS INAUDIBLE   the twittering
he makes blew it away.
The left wing is broken   his helmet remains.

Pieces of chipped paint litter the dock.

Memory goes backward and forward.

A painting by Ingres relates Ovid's story of the rescue of Andromeda from a rock by
Perseus.

The *Strum*

What is fraught and undenied travel in rare
dayishness   supplication in ermine an approach.

Landscape treated
to remoteness.

Newish place, ferns, gracefulness.

And excavation on
the edge of attendance.

Weed dangle in hair.
Do not reverse shapes
go scared
ermineless.

.

Ripe in default
what preceded
old root tree.

(detail starts to blur)

Nightingale
and human outline
landscape behind landscape.

Spill of ink not enough
lather

        bottomless
        passage in the *red strum.*

        Dream of effervescence
.   pine and mountain gear.

        a different appearance, new
        imaginations
                here and beyond.

                                                                        •

Music History

                        i

        The rhythm of the section
nor said to be withheld
a credible garnering
a natural context of
        mountain property
nymph on the ground
fountain attached to
grotto.
        Mind you the soul of the piece
a tight operation
and viols
wilful counterpoint.
        Addresses the Mass
and far off Celtic tuning.
Wolf chorus
then bells lavender bells.

                                                                        •

                    ii
   Twittery business
at the waterfall
animal noise snow
snow cutting teeth.

   The awe of
friendly speech.
   Edenic viols
no promissory masterful
explanation of
   the reprimand scene
a non-turbulent
withdrawal.
   The camomile fades,
breeze off the lake
preparing lemon trees.

                    iii
Audacious idea
empty left hand,
Die Glückliche Hand, *
interrupts the idyllic shore-line
   light bulb
       mobility.

_____

**The Lucky Left Hand,* Schoenberg

Sideways

    Sideways
become what is
      thoughtbred
and steeple.

Is true this bodie
has a surpass of beautie

thief in that heart ladle
ladle historic

         supergreen

printed in darkness.

No chill no vapor
unroll or unwarm
the skeletal

underground plenty
warmth of plenty
    is
       warrant.

Or gobble the soil

flavored

as if warm

ingratiatingly coated

invisible.

With sharpened

cornice

and is of

cheek bone

a tame animal

    scentsuet.

And tame animal

slungover his shoulder

wet autumn

of palette cloth.

          •

Ennobled with surprise the root

deepens and the sprouting,

the pagan sprouting,

   small packets of marble,

   grains of it torture the eyes.

   A greened-over tree years

         (mourning)

   of mourning and exploding.

          •

 of altering!

of "unmuddied visage"

     (sideways

          •

The Confetti Trees

Overboard

my first Motion Picture story derives from a
sequence in the classic   *Art of the Film*

Nothing is shown except the quivering surface the woman standing up and then jumping overboard in which is seen the reflection of the boat the woman indirectly shown by her reflection in the water she is seen falling into water where the reflection lies of herself standing up and jumping off the boat; at the next moment the woman herself is seen falling into water at the very spot where her reflection lies the boat is not important the boat with the woman on board "reflected in the water" is important it creates "unusualness"; the suicide reflected in the water catches the eye that with only a passing interest might have watched the woman jump into the water the eye is caught by this "artistic trick" when an adolescence is passed viewing these "artistic tricks" the woman jumping into the water could never be as significant to this person as "reflections in water" the reflection in water is "poetry of the moment."

The Tear

She walks up the slight incline of a hill fatigue conveyed by the way she bends down to loosen her hiking boots. The sun is high, there is an absence of wind, and ripples of heat arise from the distant sand. The heat is given a further tonality when a cloud of bees swarms over the horizon. A tear collects in the woman's eye. This *close up* of her eye with its tear is purposefully designed to interfere with the camera's exploration of landscape. It signifies that a tear collected in a heretofore dry eye will convey a possible sadness entering the film.

There is a further purpose to the emphasis of a tear in her eye. The Director desires to wrest our attention from the landscape! The camera "says" it is no longer interested in the details of nature. Our full attention must now flow to this long-haired woman.

In a rare static moment (rare to a camera) the camera having removed itself from its *engaged closing in* on her eye, we are permitted to follow the hesitation of her arm. Only then, (an almost invisible moment of time) we recognize that the camera *is* "intimating," *not telling* that the *dramatic* action of this film is about to begin.

The Cough

He felt an uncomfortable sensation in his throat. Perhaps his throat was struggling with words. Seated in the car next to this Japanese film director, Wilhelm began to cough. He feared the conflict going on in his throat might not stop. It might continue and interrupt their conversation in the long drive from the Japanese airport. He threw his body against the seat in an attempt to shake off his embarrassment.

"Allergy," said Nagao with confidence, "Allergy to our film." On Nagao's unwrinkled skin were little ribbons of smile.

At the intersection of the road in Nagasaki where in Japanese films a short dark woman usually squats, Wilhelm pointed out a break between two buildings where light crept through like an oyster. He said he would like to use that oyster light. *"Cliche,"* said Nagao.

(Observing Nagao in his dark blue denims, he wondered if their film should be called *Dark Blue Denim.*) He wished the noise an oyster makes could get into the film. Nagao shook his head. "Better noise the eye when it blinks. *'Pachi Pachi'* in Japanese."

Wilhelm suggested the sound of creaking wood for the scene of the two people lost in the garden.

"Pachi Pachi better," Nagao said. "More subtle."

The action was too slow and Wilhelm wanted a more violent crescendo. When the body fell down the cellar stairs, perhaps another body could fall on top of it?

"Could be liquid soap on stair," said Nagao.

In the middle of a film, Wilhelm always had the feeling he was being chased. He complained that when he directed those shots up in the sky with two planes flying parallel to each other, he also was in a sky chase. "Flower petals putting on the wings of the plane," suggested Nagao.

Perhaps he might return to his home for awhile and the scenarist could work with Nagao. She could put her own story into the script, how she got hired, etc. Was there something going on between her and Nagao.

He thought of home as a possible sequence and *Home* started to roll with its camera views. *Home* needed editing, especially the scene with his analyst when they discussed his cough that now seemed like another room in the movie.

Nagao believed the film was too slow. It was old-fashioned to explain why gangsters upset the fish cart.

Wilhelm disagreed and told him the fish cart was like a scene by the painter, Utamaro, a capsule of real life. He suggested a new title, *Dreams of Real Life.*

"No," said Nagao, both eyes blinking, *The Cough* is better.

Trousers for Extras

It was the scene where the toothy actress takes a glass of water and places it on a table next to a bouquet of flowers. The glass of water was merely a prop intended to remove the camera from her ambitious arrangement of flowers. The camera, following the rhythm of the water, picked up the shine of her molars as she brought the water to her face. The shine remains in the shadowy fade-out to a mansion where the star of the picture under a canopy of ice green purple red lay chained to an enormous burlap bag. "TROUSERS FOR EXTRAS" was written on it, and there were many many people in the chamber all dressed in trousers, with "grips" handling extra lights and extra food and extra "quiet" cards for the extra stages in what was to be one of the most gigantic productions of the studio.

Nostalgia

A need to film *Nostalgia* crept into the studio and *Fade In*

Les Grand Boulevards, umbrellas and personal sky, ambition and secret desire, "stiletto" of rain. *Dissolve* to nostalgia shots ambition and secret desire *plaisirs* of visual kings: knees, masks, intolerance, greed, ballrooms, Bucharest, Vienna, slums; barges, wars, candles, airplanes, deserts, California, New York, railroads; gangsters, light bulbs, aprons, swords, horses; the Riviera, Russians, madmen, births, Christ, weddings; *Fade Out* dissolve into an earnest documentation; *Fade into* "Overview: "*Now*"

*

Now the pain has left the body. Only an outline remains. Down by the bathhouse where the soundless waves tumble the *Montage* ends in an unfinished tree. Nothing is alive. A writer sits at *Windows,* a woman on his *Screen.* He puts her on a reef with the shipwrecked sailor. The feeble sun he paws will not burn.

The Guerrilla Reporters

The guerrilla reporters move into the first reel and "Scanty Panties" moves out. Over the hill slowly a mass of shadow lights up as on camera facing front there floats a pink tutu. We never tire of this scene it crosses our eyes at night mixed with the director's sweaty palm holding onto the tree while the mobile camera moves toward him past a sack of rice.

There is uplift everywhere there is no darkness the little screen the film will play upon is not frightening. The millimeters are small tongs catching fireflies in front of the rice. Printed onscreen a revolutionary alphabet interweaves with the action and they make it happen again while guns run up a hill then down and the dummy soldier falls several times. The momentum of the film is so swift we almost miss the counterpoint of Guerrilla voices accompanying the ghostlike drift of the tutu as the gallant camera moves in little steps behind it. Then with a sound crisp as an icy tear, the soldier falls again as the tutu fades from the screen.

Confucius

The actress was washing her face the camera picking up her motions slowly with great emphasis on the wrists, she had a way of flexing them that was unique and the director wanted the camera to catch this movement. The cameraman was from Sweden and he understood the delicacy of piecing together snow floes. He understood the scenario, how snow rinses her wrists slowly, without being told he slowed his camera, so that the audience might grasp the meaning of snow on the wrists of the actress, and the snow that the wrists moved through. He was filming "slow whiteness." Lighting was important and the lighting assistant, Swedish, also, was selected because he understood the business of snow as it enters the atmosphere. The dialogue that takes place between it and day as it begins and as it ends gathering a momentum of whiteness. The film becomes more than a contemplative movement of wrists. In the beginning water that fell from her face to her wrist served as an introduction. At that point the story line needed to be photographed from far off. Only later in close-up details were sharpened to pick up the signature of a woman's face. There seemed to be no misunderstanding as to who indeed was the star and what role the camera played, each subsisted on snow. Within the screenplay originally fixed solely on the ability of the actress to flex her wrists (camera shot of wrists) (camera preys on face above her wrists) a secondary plot was now beginning to develop as snow and light crossed the face of the actress. The actual fact of her washing, the Director now realizes, has become a subsidiary plot in need of more complex artistry.

The Director is a difficult man. His sudden changes of mood often cause alarm. In exasperation he picks up a book lying on a table nearby and throws this book hitting the sink where the actress washes, narrowly missing her wrists. It is silent film so we do not hear a plaintive voice, or the sound of the book striking.

We see the trembling of the actress as the book narrowly misses her wrists. Without any prompting she picks up the book (no sound to delude us) and guides the book up to her face where we see written on its cover *The Sayings of Confucius.* "She is reading Confucius!" we repeat over and over, as we savor the Director's silent applause.

Color

He believed if the woman on the right moved over to the left he could place her into the frame where a meadow lay beyond her. But it did not work out that way. The moon came up too early. The glow the moon cast lit up the shadow behind the wheelbarrow. No one could advance in the shattering moonlight. The film begins to take the shape of a milk bottle with the heavy cream on top.

He blamed everything on the use of color. The heavy woman who played the woodcutter's wife wanted to lay some emeralds on her bosom. They are the color of trees, she says. The skin of the leading actor was the color of ferns which do not blend with the pastel process that turns the clouds to pastel. The girl's knee is supposed to be grey when she bends it, not the color of blood. The voice coming from the elderberries is colorless, indicating melancholy. He remembers the alluring depths in film without color when tears were dark as drops falling from a raven's mouth. Once again his efforts have been emptied of meaning.

Nuns

The story was about nuns shedding their "Habits," it was supposed to be a documentary with a close-up in the cloister of one nun walking in the new dress of a nun. "Something simple in cotton or wool with a cardigan and low shoes" were the orders given to the wardrobe department. The other nun would wear the discarded nun habit with rosary at the waist. Unfortunately the wardrobe department had packed away or sold the original habits and had not ordered any replacements.

The picture was about to be cancelled when the director had the idea of taking his crew over to a convent and filming his picture there. At this point an argument began about where they would find a convent. A member of the crew told them the nuns lived on church grounds, or so he thought, and why didn't they move their equipment to a neighborhood Catholic Church.

Then an argument broke out about whether they should use the actresses who had already been chosen after much delay and search, or if the nuns in the Church that was yet to be located would permit themselves to be filmed. The nuns would add authenticity to what was proposed as a documentary. At this point the actresses said they would sue the company, because their contracts were already signed. It was also mentioned that there might be a clause in the contracts of nuns that did not permit them to act for commercial purposes.

"Commercial purposes" was familiar to the production department and after no more than an hour word came from the head office saying the department would be delighted to make a gift to the "church of choice" if one were selected as soon as possible as the production manager was already annoyed at the delay.

The director idle during these conversations retired to his van and was reading "The Counterfeiters" while he sipped his afternoon vodka with orange juice. His assistant climbed into the van and they began to discuss Andre Gide and how seldom in French letters did one find a writer who was a Protestant. The Director remarked it was quite a coincidence that he, the son of a Protestant minister, should be making a documentary about nuns.

Old films about nuns used "star" material like Ingrid Bergman. It was absurd to make this "documentary" with third rate actresses and local churches. They were deciding to take the company to Lourdes when the telephone rang cancelling the picture. The church in Beverly Hills wanted too much money and the priest of the Church of the Angels near Olvera St. was in Mexico.

Corelli

The more the scenario relies on Corelli the more fluid it becomes and moves closer to the idea of a master scene whose nuance is fixed in a shadow kingdom which the music of Corelli will underscore. Within the scenario there is built an incredible gaiety that may or may not take place. It is "a strrrictness within fluidity" which will complicate this movie now experimentally called, "Bird on Nude Girl's Hip."

The Vanished Library

They were in Alexandria filming *The Vanished Library.* This film was assigned originally to Petaluma, but she was in Minneapolis making *The Life of Hiawatha.* She kept faxing suggestions to the new director who was already intimidated by her. In a re-run of the first reel of his film there was a curious rush of water, "like the Mississippi," someone said.

The film was barely off the ground when the wardrobe head decided to redesign the costumes of Aristotle and Pliny. The film began to act as if it were haunted when the crew was forced to destroy the plywood copy of the Library which an historian told them was incorrect. Also, there were too many ships in the harbor. Another consultant from M I T recommended an Egyptian director.

They put in an emergency call for an archaeologist from Princeton who happened to be on a dig in Turkey. This archaeologist, when he arrived on the set, laughed brutishly. He told them the scholarly debate was not over the size of the library. It was whether the *Iliad* and the *Odyssey* had each been written by Homer. He reminded them that the library had been burned several times. What they were now working with was a false copy of the second burning of the library.

By this time the crew and the actors had decided Alexandria resembled Los Angeles. Why didn't they take the picture back to the studio in Culver City where they could live at home, comfortable and mosquitoless?

Los Angeles had a burned library and an Art Foundation that could supply them with drawings of historical disasters. The sea of Los Angeles was also poisoned, like the waters of Alexandria. It was decided to move back home.

Petaluma had completed her work in Minneapolis and was reassigned to the film. It turned out that midway into *Hiawatha* she had converted to Social Realism. Despite groans from the accountancy department, which had approved *The Vanished Library* as a "prestigious property," she announced she was not going to make another A R T F I L M .

With her fabulous eye for detail, she now focused on the illiteracy of the populace. "Starving" extras now filled the streets, in rags the locals wept. The Stars weep also for the fragile gowns they cannot wear, the specially cut jewels, forbidden. The actors sigh for the silk and fur of their cloaks, the flagons of wine now missing.

Then begins the actual conflagration when the Library like a mighty ship keels, its marble columns are felled, the precious literature destroyed. Historical records burn. Petaluma jumps up and down tearing her hair clothes skin throwing volume after volume of books into the fire, urging the extras to carry more books.

MORE FIRE MORE FIRE   BURN MORE

           BOOKS   MORE BOOKS BOOKS   BURN

"Lonely Mess"

A fully dressed man with the mobile face of an actor of the 1930s is standing on an empty beach. He is reading a letter. The sea gulls screech above him. The camera pans in. Looking directly into the camera he repeats over and over: "I refuse to get whipped up by your lonely mess"

Lubitsch

She was handed this beautiful opportunity of directing a film she truly believed in. The "truly" had been written into her astonishingly female-oriented contract and for days she had been considering scripts, even books. Now she was in a blue funk.

The color "blue" flew under her lids as did a passing memory of *Erwartung* by Schoenberg. A pink tulip was added to a painting by Tiepolo. She noticed a bowl of raisins placed near her desk. Did they belong there? All at once she remembered a little girl with a cow and she believed the little girl once belonged in a nursery rhyme in a book called "Smooth Realities." The pink dress of the little girl, even the bows on her dress went with the tulip that went with the room.

Meanwhile the postman delivered a large package wet from the rains that beseiged her city. She put the package on a table and a plum rolled out of a grocery bag her daughter carelessly had placed on the table. The cat came downstairs and bit her leg. She remembered the blue cat who had fallen out of the window in Switzerland. There had been a tall old tree under the window and the cat had lain in the tree for days alive and meowing while the people below in the first floor apartment had told her the cat was dead and had been carted away. She looked at the palm tree outside. She began to weep a little and tears gathered in her eyes just beneath the memory of *Erwartung*.

The door opened and her husband walked into the room. He had been away on a trip. He put his suitcase on the floor and embraced her. His gaze, however, was not on her, but toward the open door of the kitchen from which came the warning smell of burned chicken.

"I am going to get rid of this," she said to herself closing her eyes. When she opened them her husband was gone and so was the odor of burned chicken. "That is real editing!" she said out loud.

Then she talked to herself about Montage Montage and how people neglected it, etc. She really began to believe she had completed a picture and her husband was home to celebrate with her. Her daughter, or the cook, she added, as she liked to think the studio paid her more than it did, had made a *coq au vin*, the same kind of chicken they served in the films of Ernest Lubitsch that took place on the Left Bank.

She remembered the champagne they served in Lubitsch films even when faced with poverty and bitter times. Then another tear formed in her eye with the memory of the chiffon dresses that floated over his shiny floors. She heard the music. The music that lightened his touch. Moody but not sad. Doors that accompanied his motion pictures. Shining like the floors, promising secrets.

You climbed up his handsome stairs to the great doors that swung open to men sitting in chairs and drinking, laughing, lying. People lied in his pictures and you never minded. Only betrayed people opened his doors.

Dreamers in Lubitsch films. Gifted people, like herself, determined to exit the snare of everyday life. What did dream-laden Lubitsch know about everyday life! Then she recalled the eyes of a former Hungarian Baroness. She had played with a little fan tied to her wrist as she confided her life story tears, international tears, of loss and regret lay nested in her eyes.

Now it occurred to the Director that she was not in need of a script. All day she had been "montaging" bits of stories. Her script was already written. It was composed as an *Intermezzo*, a breeze in the middle of the day. Her film would be the length of an *Intermezzo*, whispers, interruptions, innuendos, a memory confided across the table, before the half-bottle of champagne is served.

Noise

It was midnight and the chief cutter was turning out the lights in the cutting room when he heard a noise. The noise seemed to shift around the room like an obscure cloud. From the open window of his house he often watched the *montage* of these clouds.

He had been in this country so long he was accustomed to the continual shifting of noise. His native home was in the Black Forest as it edged around Freiberg. Later in Berlin he learned to edit out the city noise. He became a film cutter because he could control the little shifting sounds that attempted to warp his life.

He remembered an actress in Berlin. On the set her heel caught on the hem of her gown. She fell as the camera turned. The curls of her hair were spread over the nape of her neck. The Director murmured "Lovely," then he called "Take."

Later the cutter had rerun the film in his machine and decided to delete the fall; to use only the moment when the actress lay on the floor her hair spread around her. He noticed the cast had gathered to watch the fallen actress and he left them in the film.

Now he recognized the source of the noise in the room. It was his scissors cutting into the woman's hair.

Preparedness

They were on location in the hills above a small California town and before breakfast the Assistant Director and a member of his crew were scouting out possible locations for the movie they were going to make. It was tentatively called "Preparedness" or "He Is Prepared" or "Without Preparedness"; the word "Preparedness" or "Prepared" was ordered to be in the film title. This had to do with an idea of the Producer's that all bad things in the world happened because people were unprepared. "For What?" This was asked all over the set. But no one had found an answer.

The men had climbed to about three thousand feet and were surveying the gentle land that lay about them. There were wildflowers amid the eucalyptus trees and there were chestnut trees with the pale rose colored blossoms at their long fingertips. An azalea or two became part of a disordered group of cultivated flowers blown there by the bay winds. All was serenely natural and even stately with the yellow Iris, and the browned Peony buds, a straggling Rose and the carpet of Wildflowers, violet and pink sometimes yellow. The flowers, the soft breeze laden with scent, trees changing color as the morning passed and light filled with yellow charmed these Hollywood men, their talk became less indignant.

They could see the water of the Bay below them with small boats anchored at its shores. A cloud rolled over from a mountain above the Bay. The light changed on their mountain to a dark grey. The sun slowly entered the cloud and the cloud was mottled with a yellow glow from the sun forcing its way through the grey cloud. On top of the far mountain there was a contest between the color of the sun forcing its way through the cloud and the dark cloud coming from behind the mountain forcing itself into the yellowed light.

The movie men noticed that the ground below them and beside them was mottled with this color coming from across the bay and the leaves on the ground began to pick up a little wind. The flowers began a slow nodding and what had been simple now began to turn into a darker more complicated color; the breeze was picking up and this caused the leaves of the tree near them to flatten and show their dull greyish green sides. The odor of flowers began to penetrate this slow changing of the guard on the mountain. The odor began to enter the new stillness and halt there.

One of the men sensitive to attacks of heat and cold began to shiver. Another took out a package of cigarettes and was going to light up when a hand reached across and closed the package. He was reminded that smoking was forbidden. The land had been too dry, too crisp and eager for fire, and they began to discuss the terrible fire that had ravaged a mountain nearby.

A bird flew across the horizon. He was large and the swoop that his wing made was slightly disturbing. Yet the dipping of his wings as he sailed across the canyon created no disorder in their vision, but indicated a calmness as always in an elegant finesse of nature. This brought the men to a conversation about elegance and how sometimes it was needed in a film. Just enough of it might save a picture from the tawdriness it willingly fell into. Elegance, as in the length of the swoop of the hawk's wing. One of the men looked at his watch wishing to time the swooping, if possible. The hawk obligingly flew over them again even as the first drops of rain fell. With the beginning of the rain the hawk began to fly higher like an airplane, it was remarked, seeking another altitude. So they were unable to time the hawk and its elegance became a memory. But memory is useful they remarked. They were talking about memory in a film, of course, because none of them had much use for anything outside their work.

The rain had by now muddied the hill path and the color of the flowers became more brilliant against the ground before their soft heads were utterly destroyed. Across the bay a streak of lightning hit a mountain peak and they watched the rain pour from a cloud and into the bay. The men had brought no umbrella or raincoats they were unprepared for this natural seizure of land and color. They were unprepared for the sudden swirl of water around their ankles as a torrent got in their way going down. But they were laughing. Their teeth outside their mouth in the widening of the mouth for laughter getting wetter and wetter until each of them was swallowing the rain water. They had been unprepared for this torrent of water but now they knew how the scene would play out.

"Moments Before . . ."

A surprising order had come down from the Producer to make a film "on/or concerning the subject of Death, an accidental Death of a person of importance."

This caused much speculation as to the mortality of the producer, himself, until someone pointed out that lodged on the sparse soil of his mind, like an Icelandic flower, was a fondness for the films of Ingmar Bergman. This faith in Bergman, who many of the studios considered "finished," must have established itself when the producer was an adolescent, as no similar evidence of this affection existed in his harsh demands to make more "gun shows."

After the usual studio squabble, a woman came up with the idea they film the death of Margaret Fuller, a noted Feminist, who died at sea with her lover, an Italian Revolutionist, and their child in 18—. "Don't make it too sad, Make it inevitable." The producer envisioning a Joan of Arc film, said to the Director.

The Director was surprised to be pulled into this film. The elegance and nuance of his direction was out of favor. (*As if the Producer decided to open his last case of Lafitte Rothschild.*) The Director was not interested in a shipwreck. He had come to America in a packed ship just before the Nazis closed in and he was not interested in recalling any of the details.

He decided to avoid the shipwreck altogether and to concentrate on filming the hours before Miss Fuller went aboard. He believed that in a film it was the moments "before" death that counted. (It was odd the young people considered this a "feminist" film. Death was no divider of the sexes.)

A snowfield was created. Margaret Fuller was seen wrapped in a voluminous cape cradling her child in her arms while her companion struggled with the luggage pieces that in the wind were losing their careful wrapping. There was a close-up of the man struggling to bind them.

Margaret was facing the wind her high boots covered with snow. The camera was ordered to zoom in on the woman and then close-up on the child burying his little head in her billowing skirts. The camera moved to the harbor to the frail ship plunging and tacking in the wind. The grips were ordered to raise the wind noise and it grew weightier and a word to the soundman brought a wail from the ship's mast. Then the noise was cut back. The snow stopped. A silvery moon began to climb out from behind the clouds. The silver touched her shawl and the forehead of the child.

The Director motions the Captain to climb aboard with the silvery moonlight now full on his face. Moonlight flits from their heads and their shoulders and spotlights the luggage now mysteriously aboard. The Director shows the child wrapped in his bundling how to fling his hands outward as if to catch the rays of the moon.

Margaret looks through the moonlight (a few flakes of snow fall gently upon her) to her lover standing aboard the ship, and we see there are tears in her eyes, snow tears. A small cloud begins to cross the heavens, the cameraman films the cloud as it passes across the ship and he continues filming as the cloud smudges the figures of the protagonists until the sky completely darkens. Snow begins to fall once more. There is no sentimentality in this scene with Fate in the turbulent air.

The ominous moon moves out of the cloud. Death crosses the foreheads of these people even the crew and the child. The Director has perfectly understood the requisites of his film.

The Dream Motion Picture;
A PROPOSAL FOR ANIMATION

A sword is thrust between sheets while a choir of robins sings, we then hear duel noises mixed with musical bells.

He dreams of a crowd and in his dream becomes detached from the crowd, next he becomes detached from the dream, and he struggles to return to his dream of the crowd, while in a corner of the same dream chamber a man hugs a book bound in vellum as he reads by candlelight.

The dreamer sees upon the green a mighty cavalry and fairies floating over-head, one a queen, and on her hand is a purple ring, and at her throat a scarf with prophesies woven on it.

A wind springs up and the carpet upon which people walk is filled with flower-notes drifting in the wind; above sails a planet with stars attached to a frail motor, and from the stars fall these flowers.

We see strolling down the hillside a band of stragglers laughing, they are all laughing while the man they follow never ceases to talk. On his embroidered sleeves that plough the air as he swings his hands above his head is written: "Philosopher."

We are led into a library where sits an ancient fellow poring over a map that is the Map of the World and over the Map dolphin swim.

Another chamber in which there is a person dressed in velvet with rubies and emeralds falling from his neck and over his shoulders is placed a fur of the little ermine and sketched onto this fur in thinnest ice is the word: "Alchemist."

All things in this dream sequence appear of a great and kindly Order and the rhythm of the dreamer (his breathing) seems moved by this Order, and no thing artificial reaches into the dream chamber. The dreamer is passing through the gate over which is written: MODERNITY.

Nemesis

The film she was working on was filled with an odd, an unexpected grief. She could not rush past it. The lines on the face of the actress showed up clearly and her eyebrows puckered in a frown, even as she read the scenario that was sup-posed to be sophisticated and amusing. Her little dog lay with his head thrust down; his long hair fell in front of his eyes, from time to time he moaned. Her flowers wilted in all their vases. The piano became mute. The boy who was to enter from the right tripped on a rug and fell sobbing in front of strangers. Even the midget so full of jokes, near the piano was heard to say, "I've had my share of sorrow." The automobile to be filmed in front of the white door to the mansion developed carburetor trouble and had to be removed. The actor who was to drive the car stubbed his toe on the big rock that sat at the end of the driveway with the name of the house painted in black letters.

And it rained. Los Angeles rain, like no other rain, overflowed the gutters. There were mudslides and lost houses. The Rose Parade to be used as a background shot to give the film *authenticity* was cancelled. A month before when the film was in its earlier stages there had been a fire in one of the canyons the production unit was going to use. And the planned filming of a famous Buddhist who was to land at the Burbank Airport near the Studio had to be scrapped, because he was taken ill on the East Coast.

"The spirit of Nemesis" was heard on the set and rapidly picked up. The studio head moaned, *"my Nemesis."* A bright and neglected writer asked, "Why not call the film, *"Nemesis"*?

Few knew what the word meant, but they liked the sound. Its sound might improve the imageless desert on which they were stranded.

The Aromas

It was the beginning of the picture, a few lights were winking in a great dome and cars were running below like small butterflies arching their limber wings. These were known as Aromas and introducing them in the first advertising reel was difficult because they had no aroma and were difficult to catch in the huge sprayed nets spotted around and above the tracks.

An anonymous noise issued from loud speakers and a nondescript filter equalized the light meters in an attempt to project an air of anonymity as if it were a separate chemical property. The idea is that it is possible to reduce subject matter to a form of chemicalization and the intent was to spread a monochrome over the entire area, allowing even spectators to be alloted anonymous positions, poised in a world losing the individuality of its personnel. Thus anonymity will act as a lubricant in personal lives, adjusting salaries, easing relationships, etc.

The film projection circling around the idea of a civilization directed by chemicals created difficulties on the set, even highly emotional ones. The director and his assistant, while clinging to the established historicism of Cinema production, welcomed the advent of computerization ordered by the moguls in control of this picture. Their task would be lightened if the plot were developed through computer graphics, rather than an actor's characterization. Signs would replace screams, or lengthy conversations.

The main office was thrilled to have its employees welcome an innovation they were eager to pursue. Within a few days a massive group of computers had been rolled in with their attendants to assist the *grips*. Specialists were called in to explain the machine's elementary usages. Over a thousand computers were to be used, each personalized to fit the directives of its controller.

It became necessary to make several changes in the script at this point in order to reduce words which gradually filled up too much space. Hence a series of periods (. . . . .) were introduced to replace this superfluity of words.

Meanwhile the Director had changed into a chemical proof overall. (It was remarked in hollow voices by men standing farthest from the computers that what they were preparing had already been accomplished by Eisenstein when he filmed Russia's massive chemical factories.) An argument broke out among the aging production crew as to whether chemicals or people caused the defeat of the Germans in that terrible winter no contemporary graphics could reproduce.

Later another argument would unfold in the studio's promotion department as newspapers and magazines were fed stories of the phenomenal use of graphics in this production. Like warriors falling on the battlefield, so did the faces of actors now disappear in advertisements to be replaced by computer O's, a form of camouflage distressful to the film stars, yet considered a radical break through in computerized studio promotion.

The same idea was seized by the computer companies, who ordered that the O's inside their computers in radical situations be replaced by *faces*, a substitution forever associated with this award-winning motion picture.

Falling in Love

"You have to be on your toes," he ordered, so she obediently tiptoed out of the room.

"Cut" called the Director who liked small body movements, toes turned outward and knees hidden under clothing. He had seen her knees knocking against the fabric of her body. Knocking knees disturbed him, although his own walk was odd, with one foot hitting the other.

She was back in the room, obediently on tiptoes, her head in a cloud the effects man had built, but her body was off balance. Standing on one foot as she was told to do, her torso was off center. When she fell, with that little look of surprise one always has, unfortunately she was outside the camera range. This deeply annoyed the Director who wanted to stress the frailty of the body with this fall. The whole company would be surprised when later the front office titled their film, "She Falls in Love."

Details

" . . . the stream upland and you in your overcoat a tender brown the mood of the landscape yet a storm treads its way and thee Oh wanderer who seeks the real storm pauses for this apparition to disappear."

He was the same Director as in "She Falls in Love," with the same attitude toward his actors, sitting in his poncho under an umbrella reading the script as the storm approached. The actors in the distance were gathered near a barrel. Taking out his binoculars to see more clearly it turned out they were next to several low barns. He had told the actors to gather by some barrels while the cameraman adjusted his camera for a distance shot.

No, it wasn't barns they were standing beside, it was a house he now discovered. These mistakes were unusual for him. He was noted for his meticulous use of the landscape. His actors appreciated this in his films. A house in the distance changed the whole concept. He had ordered the barrels, because they lent an impermanence to the scene, and he wanted to introduce this into his picture. He didn't actually use the word "impermanence." When speaking about this new film he sometimes said he wanted the film to be symbolic of a world that was "a bit shaky"; apt to "roll" away if not watched.

The action began in heavy mechanical studio rain. An actor in a brown overcoat lit a cigarette and detaching himself from the group entered the house. Other actors in brown overcoats with lit or unlit cigarettes entered the house. One by one as the director watched, the actors reappeared. Each carried a barrel he then pushed down the rickety steps of the house.

One more detail decided the Director. Over his loud speaker he called to the actors to put out their cigarettes. "No smokes! Not in this rain! Keep the unlit cigarettes in your mouths. Keep pushing the barrels! In and out of the house more and more barrels! Four more times. Before the real storm hits."

As he turned back to go to his car he was dissatisfied. The mechanical rain had looked too mechanical. The script has said something about "apparition." Wasn't the landscape supposed to be like an apparition while the men in their raincoats going in and out of the house in the studio rain were supposed to represent reality as opposed to . . . he had missed something. He lived in the real world too much these days. He hated reality. His raincoat had already dampened the seat of his expensive car and there were puddles on the floor. Puddles! In his beautiful car! That was what was wrong. You had no control over reality. He sat back in his seat, prepared to reconsider the film in terms of an apparition with absolutely no intrusion of the physical world and its weather.

The Confetti Trees

A wind was howling in from the desert, strong for that time of the year in Los Angeles. The woman being filmed was walking up a Boulevard, the wind blowing her hair, her skirts also lifted by the wind. The wind was dry, having arrived from the desert with no scent of the sea upon it.

It was, however, performing strange tricks with the camera. The wind spilled into the camera streaks of color, like peals of hysterical laughter.

The landscape was now speckled with color. Looking out on this curious forestation of color were the palm trees. Their heavy heads and long thin trunks were speckled with green. The green of the palm trees seemed to grow more intense with each moment that passed. The camera began to overflow with the heaviness of all that green inside it overtoppling the speckled color that jammed it.

The figure of the woman became a dark green as one color passed into another. Suddenly her coat turned black as the colors mixed together. What was happening to the cameras was now beyond anyone's control. What was happening to the road in front of the woman heavily laden with color was also beyond the camera's control.

The men carrying the cameras and those on trucks following them began to behave in an odd abstract fashion. There was an illusion of heads becoming heels and waists became arms, as if a circus bounced along a road distributing colored announcements of its arrival. As if there were clowns in the melting colors whose cheeks became more and more highly colored, their rouged lips opening to swallow the liquid color that flowed around them. The royal palms, their long necks entering the sky, were like gaily decorated elephants from whose snouts colors flowed.

Color weighed down the heavy burlap of the short scrub palms intruding into the burlap around their waists. The palms appeared engaged in a practical manufacture of color. All this took place within an hour. Color crumpled the pavement, then mounted upward making its way from the soft centers of the palms to cover their features.

On a nearby hill was a camera crew whose lens were still untouched. There the trees still maintained their silken royalty. Suddenly one tender palm winced as the first ember of color fell on it. And as the wind gathered strength a shout rose up on this commandless battlefield. Packets of colors like confetti began to pellet the trees. Anticipating a final explosion the isolated men hasten to adjust their cameras in a final hope this shot will alter their careers.

Romance

The director had led his cast to a viaduct of a dry river and the cast resented this overture to reality. They wanted to be seated in green with blossoms. The leading actor had thrown his motorbike on a slope of the dry hill. He wished the bike were a grey palfrey resting on green. Having to play the tough guy was annoying. It betrayed his true character which was romantic, like the grey palfrey.

The actresses, given names like Dessie and Brunnie, wearing harsh leather and gun belts, were also annoyed. They, too, were romantics, believing their true names to be Desdemona and Brunhilde, even Lotus Blossom. And the tacky sodas they were forced to sip, all because the Director believed the sodas would "underline," that was his ridiculous word, "the level of society they belonged to." Stupid.

The Director, putting a pinch of snuff in each nostril, was likewise engaged: " . . . Norma Shearer . . . John Barrymore . . . Conquistadores . . . silver armor . . . Norma Shearer . . . daughter of Emperor . . . expensive hotel . . . Barrymore . . . beautiful voice . . . thick oak door . . . Norma!" ran through his head like the sips of rum he remembered from the the old days in the screening room, the feel of the glass in his now shaky hand. *Tacky soda . . . laced with gin . . . ugly Burbank.* He floated away to his new home in New York State: " . . . Dutchess County roses climbing roof . . . "

No Words

The Director sat slouched and disheveled in his chair on the set, the scenario in his hands. Words lined the pages, more words lay on the floor where he had thrown the pages. For hours he had been sitting in the chair reading words. They bounced from off the window onto the floor. They plastered the ceiling. They had fallen into his coffee cup. How he detested these words!

Words were supposed to explain the motives of the actors. Bah. Words told why the actor left the house and went to a river. Why he sat in his car by the river. Bah. Bah. Words told why the actor drove off the bridge. Bah. He threw the script across the room.

He got out of his chair and stamped on the pages where the words were written. He shouted at the cat who had been sitting on his lap and now had run cowering to the door. "Even you Delilah," he said to the cat, "make words! But you cannot write!"

He picked her up from her cowering position and held her trembling body in his arms. "You cannot write words! And that is why I love you." He held her close to him stroking her fur until he heard her purr. "A purr is not words!"

He returned her to his chair while he walked around the room muttering, first in a soft voice then his voice became louder and then louder and once again he was shouting:

"FILMS ARE THE ENEMY OF WORDS ENEMY OF WORDS!"

He went to the bottom of the staircase where the steps went upward onto a false landing and shouted: "It is written to go upstairs and kill the woman, because these damned words say so," and he shook the papers of the script in his trembling hands, "I will not tell the actor to go up these stairs because these damned words are lying. MOTIVES personal motives refuse to let the actor go up these stairs, even if it is written that he should go up!"

"WORDS ARE THE ENEMY OF FILMS!"

The Director was flailing his arms in the air and a terrible expression crossed his face, of determination and belief. "Character and Time and Space tell that actor to go up the stairs! Words, never." He sat back down in his chair, clasping his head in his hands, and now he was weeping, "I cannot direct this picture," he mumbled. "I cannot direct any more pictures, if they keep on handing me these Words."

By now he was speaking in the foreign tongue of international speech and what he was saying was incoherent to the actor who had entered the room with a glass of water in his hand.

Even in his rage the Director had remained alert. Turning around he said to the actor in the familiar way of the theatre, "Oh there you are, you darling," and then "hand me that water, if you please." A rather sweet smile was on his face.

"Now walk over to the piano that is there in the dark and start to sing. But don't," his face stern again, and he stood up, the glass of water falling from his hand onto the floor, "but don't sing any words! No WORDS. You understand. Turn your back to me and make beautiful noises. PURE NOISES! NO WORDS."

The alarmed actor, who was also a skilled musician, did as he was told. Ah AH, the Director was breathing deeply. "Ah, No Words. Passion. Only Passion."

The notes poured out into the room, just as the great *lied* composer had written them. A smile crossed the Director's face. "Passion and no words," he breathed, "passion and no words."

Screening Room Notes

(explosion)
HE MISTOOK THE HANDLE IMPLIED
GET OUT OF HERE (CUT) next stand in line alphabetically

You under the purple cloud   as witnessed the shooting of this film
drawers open at the seam ("What a director!") speaking   over there
sound widens   like the opening of an egg (graceful)

                              Sad Hop-hoppers (use left aisle)
        "elbow touches the desk"

cottage divides into two dwellings   blown image EDGE OF SINIS-
TER TRACKS
        internal rhythm: repeat as it shifts toward window

rejoin the others with more laughter and cat-calls
    climate changes   moon sails upward
wearing stripes   remember the mittens   like the side of a shelf
the interior more grandiose, but with less furniture   where they can sit
stroll   aimless postpone the action "figure it out"

                                other rhythms erupt
physically not too strong so the moment collapses
you like this car

use a REMOTE   feeling tired with fading vision

                    the key is in the door
    move slowly   a lizard slides into your bosom   Nice Title
        find the screwdriver

"I believe her name is Dora in the first re-write"

            this lovely lack

think EUCALYPTUS

                AND THE IDEA OF A MOTHER AT THE PIANO
WILL SMOOTH THE TRANSITIONS AS YOU GO OUT

sand on the floor mixed
with toes near the door

move in to CLOSE-UP
EVERYBODY KNEELS   WIND SHUFFLES THE SAND A
BRUISED KEY DROPS FROM KEYHOLE

The Minus Ones

She submitted a few stories she called *The Minus Ones*.

They came to her as short signals, as if they lived on her rooftop. They rolled off the roof of her mouth climbed there from memory or from a table where empty cups glistened with tearfulness. Also menu-like out of her stung heart came surprising plots: Spanish women and high shoes, stories of valleys and boatless seas no cargoes. Rocks similar to the porpoises in her marine story appeared. They were made of coal hard yet they chipped flakes of coal dust blew off them soiling her clothes.

From her reading she borrowed a lake bottomless and a body without gravity flying over it. This appropriation brought on a serious malaise; she became plotless and her stories were bound without the usual wrapping of ribbon.

Seasons became important, ivy on green trees and the mournful rhododendron, icicles appeared more frequently. And meadows with horses. She neglected to include the rituals of contemporary life and the Scenario Department complained. When she wrote of wood burning she said the devils inside the fire were excited.

The fire scene destroyed any chance she had for her new stories to be accepted. They told her they liked real fires and not those of the imagination. Imagination was harmful and always messed up the set.

Scenario-iste

SCENARIO. She loved the word. It was like hearing *Carmen*, perhaps. Scenes passed before her with red curtains upon their shoulders. "Scenario vicissitudes." As if she were pouring iced water on vari-colored capes.

She repeated to herself, "I am a scenario-iste." More drama intervened. Caparisoned horses drew near. She stroked them with her red nails.

A willow suddenly put its leafy arms upon her breast.

A sound of broken glass and a man in a domino entered through her window accompanied by a little person who wore a sign reading, *"Modiste,"* who handed her a lovely veiled hat.

There was pepper in the air and spice. Birds sang, "Oreos, Oreos."

"I am filled with Air and can float," the scenario-iste said to herself as she stepped out the broken window onto the browned Culver City grass.

Celluloid

She thought of Celluloid as a silken twist of rope one held climbing to the starry dome of a motion picture theatre. An acrobat lady crossing back and forth under the starry dome to show off tricks that even on paper were chilling ideas for performances on celluloid. The silken twist of Baudelaire, dizzying, entwined with collapsible fruits that will fall into the net stretched below.

She holds the silken twist above an audience stretching its neck to feed on the golden light of celluloid, that silken twist laid bare in her scenarios.

Ars, Longa

The actress is sitting in starlight her head held up by her hand, she feels as if she is slipping away far away to the clouds that briefly hide the studio moon. She frets under the weight of the camera as it edges closer to her. The lights are brighter. They block the moon. Her head shifts in her hand. Gathering inside her, more and more tumultuous as her body leans heavily on the chair's frame, is the need to resist this light under which she is impounded. Sweat is gathering on her made-up face and someone bends over to blot this face which is not hers, but belongs to the camera that is breathing upon her in the silence of an important scene.

She has been in pictures since she was a child. She knows the reasons for not interrupting the film's continuum. In her early pictures both camera and lights were friendly. Struggling and modest like herself. But now is the moment of injustice. The camera has a different life span. The camera examines her mortal face and body harshly. Lights are attracted to its cruel discipline.

Sliding down in her chair, she struggles to keep her body within the frame of the picture as the camera zooms in. The lights moving closer are more powerful than she can remember. She opens her mouth to beg them to go away so she can breathe. Now! From under closed eyelids she feels their terrible brightness beginning to dim. And she understands. Seized by fresh stamens of desire the camera is moving beyond her frail body.

Metropolis

He had been sitting in the dark for a long while in that chair he brought with him from Berlin, the wood preserved unlike so much else left behind. He was thinking about Lang's *Metropolis* with which he had been intimately connected from the days of its first sketches. Now after reading this obituary of the last person to be connected with the picture, besides himself, he felt an emptying of the air above him. Emptiness continued to pour into the vast low skies and lights above Hollywood and he willed it to flow into the minotaural labyrinths of the valley malls.

Metropolis would never again be constructed on a film stage. The idea would not enter anyone's mind today to build a skyscraper whose hidden powers lay concealed under ferocious mechanical wings. The motion picture, he let those words roll over his tongue, had been the epitome of motion. *Metropolis* could be said to have originated in the ancient belief in the power of the destructive Unknown.

The American Studios, disturbed by the volcanic mechanics of the picture, had cut some of the best scenes, the ones most Futuristic and daring. In particular the costuming, salacious and full of a mad gaiety!

The air of Pacific Palisades curled around his shoulders, moist from the sea. He was beginning to experience the first approach of a California dawn to whose cold he had never accustomed himself, nor had his wife. Lili had worn one of those marvelous costumes vibrating with false realism. When he kissed the soft down of the bird on her ear his mouth had filled with paste. On his mouth now was the original tremor of a dusty paste that had looked like a real bird.

Enchantment

Each day emerging from the grit-grey skies of Los Angeles he would enter a motion picture theater. He was not seeking shelter or escape, he wanted to immerse himself in the world of film. The celluloid must roll in front of him until it exploded in his mind. If what he saw was totally innocuous, he crept out of the theater with bits of remembered location and dialogue in his pocket, so to speak, and hastened home to salvage them. Frequently he became choked by the splendor of the celluloid images.

The primary purpose in his movie-going was to gather material for the daily dialogues with himself about the construction of a motion picture and its metaphysical position in a physical world. He liked to take a particularly bad film and rip it apart seam by seam until the pattern lay unsewn in front of him and then he would sew it up with what he believed was the ideal seam.

He wants more than anything to become an acknowledged expert on the making of film, but the field he selects is made of incantation and illusory objectivication. He promises to exchange his not inconsiderable knowledge of philosophy for a study of film as an Art. The theater repays him for his excessive interest by introducing him to its secret visual life, which now occupies him completely.

He quickly learns that this world of imagined scenes needs help in its masquerade of the real. And so he nominates himself "director" and introduces into his study of this art a portion of his philosophy of the "real" diluted with the film's potion of enchantment. It is at this point that everything becomes mixed up. As a consequence of his involvement with film he gradually is less realistic in his expectations of its scenes. This subsidizing of his life by motion pictures results in his gradual separation from the classic depictions of "real life." "Real life" dissolves into a motion picture frame.

The only thing to do is to write his way out of this dilemma. He appoints himself a film critic. In the darkness of the theater he scribbles. When after a few months he reviews the rapidly developing notes, he finds he has written only about himself.

Simultaneity

Having followed the fox over the dry hills of the canyon, he thought it might be here the fox would eye him. Because his skin always felt a mixture of thumbed wool in the seasonal wind of Beverly Glen, he considered this skin an entrapment for creatures who cared for dry weather.

It was here he had found the enjoyment of his youth in climbing the rough passages through the hills of Beverly Glen. They dressed in hiking britches in those days with hiking boots that went to their knees and required laces. This lent a certain Alpine air of sport to the trails. He liked to pretend he was traveling over glaciers, seeking a more remote place than his canyon.

There were Mesozoic outcroppings that proved earth had suffered huge earthquakes, and this evidence of the volatility of time was part of the excitement of the excursions. Volatility would be an addition to the genius of his camera.

He fingered the grasses, rubbing their pungent smell against his nose, remembering how his eye once moved over the landscape, learning to measure its contour. He often said his camera had been spawned on the browned grasses of the hills and its soul hidden underground. He was aware of an arrogance in the underworld of his camera. When he entered it to capture simultaneity this mountain was edged out of view.

Sitting on the stubby earth, dressed in those antiquated pants and boots, he brushed away the red ants and prepared to wait.

He had summoned a wave that resembled a geisha from the films of Mizoguchi. While he waited he began a projected script about Portugal, because Lisbon was passing in front of him its winds tossing the grass and the sea and from his mountain he looked out on a Portuguese port. The boat that was anchored had a Portuguese name. It was the name of the poet, *Pessoa,* he decided sleepily, as he read the name on its hull. *Pessoa* seemed to cause a neurasthenia in the water, slowing the wave that was sure to arrive, but now more experienced.

The Spell of Beauty

There were endless searches for beautiful women who, it was believed, could be taught to act. The search continued because Hollywood had never determined its own canon of beauty. For this canon to remain indestructible one had to be fanatically aware that the skin that presents itself as beauty is part of the fairy tale that envelops the studio while it continues to sleep in its palace under cobwebs.

Since the "giants of the industry" were always under a spell, a certain type was displayed in their films, not beautiful at all. Pure beauty eluded the industry, being so emphemeral it refuses to show its face. One of the producers defined this elusive canon of beauty as unbelievable, undefinable, and utterly necessary. Stripped as he had been of money and wives in his continuing fairy tale search, he attended all the unproductive meetings held in the early hours of the morning when these men liked to hold their meetings. He was the most voluble of the unhappy men at the unproductive meetings held at the yearning studios where unhappy powerful determined magnetic men discuss a subject that eludes them and will continue to do so.

The fault lay actually in the camera. A truly lovely woman is an enigma to its lenses, she is beyond the propriety of real life. The artist knows that beauty lies in distortion as Ingres, a favorite of this studio official, the one who had lost so many worldly goods, discovered. Of the distortion that exists in rare beauty the studio officials did not wish to hear, the subject made them restless and domineering at the same time.

There was only one Director who, marked by "the wound of artistry" as he described it, would be willing to cope with ideal beauty. (Not once had this Director, despite harassment of the most vulgar kind, permitted his work to be finished on schedule.)

He acquired a meticulous identification with this "wound," a kind of gauze wrapping surrounded him. Regarding his committment to the projected film, he asked if before they brought him into their discussions, he might be permitted an interlude to listen to *Ariadne in Naxos* with *Elizabeth Schwarzkopf* singing the title role.

There was something harmless and melancholy about the studio's reaction to this proposal. One person fell down, another broke his little finger. The woman present quietly pulled out her eyelash. The spell of beauty began to work.

The Utmost Unreality

The night was warm. Schoenberg was sitting in the garden in his canvas lawn chair. The smell of mesquite drifted off the canyon. Earlier the drop of a tennis ball had reminded him of his beloved children. He pulled his sweater closer around him. He was always chilly on these sleepless nights when he sat outside. There was the choking matter making a percussive sound in his throat. To distract himself he turned to the little writing pad he kept near his chair. He wrote on it the name of the man who haunted his sleeplessness: KANDINSKY. Next he wrote, MURNAU, the town near Vienna where he and his family spent that summer of 1914 with Kandinsky and Gabriele Munter.

A voice from the film studio had spoken to him yesterday. They wanted to film his opera, *Die Glückliche Hand* (*The Lucky Hand*). To follow-up, they said, the success of Stravinsky's *Rite of Spring*. They wanted to show it at the same theatre. It was an expressionist opera he had written before the First World War and to it Kandinsky had lent the flowers of his genius.

Did now a tear drop from Schoenberg's eye? Was the angst, a racial angst, that separated him from Kandinsky, at last to set him free?

It was Kandinsky who had understood the wish that in *Die Glückliche Hand,* with its ambiguous title, the cast and director should maintain the *"utmost unreality!"* Schoenberg's instructions were ambiguous as the black veils he directed to sink down on the hero: an idea of "darkness in motion, like deep chords!"

And at the beginning would be twelve light spots on a black background lighting the faces of six women and six men. "These faces represent *their gazes. These faces* are a chorus of *stares."*

"Words are sung. Colors cross their faces." Gestures, colors, movement and musical tones, like colors. As if the plot were composed of pasted gestures. Music plows its way through floating lights and the fateful (*Glückliche*) *Hand* "which does not hold what it promises."

In the years after that first war, hatred still alive and recognizable, what was *kindly* in him had been replaced. And in his music tender Melisande had faded. He made a clicking sound with his fingers. Atonality.

He would so much now like to share with Kandinsky the Utmost Unreality that tomorrow will knock on his door. Together he and Kandinsky could allow a new genii to escape from under the aged veils of their magic.

Disappearance

What was seen was at an angle, bits of blue smoke falling from the ceiling and into his hand. The paper in his hand contained bits of words that mingled with blue smoke as they became smaller, until he knew the words were vanishing from the paper.

Time passed, the words grew smaller as they lay on their backs. The time passed on their backs was like fingers. Very thin fingers. They became smaller, these fingers, and could not hold onto the words. Now, too feeble to make sentences the words clung to the cameraman who examined them with his camera.

The cameraman was puzzled by their casual vanishing. They were losing their clarity. He could not put them back into the mouths of the people who waited with their playing cards whose numbers and scepters were vanishing. This was a terrible scene. Words tumbling from thrones under a green light.

The cameraman or "cinematographer," as he elevated himself, was famed for his ability to grasp a scene at one Take. Now that the words were so mixed up, falling from thrones and onto the floor, the cinematographer realized he would never win an Award for this picture. He lost interest in what the words tried to say. Order became disorder tumbling around him as words grew tinier.

He thought of Deauville all of a sudden. He saw Deauville in green lights. He began to move in the direction of those lights that spelled "DEAUVILLE," but they became fainter. After Deauville there was another word SEEKING and he began to run after it foolishly, because of its meaning.

He had sought this studio, because it was here, within its walls, that reputations were made and cameramen called themselves "cinematographers." They became famous as a string of pearls can become famous. But the row of pearls etched on the walls was vanishing in a rhythm that matched the fading letters in SEEKING.

The cinematographer needed more air. Frantically, he began to clear the space where tiny words lay on the floor, to make a larger space where he might lie down and breathe. As his breathing became more difficult, he began to comprehend that he was going to disappear with the words on their journey into smallness.

Rocks on a Platter

Notes on Literature

I

To live is to defend a form . . .
HÖLDERLIN

Ideas. As they find themselves. In trees?
To choose a century they are prepared to inhabit. Dreams set by typography. A companionship with crewlessness — shivering fleece —

Ship
shoal   rocks

to approach this land raving!

Rocks, platter, words, words . . .

mammoth teeth.

Mobility interseamed with print: "a small car beside the porch and wind with a harsh caress . . . "   another STORY BEGINS:

A DONKEY DRAWS A CART TO THE FURNACE AND
THE CHILDREN PRESS AROUND, THEIR SMALL TEETH
GLOWING.

I heard the wolf.

It had been a vagabond voyage and the entrepreneur was fatigued, yet held up his head inflamed with "LITERATURE, the ABSURD." Ideas dropped off vines and into his mouth. An idea fell off a SECULAR vine roaming his head: BAKED APPLES!

Among his listeners, a waterer of his vines, was a beautiful girl who hand-typed A BOOK CALLED "BAKED APPLES." THESE ARE STORIES THAT "MELT IN THE MOUTH," said the critics.

THE KING   READ *BAKED APPLES 100,*
AND GAVE HER AN APPLE TREE GROVE.
THE KITCHEN MAIDS, who had written JONQUIL TALES, asked the king for a jonquil grove. "I prefer BAKED APPLES," said the King.

TEARFUL, THE KITCHEN MAIDS CLOSED THEIR KITCHEN AND OPENED A JONQUIL STORE IN BUDAPEST, WITH YELLOW DOORS, and GREEN CEILINGS THAT VERY SOON APPEARED IN A FILM "THE BRIGHTENING OF BUDAPEST."

(The King, who liked the film, donated 25 white Palace chairs.)

        Passivity . . .

       pollen indoctrinated AND fragrance.

She digs with her fingernails into the earth while speaking and

weeping. Her face is also

introduced into the story:

a fragrant narration.

"ASTOUNDING BEING ALIVE!"

Pockets jingle   highly responsive place in the shelter
     of those rocks   at last the jingle of your pockets

HEARD ON THE PAGE.

     . . . in its contiguous
treatment of time, literature:

     is inclined to divorce
the uninhibited   aroma of BEAUTY, OR
     SPECTACULAR LEAP

     suspicious
of fragmentation,

or *sweet reproach of invisibility.*

Tradition

Tantamount to theory

   treacles
         of tender truckland

   near Trebizond.

        TRIUMPHS.

   A TREMENDOUS TUNE-UP.   ORTHODOXY.
 tremendous   tune-up

        tra-la-la.

Wet earth disinters itself.

With aplomb

   bestows

      "The Kiss behind the Counter."

     Implacable poet.

Shattered rocks

　　　　　　　　　　　hid in the rock?
Deft, vehement.　　Amulet cast from the pocket.

And wind over red-tiled roof　　and we grow closer
to the moss of subjectivity　　guarding an iron basin
　　limed,　　　　　　　　　　old stars.

　　　　Rays　　modern rays,
　　　　　　　　　modernly, so be it.

Noise of the shattering!

　　Behooved us to welcome tonality,

　　or succumb to the theme of inharmony . . .

　　"where we once were."

　　　　Fiction and Complice

　　　　torment the mineral kingdom,

　　　　　　　feathering the page
　　　　　　　in the merit of feather.

Of brokenness —

brokenness   resembles
            evasion (although not separate), and
with a coat of arms,

"afloat with the telling."

II

To invest abstract ideas with form,
and animate them with activity has always
been the right of poetry . . .

DR. SAMUEL JOHNSON

' And the words linger, deciding which direction to take.

Will they remain with the middle chord? The atonal section is

fearful, running along beside the pale brook, clouding and declouding.

Aching

time interrupted   discontinuous treatment.   After the piping
MURMUR unlocked   inclined to advance toward the desire
to hasten an ending or

avoid the spectacular jump —;

drifting into invisiblity,
as does remnant of self.
A blow is merciless —;

solid objects are merciless.

OLD SHOE.

Hullabaloo, Hullabaloo

Again, are you more *tactile in* handling

the body

pressed against you?

Is the pear-shaped manuscript

endangered?

Alas, its honied drip.

The honied drip.

The empirical sun

on the disturbed border
in the animal-clad wood   gone down,
magick within   begs extension
disappointed   at eye level:
grey-streaked sky, sea.

Less
less mourning less
sandy mourning!

Frail sentence moved by

the seismic sway of existence

under a shaken tree

is cultivated outside us.

Words, inflammable,

          lie   in bricks

             this changes.

                  White
perpendicular lights   attached to the shoulder
I touched the wrist with my writing finger   and from the center
the orb of the eye was enough fire   to light the writing lamp and
afterwards   the blade   withdrew from the writing shoulder ·   and
that writ
blew away   flame lit with nothing   and nothingness stayed.

        Skin of the lost paper
           Knuckle smooth   (touched the writing).

            Nietzschean   thumb on
                 the trout
            and they disappear.

III

Intimacy of tone

and form

beyond the tangible itinerary

mirror trap

at 30 degrees

I have the impression of a long body;

of loaves and fishes,

of "belles lettres."

Wisdom in travel several palaces

latitude without margin —

silver-toned blow up —;

arm in a sling and hawk chin

you are also a hawk —

you walk in hawk shadow a guise —.

Sad rose, Rilke charm

lodged in a castle —

bone button sewed to a coat —;

snow footprints adieu

cold tears splashed acre is intimacy,

and many chimed things,

future's conduit.

... to recapture   early days   cats-cradle.

Mont Blanc   Childe Harold

demons. a tooth bends down on the "d."

Transubstantiation   only a web

is permanent dent   on the body and ablaze.

                       Shoulder ablaze.

             In a room

                "not alone"

          enters

               midday

               appears

          massive.

In the faded game you won the top with the green scratch you win,
I alter the text "did not win the top" put "earned" white flag.

Four in the entertainment room, you and someone with a foreign name,
I forget.

He has written out a plan and glued it to the text. He told me he is a king himself entering life on a whim,

language attached, gerunds.

In the loneliest hours to share a flamboyance,

an attraction to distance and disappearance.

Beyond the roof tiles,
lap of a hill, *fleur d'or,*
gold ass on the threshold
Apuleius' other.

Cannot dream except in "two's" or be alone, is hollowed out.

Of many colors   porcelain

                 with faerie glove

you betray   (biography).

dissident morning!

with no ulterior purpose

image exchanged for a feather

le poisson on watered page.

Apparition shape of thy head

finds its verve,

        ivy the poem

shoving it into the stain,

        weight in the room,

        I promise.

Here the dream began, two voices, one joking, this took place in sleep, you re-
member, and the other caressing, a tussle between the joking and the caress,
points of view caressingly and jokingly; they often sighed between joking and ca-
ressing, the hiccup, an odd note the hiccup, between the joking and caressing;
perhaps a lapse in the dream.

PHANTOM

        (reverie)
        (passion)

in canoe

of twelve-tones

or *Helen in Egypt*

                                                  •

Bar of silence crossed the mouth

decorates it.

She watched skirts sweep the floor,
from that day of her sixteenth year
her skirt brushes the floor. What she is after

"trailing skirt," blossom
in mimetic hair

fills some other Body.

                                                  •

IV

The Moment a limit is posited
it is overstepped, and that
against which the limit was
established is absorbed.
ADORNO, *Aesthetic Theory*

Without shyness or formality:

"a gesture of *allowing oneself time*"

Remember how starry it arrives the hope of another idiom, beheld
that blush of inexactitude, and the furor, it
will return to you, flotsam blocked out.

compose, like Schoenberg, *poem* music

"robustly"

"flotsam of the world of appearances"
drifting by and out of the picture,

where the throne disappears . . .

now in robust position,
NAMING,

naming the throne, *"flotsam of appearance,"*

ALLOWING TIME.

                                                         •

Is evanescence the wool beggar?
strike that simpleton

                            "Bafflement."

                Thee   GLOSS   GLOSS

            point to the Mix, and

                there! it slides into view
                    the Dolphin,

                before the moment oversteps, ·

                          into

                  the *hum* pour his ivory.

                                                           •

And is this what they mean by *transfuse?*
the hum pouring into another,

the furnace turned down,

snowy apricot furnace
of the dolphin.

And the rage disappears,
intellectual rage over grandeur.

Swimming off in the twilight
is the Dolphin, what occurs
absorbed in the skin.

Grandeur oversteps,
artificial and strange, lifting

a leg above *glitter* . . .

The rule of thumb under *glitter*
is that *glitter* disturbs, and

paled, finds painting

a wild grape loosens

glitter
from the *rock platter.*

Ovid writes,

"Earth, painted with flowers, that *shone brightly,*"

Pictaque dissimili flore nitebat humus.

•

How does the pickled axe maintain itself . . .

is the desire of the stone figure
                    to outlive a sheepfold?

    Bittersweet and decisive the urn
                when showed a technique
        of maintenance in the dark field and modernly.

That pickled axe

is the anima, entry into waterfield,

is the wax waterfield,

and savaging.

. . . pumpkin glazed in the sun
no alphabet, no grief.

Overstepping the farmstead to make way
in the underbrush for a faun-like portrait,

sweet pumpkin.

The sight of the arm
even in the cornfield there it is found
with three racing women   hair grown
over the forearm   was considered upside down
and rumor of a complicated series of burials
lent a deshabillé   not usual on ancient ground
no one could have foretold   uncovered according
to various ideas
about sacred places.

And ingenuity   follows the silvered
   montage into a new elevation

      As if whispered.

      An episode with new palm trees.

      Words in magnetic order

      Words in natural order.

         Vulnerable Dolphin skin

         and magnetic skin.

In the new part about palm trees

   stumbling to multiply

   tall palms, to replace

   a fanatical order (*Orlando*

   Furioso or *Dolphin Empire*)

sensuous *en effet,*

and near the sea basin

rustle of the palm trees

introduce   (and a similar movement among their
leaves)   then the Dolphin slow.

Where are they, wood nymphs and the glittering

Beings — do they overstep each other . . . ?

The Dolphin God — does he swim on the page?

* * * * *

"*In ancient times*
Heavenly Beings made sense of themselves and how
they have made off with the strength of the Gods."

Hölderlin

Symbiosis

Symbiosis was originally published as a collaboration between Barbara Guest and Laurie Reid.

A writer and an artist working together establish a Symbiosis, as in Nature, where dissimilar organisms productively live together.

     Hiss
the wool
        fable,

        close and away.

        Hiss in turning wool,

           and envied the circle
               and volume,

        working in layers.

             The spirit
      sails along,
           amid live speech.

      "Ripening beyond sheer height," calls itself.

Is symbiosis aflame   stroked

each line   power wound up in volume,
when spoken to, fear in place of the woven,

often, it says, in place of the line.
Thinned down, staggering   looks up to the drawing;

bodies all the way up the hill.

Will it belong, or is symbiosis aflame each pine stroking,

symbiosis aflame,

each day autumn. Day awakens, no break in the
thread.

Needing, needing, needing

over the surface perpendicular

is not something to chat about filled
by iridescence.

They talk about
loosened bones. Could be a shuttle

if it worked in direct light.

        •

The thread loose

as any from the underworld,

more in iridescence, hidden.

A suggestion in mid air

dropped on the hid body, no nerve blinding nothing
attached,
      no weight,   no thing to litter,

free as unusual.

        •

Plume of impatience the petal,

a clue to ensnare the undrawn,

O valley. O wine.

        •

This is the point where the strophes meet,

one line interweaves with another,

room of liberal fountains,

a different speech and metabolism,

•

near an ancient site of accord

and priority.

•

In no climate whatsoever

noise traveling up the tower

•

bronze green in the tournament,

each player hit a wood ball.

•

Positioning the strophes
ended in calm,

after the strophes are positioned.

Knitting or singing a song, hair let down

from the blue—ranging and tumbling the blue

magnolia nestled, the wild berry, also.

This is a strange way to tell a story being

where one does not wish, in the midst of a storm . . .

Gas lights and lost

the cares of thought,   an oil lamp,   Maupassant

put it there. He stands at the window.

She places her hands on her hair.

She looks at a Poem-Painting

"The walks of Saint Cloud

are open,

the eyes of the fish

are closed.

Remarkable basins,

you give me ten years."

The difficult! the difficult!

loosen the ropes that entangle it,
tear them down from the mast!

The schooner off its route,

adios to the bird of prey,
flies in another direction,   the nineteenth
century

wears a plaid cap.

Say *adios* when you see

the figure from the mainland crossing on tiles.

And they have no intention to avoid

the gaze of symbiosis,
or the century,

pasting and printing in the same room

— sharing

the furry moment draped over their head,

light from the transom.

A sign of being gentle,

the scene is more mature.

She is not so silly

as they thought in her mantle,

coming from outside

studying to be someone else,

why not? And write her own script,

write it then she did

first learn about pretense   the make-up and lounge dress,

authority and the syllabus.

.

A tendency to respond (lacquer) near the driveway, she was

thought not pliable or overtly sensitive.   She is more
fluid,

she is outside.

.

Coming from outside,   fluid orange.

Rhythm

and festivity.

A sign of being gentle, plain orange.

She can read the image in the overlapping

even from outside,

those parts that overlap,

lip and facial movement,

color of the image as it changes —

pushed her leg through the rippling

image changes.

Miniatures
and Other Poems

I, too, am an ardent defender of Miniature Pieces.
ANTON CHEKHOV

MINIATURES

Shabby Boot

"There is a shabby boot

O whither does it wander?"

Earth has   gala momentum.

"Be not lachrymose,

tear-streaked.

You are out of reach

of fakirs.

On your boot

the King of Naples inscribed

footprints of The Aeneid."

On the manuscript are Dido's tears,   from Dido.

Bird of Art

THERE CAME A CLOUD IT SETTLED ON YOUR
SHOULDER.
 The cloud seeks high culture, after Ovid.

 To soar through domes, bird of Art,
 Halfway to icy heaven.

 Halfway to heaven search in high space, in deep
 crevasse.

 Knighthood.

 Poesie be engendered after OVID.

Spirit Tree

LO! It shakes boughs Spirit Tree.

Plenty of wonder here and miraculum.

Pleaseth shade with lark!

Immortalis makes entry.
Small feet carry chalice, Domine.

 Swete be sound and soothing.

Lady and gazelle, amitié.

Turret

 What is your version, raking hay, reading law
 In turret, transferring documenta?

 What is origin of miscellany, misdemeanor,

 from whence doggerel?

Whose profile in margin

where small animals lie, toad, minnow, book of Saints,
olives.

Negative Possibility

It is not your physical appearance or hazelnut
hollowed out by sorrow,

or landslide of poetry.
Paying duty on one place,

language or tidal property.
Belonged to library of small estate,

Taxfree, built into house.

Camisole

The heart knows.
climbs stair to reach
basket of Heaven.

wintry Heaven strikes arm.

Your viol shall release thee, is said.

Beyond steeple. Animals. Lather runs.
Fabric sewed into blood.

Moldy day. Leather gaiters. Warm camisole.
Slow measure.

Tiny Foreign Tears

Tiny foreign tears in autumn,

Finnish architecture! Handshaking!

The right-handed cloud is
lower than the left
where a spirit hides.

In his dwelling Coleridge
handprints ghostly elaboration,

the notion of subject to enlarge,

he goes all year without.

Word akimbo,
lined with wool, even in far off place.

Transcription

Go sit, listen. Two feed earlobes, with wildermass. Slowly partake
of uncrippling. Part of transcription. Sleep of transcribing after long day
In honey cave, sans emotiveness.

There is lip descendant placed on wood for viol outside
witherglass. Here is plentiful lambswood fife for thine, we pass
upward in front of mere clumsy, Knight of Andorra and pony.

O sleep will be shiny apres plentiful unrehearsed   their sheaves, yon
Magnetic fleece nestling   while it chew
fertile green stone. Coxcomb be schon.

Alliance with bickering   be wrestled and
fielded on gold champs.

Lost Speech

Archaeology

> with a lift of brow and occupation,
some of it mixed, as in that speech germinated
on layers of limestone, protects a lost speech in thick
wood plundered.
> A search for past occupational diversions.

> Let history commandeer your tongue at this elevation.

> It is nothing to grow wings. To be La Favorita.

A girl wearing satin and wings makes a speech, then ventures
outside, a cloak thrown over her shoulder. The Macedonians
know how to plunder, to thieve, yet they lifted La Favorita
from the overturned ship, and send her back to the Lycians.

First Prints

> balanced on leaves green-toed
> suspension
hard to pronounce,

> to recall.   Pulled-up air evaporates.
here and in color.

Woman in field
light-toed.

Goddess category.

Yesterday

Light still glowing through the iced-over window, city
     silence and glow. Ice on Harbor Street.

        Twin points of light in darkened harbor.
    Winter slumber. Lone tree. Shadow on empty beach.
Piece of ice. Daughter of an Elf.
            "Clouds afloat in Winter."

Red dots. Circular movement. Common life joined to emotion.
    Groaning roof sighed in sleep.

He wraps her hair around his wrist   a cloud   human hair
smothering the universe   in a mist dogs bark inside it.

Moon
in their sleep.

Pilgrimage

    Start at beginning   in early morn
    move through streams. Observe in district.

    stripe of clown in vestibule,
brief rummage

    Dove on mule cart.   Hand is homeless far from St. Jerome

    and harping.   weightless, in Sacred Wood.

Finnish Opera

Grass grew long in the story.

Pieces clung to bedclothes. In the night he believed he grew taller.
Grass covered the dream of a serpent, eyes sunk in his head, tail of silk
clover. The dream translated into silver tone. More serpent heads and the
dream turned into an opera.

It was the opera that made the dreamer famous. Location of opera could be
in any country, could be Antarctica, more likely Finland, where they believe
in silk clover, it is gold in a land of starved desire for summer.

The opera had a clover leaf copied in porcelain by Aalto, the famous
designer, who sewed the clover leaf into a white curtain. He designed a
window for the man when he looks out to sea in his serpent costume.

This opera that begins with a dream traveled to Rome and Zagreb, traveled
across continents, once by camel. The travels became more famous than
the opera. People began to forget whether the grass really had grown long,
and where the serpent came from.

The opera was called by another name and included a gold limousine.
Somewhere in Oceania they added mermaid elves.

Photographs

In the past we listened to photographs. They heard our voice speak.
Alive, active. What had been distance was memory.   Dusk came,
Pushed us forward,   emptying the laboratory   each night undisturbed by
Erasure.

In the city of X, they lived together. Always morose, her lips
soothed him. The piano was arranged in the old manner, light entered the
window, street lamps at the single tree.

Emotion evoked by a single light on a subject is not transferable to
photographs of the improved city. The camera, once
commented freely amid rivering and lost gutters of treeless parks or avenue.
The old camera refused to penetrate the unknown. Its heart was soft,
unreliable.

Now distributed is photography of new government building. We are forbidden to observe despair silent in old photographs.

Petticoat

She ran down the middle of the road throwing her hands up to Heaven.
Longinus, Leviticus, mathematical wonder.
              She believed whole buildings might fall on top of her.

                     Pollen filled the air.
It was her duty to plunder the ant of air, beasties of calico.
        The Morse Code arrived in petticoat blue, the steam engine.
          She read Leibniz before she visited the pastor.

Blue Arthur

           Aroused from bed with movement around him.
    Fasted and lay with malade.   Waited with poem
                         folded into sorrow.
Hollow, blue morning.

          Cloth overhangs daytime

                  Kingdom of Blue Arthur,

       Dismayed lightness.

Woman walks solitary arrayed in grey velveteen, doors open for her.

Autobiography

          Underfoot is secure,
              part of made up plan.
            In middle ground,
        Coconut tree.

The coconut tree grows beside warm
house, hard fruit has softened center.

In winter trees enter firm sand, barrels
are protection from salt water.
most of the work elective.

Air without salt is different, moves upward
from red evening sand.

Bar of ivory light suspended,
numbering of ivory bars.

Noisetone

Each artist embarks on a personal search.
An artist may take introspective refreshment from green.

Or so they say in Barcelona when air is dry.
In our country it is a water sprinkler that hints, "rinsed green."
Colors often break themselves into separate hues

of noisetone.   In a Barcelona cabaret when green is overtaken,
it is stirred into the mint color of drink.

The spirit is lifted among primary colors. Nine rows of color.
The future writ in white spaces.

Fourteenth of July

Automatically
at lit dusk,

path of camera
veers into goats.

Alpine

camera allowed, vendor of cockades,

cockades, and nearby

taper of
dried glass, mountain tapers.
Fire in snow, dazzle of film, raisin-charred, described later,
and under waterfall icicles.

Walked with goat, shared
scheme of Revolution,   thread   homespun
In open place.

Chekhovania

En pointe in the *plié,* she greets monster sailing ship. Sky is overcast this day.
Bell of last regime trembles in an overcoat. Worms wear old rings. "Here is
where they were!" she says. "A bag of apricots hidden in the chair . . ." He
listens to her sing "Bitter Avenue." Her boots are covered with caravan dust,
broken seams.

Roofs fall in, no grapes grow in the harbor.

They only have their skin and old satin shoes. "It's the luck of the road," she
moans, and puts her hand on his cheek. "Look at our russet wind."

Coal

The black curtain has fallen over the moon, yet stars are out tonight. Dust falls
through the curtain. We are asleep. Night descends into another part of the
house, coal shifts in the bin.

My grandfather shuffled the coal veins that come from the deep shoulder. My
eyes are closed, flecks of coal fall onto my cheek. He brushes them away. He
brushes my shoes with a little shoe brush. Soon his eyes are closed. His eyes
shine red in his kingdom. I view the coal God through dust, darkest dust.

Colonial Hours

Slow moving and daybreak,

an eyelash trembles. Cat in mouse coat and thunder, the lane shivers. A branch falls as she listens. Weary of effervescence, pickling languors and knitted on the way to Princeton in a phaeton, dark blue splashed, mud from early rains. Bon jour to the Count. "bonjour" Benjamin Franklin, we've memorized the court order, legalized the tunes. An
odd evening. Dark in the middle where the berries stood.
The spinet was out of tune.

Sound and Structure

"Sound leads to structure." Schoenberg.

On this dry prepared path walk heavy feet.
This is not "dinner music." This is a power structure,
heavy as eyelids.
Beams are laid. The master cuts music for the future.

Sound lays the structure. Sound leaks into the future.

Musicianship

How far are you going in the culture program? Liszt draws nearer. Wagner overwhelmed us in that last demonic song.

Where the snowline fell on its supple track, people lost their maps in advanced culture. And the faces, on the back row singing: rare tonalism, lying on its sides like a walrus, chords broken and chewed in liberation.

PATHOS

Arms flutter close to the body, skating on pure ice, harmonious
composition —

        body in mellifluous line —

      face in profile withheld itself, thin smile,
self approval.

          Lithe her romp!

lithesome her romp upon the indignation of ice

        She is falling!

           Shiver of the fallen,

  of the tulle skirt.

       Disarrangement of composition,

      Snow falling from tree.

So young in this electric world —,

   something Katya needs to know. Something is needed,

     fiction is overturned.

   Something she must know about hazard, what spills out —

      — disturbance — pathos.

Equilibrium never fixed —

losing momentum in the trials — boot tossed away,
    a gesture she made.

Making difficulties for herself   in the wrong direction.
Fear of the word, haunting of fear —

        the word passed through that haunting.

        Weight of the useless word,
            mirror moving backward,

        impromptu surface of the alphabet when she fell sideways

    with irascible measure — the pit of the plum
    rolled onto ice,   and her silhouette   merged quickly
            with ice in that chapter.

    Opened the entrance door,

    and make-believe arrived   with a doll on its surface,

    arrived with the soil of the moon,   it was impermanent

            living with shifted screen life.

Lived not for pleasure,   to hear the cry

        in a small coil
        of ice.

        And heard through the oak panel —,

amazing to listen to speech
by way of adulthood.

To articulate velvet,

without noise or spectacle.

Life in that eccentric balloon.

To scribble ice figures,

and drink out of the cup when bolder.
The electric world sends its current through her legs,
a global concern for her being.

The globe is drawn into this, and the frills,
the sorrow of falling

into an historical position, the legs will finish
this position, music
uses up the irresistible current, lived
with the shifting screen.

Lived not for pleasure,   to hear the harp-like
cry in a coil,

to live in an eccentric balloon.

To scribble across ice

and drink from an orange cup.   When they were nearer

historical legs used up this position,

falling down historical legs, anxious writing.

Foreignness enters the hallway in the Berlioz —

hinting at the fable
                    resisting her.

Do they wonder at her pathos/ dressed in tulle,
    athletically inclined on jumping bars.

                    One at a time

    misleading her./

She is part of *the moment*/ unrequited amour/

                    Icing machine.

    This motion in her eyes,

going outside,   the red brook
            flowed into her eyes, winsome eyes,

        drawstring of light.

BLURRED EDGE

It appears

a drama of   exacting dimension.

Anguished figure,

reign of terror.

Craft and above all

the object within.

Softness precedes

blurred edge.

A hint disappears   inside the earlier one.

Softness still nudging,

A different temperament,

inside an earlier plan.

Upon this stool is draped material
arabesque of an iron stool,

bare bones of the iron seat.

The arrangement of objects   announced

more firmly than before.

Observation.   Candor,

where candor approaches the cube.

Dark siphon bottle   mood

of blurred edge.

Life permitted no privilege

no exegesis
no barnyard door.   The feathered visage   the domed hat

allowed no strange air or music.

An attempt to get beyond the arrangement,

the vibration of a peculiar touch.

It changes between eye and alarm,

the hibiscus,

more gifted.

Part of the tension,

is illusory.

A hint of what was going to be.

Covering and uncovering necessary.

Self pouring out of cloudedness.

If views of the lower body

do not conform,
a risk of being exposed,

Rain and altitude.

This is not sand, it is drama.

The anguished figure, sand blew away
that armor. A look   extends the blur.

Other   creatures alive,
word exchanged for meaning,
moment of descriptiveness.

Sand blows away

the carapace,
in the distance,
figure passing,
unworded distance at edge.

Dürer in the Window, Reflexions on Art

Lunch at Helen Frankenthaler's

I wake up
               what was I dreaming about?
"Mountains & Sea"   a cloud
a hand over the cloud.   Is it China
that arranges itself thus?
                              Early China
before envelopes?

                    There is a figure in the landscape
no   not at all   the sea
on which an old man embarks in a canoe,
what is this?   a picnic in the canoe?
It isn't a man in that boat   the kimono
is wrapped,   how does one say   it is a woman!
It's Helen!   her face with its arbor of thunder
and laurel starts to drift over the mountain

               Helen!
we're having lunch!
                    Return
in your snow boots,
                         here's the thermos
I've poured out so many words, and the sandwiches
prepared with watercress.   Blissful
sentences begin with "Do you remember . . ."
and "After August,"   and   "I saw you in a red cloak."

               Helen!
don't jump into that pillar of statues!

                    without you there is no lunch.

On a Painting by Haydn Stubbing

Where is the sky?
Here.
And the unknowingness
Of shadows?
There.

Bracken, furze, field,
The picture bending over
To describe itself
As who, not always a
There.

The leaf treads, skies
Throng into themselves;
Water is not far off,
A blessing made of the music
Of turf.

Skimmed as frost
Forms a place on the inner
Scale, becomes easier
When it is learned
Winter begins.

The harvest
Is there in the branches
And whatever says,
"My goodness, I've thunder
In my boughs."

That person who framed
The fair weather clouds
Bestowed wisdom
To the tips of leaves,
Saying, "a chance of showers."
While you paint
The picture's skin.

So it will be robust,
Yet ambiguous like autumn
Whose thoughts tangling
With spectrum
Never recognize
Their green pronouncing,

Pampered as visionary wind
Deciding whatever burden
It will tote away
Into that space
The picture elects
To purify.

Homage

"A New Era of the Plastic Arts had begun."
FREDERICK KIESLER[*]

The world
is going upstairs
and some people
of whom Kiesler
doesn't approve
are sitting in the basement.

    Galaxies   Galaxies

You are our last jewel,
and we preserved you
in our ateliers.

A morning
was one day to open
over the roof tops,

[*]Frederick Kiesler melded large, slender "balls" of interwoven metal he called "Galaxies." They were the first "Mobiles." They may have originated in his architectural drawings. Kiesler designed the Peggy Guggenheim Gallery in New York where Pollock and a "galaxy" of new painters first showed.

and we see dawn
as a galaxy,

having in sleep
experienced original dreams,
now become an environment.

We climb into the night suit,
no longer traditional,
or isolated, the future
in another scale,

Galaxy!   Galaxies!
entering from the moon.

The Red Gaze

In each genuine art work something appears that did not exist before.

Nostalgia

Hands are touching.
You began in cement in small spaces.
You began the departure. Leaves restrain. You attempted the departure.
A smile in sunshine, nostalgia.
Beneath shadow of shadows of Columbus the Navigator. Waving farewell.
Street, shadows.

I have lost my detachment, sparrow with silver teeth.
I have lost the doves of Milan, floating politely.

           Recognize me, I shall be here, O Nietzsche.
           We have skipped down three pairs of stairs,
they are not numbered, they are oddly assorted, velvet.

           Recognize me in sunshine.
Bulletins permit us to be freer than in Rome.
Castles perched on a cliff.
Filled with pears and magic.

           I am not detached,
bulletins permit us comb, fish of silver.
A part of the tower
beckons to us.

An Afternoon in Jeopardy

Piece of tapestry with bird sewed on.
A ruin from Rome, and in the background a rope.

Old Europe declares itself.

In the banquet hall birds nest.
A stranger causes the water to flow,
the alphabet is full of sorrow.

In the passageway sits the stranger.

He is without sin or sorrow or soldiers who mount their horses
and race up and down the farthingale hills.

He will not dine with the others.
They knew not he was an emperor
described as a poor man in disguise.

He has cast away his steel to rest beside the maiden.

Shadows are everywhere.   Oddness begins.

Imagined Room

Do not forget the sky has other zones.

Let it rest on the embankment, close the eyes,

Lay it in the little bed made of maplewood.
Wash its sleeve in sky drops.

Let there be no formal potions.
A subject and a predicate made of glass.

You have entered the narrow zone
your portrait etched in glass.

Becoming less and less until the future faces you
like the magpie you hid,
exchanging feathers for other feathers.

In the tower you flew without wings
speaking in other tongues to the imagined room.

Loneliness

Wounded,
the tower and green of the meadow below.

O meadow, O furnaces, royalty passes you.
Quick steps make a noise.

She rides on her palfrey, the maiden.
Bouquets fall from her green hair.

Shadows on grass reflect a loneliness everywhere.

O furnaces royalty passes you, quick steps make a noise.
She rides on her palfrey the maiden,
her green hair glistens.
How solitary!
Lo, on the river a monument passes by.

A Different Honey

Close up shop
is what happens in Milan
and places older.
Who is protecting us,
we who were noticed by the Emperor
cruising in his vessel?
Remember navigators
tasting lemons from the trees
of their birthplace.
Do we know how they felt,
born under different signs?
Silent are honies in velvet cups.

A Short Narrative

Your painting took a long time to dry.

It was sent to Rome to give it a royal luster.

Your thoughts the evening before had been gloomy.

They would not forget rumors accompanying you.

Lo, Royalty had placed a hand on your head.

Nobles twist their rings in corridors,

worried about painting's future.

Freedom

Those at the excavation who followed the Dog Star
when he wandered, summit-catcher.
The days are unknown, the night also,
ending its speech. Sleeper on the grass,
dreamer of numbers.
Day, night, horoscope.

In the dark
we recognize
the shoreline is Vienna green.

Officials at Rome have ended the martyrdom.

Alteration

In the sky a dilemma. Fountains rush by.
Home from the tournament beasts seek quiet.

Writing covers the desk.

Your colonization of the infinite

is a romantic departure.

I ask you to permit the image

and the alteration of time.

A Burst of Leaves

A burst of leaves announces your presence

                        dropped from the frozen cloud.

Perhaps you are hiding, perhaps you have decided not to reveal

your singular presence.

            The world conceals your identity from me.

                    You once said we must abandon all risk.

You glanced at the idol

        within its burst of leaves.

A disappointed generation, words collapse around us.

Like the one who jumped into the sea. But the seas disappoint us, also.

We do not like to walk on their beaches, lined with laboratories and formula.

We are ready for a new orientation.

The Next Floor

Hours become young days,
morning wrapped in reality.
Its heel turns a corner where the game
is played. Sensitive to the murmur outdoors,
I fold you in a warm fleece —
here is its cover, it will hide you until daybreak.

Smithies, ironworks, lattices to the next floor,
we are climbing. The urge enters to see more.
Destiny peers upward into a next stanza,
resting in the nearest hayrick,
adding up, taking away.
Of what use are stanzas in the dark,
ragamuffin?

Roman Stripes

for Johannes Beilharz

What is new in the fostering world beyond.
We ask its name, created by indentation,
learned to avoid the shark's fin,
emerged from a world of fins.

Once it was thought the spiral staircase led us
to uncounted rings.
Tonight there is no other fin.
Tonight there is sorrow created by rings
tipped with green.

I saw the stair mount upward and could not stop
its climb until the heavens opened blinking,
until we felt suspension.
An odyssey parades in stripes.

The Trickster

There is no system, no one writes in Greek.
It is empty here after the seismology,
one relies on sensibility that monitors
movement on a mountain top.

Corrective light that carried shadow away
to another visibility.

Coyote before he opens his mouth.
Hidden in the canyon on a ledge
full of games and myth.

The Hungry Knight

Palest shadow on the middle rock,

Hungry knight! drifting.

O causes,

O celebrants,

massive,

comfort had ceased.

Massive night falls on the middle rock,

weighing-in like a scholar.

Heavy is the literature

bred on the rock,

filled with epiphany

night has known since infancy.

The Past

The form of the poem subsided, it enters another poem.

A witness was found for the markings inscribed upside-down.

It might have been a celebration, so strong the presence

of the poem. The sky sinks slowly inside the past.

Modernism

The dreamer enters the room wearing a garment of red cloth.

On his feet are shoes of magic, they will carry him hither and yon.

He has dipped his pen into magic ink and cleared

the ordinary from the room.

We too, have heard the midnight chime and reached for our silver spoon,

as midnight stirs a coffee cup we praise modernism.

Restless leaf modifies his poem.

Green Numbers

Others are accustomed to this hat on the furnace step,

a mild disassociation from the garment shop.

A new pair of shoes you are welcome to,

and a brimmed hat to wear in the rain.

We are accustomed to a guarantee of rain, guarantee of thunder,

the take-off that leads to thunder on the holiday night.

Green numbers, a patois we are learning to speak.

Butterflies in the house you told us about.

Stair of Our Youth

O reward us who fought in the brush,
in the deep stiletto branches grown low to the grass,
who have wandered with messages to other kingdoms,
and slept in their heavy beds.
We serve these masters and smile at their clumsiness,
as they slip on the stair. We are witness to the burned pages

of their books, to their Oriental games.
Riding over stones of borrowed pleasure
lends grace to the smooth mount of our youth.

A Noise of Return

We have seen the bowl toppled by morning crickets,

or imagined so, on our imaginary route,

it leads through the mountain.

We are walking on a shadowy line gentle in its way.

Imagination has removed the harshness.

This is a filibuster of routes,

concealed is the icy stone you tripped on.

It turns rocks into stone and promises

to listen to the morning tympanum.

felicitudes!

creating another tympanum.

Freed Color

The branches are placed in a wet cloth,
clover reaches out.

They cannot locate a blue vine.
Purple fills the agenda. Red is on the plant,
the setting of a hibiscus tree.
They are warned not to linger in the purple shade.

Are these bitter colors? Are they accompanied
by rhyme to cheer them when they cross
into that land where color is rare?

They hasten to make use of freed color
who bends to no one,
who dwells in a tent like rhythm
continuously rolled.

To stop the riot of color, to hasten the quiet paucity of rhythm,
to sleep when it is time.

And doors open into a narrow surprise.
The jingle of crystal follows you everywhere,
even into the whistling corridor.

The Gold Tap

The arrival of a winter morning unclasping its bandeau of sleep.

Marionettes are late risers. They awake in late morning,

bringing their hands to the gold tap and drinking its rare waters.

Minimal Sound

What we are becomes a memory, the hand may open a secret lock.

The poem enters on tiptoe, climbs the terrain,

weary, it listens to minimal sound, the slowed

tree branches are drawn on purpose, part of the same program.

The Brown Vest

A robin's nest being towed on the sidewalk.

Somewhere a complement to his brown vest.

He is more lively than before.

In the future we must take him away from the sidewalk

and lend him the joy he expects.

Use earth colors, they build strong nests.

He combs his throat then locks the chapel

Of the Goddess in his home.

The Red Gaze

Red, purple, brown Guardian leaf.
Complications of red enter the leaf
and it is more accomplished,
turning brown then gray in varying attitudes
after the snow begins. Colorful complications
disturb serenity, causing our eye
to wander over the shaking tree.

Morning began with a concert of white.
Blue enters later.

A Dawn Walk

Who took the tapestry from off the wall?
Who removed the silver lining?
A dawn walk in the tousled hall.

Dissolve the curiosities,
Pierrot of the mountain.
In the Alps of your being there is trust.

Search for trust.

It may be in the Alps of your soul,

young squire who tends the furnace,

who remarks on landscape finery.

No Longer Strangers

No longer strangers

in these zones of departure

somehow integrated in a

fashion to parade

and to laugh

and to write

of the old speech

in the looking glass room.

Distribute these newly sought wings of artifice,

for each raid on the moon,

we were told at the meeting of strangers

who were learning the new tongue.

Put these two meetings together!

you will notice it is all one speech,

and jocular.

Hans Hofmann

She remembers	bridges over the gorge
a rocky landscape.	Heaviness in the white.

A sudden burst of color.

               "Structure and sensation."

Going each day to the park bench, she begins to absorb
her surroundings.

Each day the park grows colder.
Who is sitting at the end of the park bench?

He is the painter Hans Hofmann, he is a famous painter.
(this is true). Talking in an atmosphere of color.

Listening in an atmosphere of color.

To invoke the unseen, to unmask it. Reality in a glass
of water. The mirror reveals heartstrings of reality.

Students preparing for the class and its famous master.

A deep red gaze through maple leaves.

Maple red now splashes the mountain.

The students need mirrors to orchestrate color.
Their master uses thick color.
"Even black is a color."

A cool purple begins to descend through increasing twilight.
The class begins to speak of cold. The class shivers and they laugh.
A pinch of red remains on Hofmann's palette knife.
It reminds him of the red of maple leaves.

Vignettes

(Hofmann classes on chill afternoons).

(Independent thinking and foreign thought).

(Hofmann explains *Narrative*).

Hofmann surrenders his brush.

                          Return of the white chandelier.

Echoes

Once more riding down to Venice on borrowed horses,

> the air free of misdemeanor, at rest in the inns of our fathers.

> Once again whiteness like the white chandelier.

> Echoes of other poems . . .

Instructions

Mood and Form. Other pieces of literature.

> Emphasis on content.

> Distance lingers in her hand.

Figure moves backward from the door.

. . . Figure modified by light.

> Remove figure from window.

Composition

Lo, from the outside a poem is with us, of another composition.

Travelled from an antique place.

Writing, narrow and sparse, pungent as the lemon tree.

Difficult, spelling and montage.

We have built no large hall to labor in.

We sleep on small cushions for as long as we wish.

Our lives are composed with magic and euphony.

Supposition

You are willing

to pass through the center

composed of independent poetics.

To rearrange rhyme,

while you gather its energy.

New Poems

Elf

Whatever is whitening the curbside. Whatever is mildew, the whitest green I knew. The disarray. They may be honorable attendants of sorrow or happiness. In my hands, in light, they crimson.

With happiness? The highway stretches before me. Wind lather? I heard elf in tree and lo! he was near and reverential.

SLOWLY HE STEPS INTO THE TREE IN KNITTED ELF COSTUME. HE LIVED ON THE BOTTOM BRANCH AND WAS ACCUSTOMED TO BREAKFAST BEFORE HE WENT AWAY.

Storytelling

You follow me into the shadowed room.
        A toy bird calls   "green   tea   green   tea   green   tea,"
a spot on the sofa of liquid brown.

Someone stumbles in with a kettle,
bringing snow and a lighted candle.

        A book is near the table,
        a hussar leaps from the wall.
        If there were a firefly
        I would write a summer idyl, but winter is on the table,
        on the samovar. A magazine rests beside the violin.

        Someone is in the courtyard, snow on his moustache.
        In the dim lighted courtyard
                wet hay underfoot . . .

        In summer ribbons of tiles are laid out of doors,
        nasturtiums and roses climb the rose tree . . .

                    "green   tea   green   tea   green   tea"

                                      by the lakeside, where the crane flies

                    longing develops now and, melancholy . . .

Constable's Method, Brightening Near the Bridge

Calm day.

Sudden commencement of rain brightening the bridge.
Sound of water continually falling like a waterfall
carved from the trunks of trees, fastidious as a garment
of silk, and we are disengaged from our revels.

                    The Universe explains this.

As far as the eye sees little garments of rain, and if it
were autumn, we would behold many trunks of trees
becoming messages over green leaves.
Night descending frequently from its map of trees,
halting and again halting this reverie.
Walking into the garden, tying one's damp
handkerchief to a tree.

More formidable last Thursday when I spoke to
the gardener, busy learning habit of trees.
The condition of sky is secret, weaving a ring
of brown weeds like a gambler.

Further into rain there were visionary carriages.
You could see them when the plain opened. And
decided to hollow out the elegance
of the forthcoming painting.

Calm night.

(Note to the painter: "*To reveal the mask. This could become a small drawing discovered in the night, and it was retained by his brother*").

Notations writ in paint, fluvial theme out of
a corner of rain. Flight of waters. Constable traced
over all the plain, heaven also, establishing a dignity
of waters, as if they rippled unendingly.
He traced with his brushes music. There is no song
in Constable, but there is the music, even underground,
when the waters have washed the musical keys
and paint is waiting.

These are the strings of masters, as if it were music
as well as painting. We hear them in the waters,
as if a large brush shifted the momentum, and
the brush used is green, water green.

We have found the bridge engulfed by history.
Four bridges tying a knot.
And he demanded this be true, holding the giant's hammer,
who was brought out of rain into the parrot-like
bridge over the raindrops he noted, not for the first time.
(He began "the rain notes" when he was young and
there was no denominator, merely a cessation of rain.
This took place on a hill, and it would become a habit
to loiter in the rain, Speechless).

Beginning of Rain Notes

Calm night.

He had found an orientation of rain that carved notes
he made on the bridge. Formerly, it was a green
alphabet of water.

Metal covers in-between the storm latch.
He discovered in the valise his brother carved at night,
going around the barn with a night light.
He would have it printed,
as long as there was rain luster.

Calm day.

On the bridge he saw "Elf Creatures."
He had known their names when he was a child making
"Elf Creatures" in the drizzle. And yet he made a
notation to be reminded of their pedigrees,
as his mother wished.

                              Spray of "Elf Creatures."

He had noted there was something child-like about the rain.
Only when the bridge was drawn did sensibility
in his drawing show.

Just to sit and draw something like a Magna Carta.
He would draw on it, unaware of destabilization,
brought on by rain.

Before he knew about amber, holding
three threads in rain. He crossed the bridge in rain.
Short-haired cat of silver independently crossed
the plank. He found another cat-like creature lying
between raindrops.

Shelley in the Navy-Colored Chair

for Suzanna

I sit so close to him, our minds entwine.

I assume his stewardship through the cold and mist.

There is no other beauty with which he is equipped.

The pain, the exclamation!

Early morning when the tide lowers

and we manipulate our choices.

To see, to feel, to engender memory

of this place where Shelley walked.

He is near.

He breathes into the alphabet I found upon my chair.

A dissertation they brought me, exclaiming why

he failed to ride the unswept sea, and like

a nautilus drowned in heavy seas, windswept

like the alphabet he enriched.

Each day a chambered nautilus near my chair.

To add more stanzas to this alphabet

is the view Shelley takes.

More haste and less worry in the words gathered around him.

A light gleaming over their shoulder,

before the ecclesiastic wonder breaks out

into praise for words he gathered,

pearls surround the armchair.

Hotel Comfort

Minutes each hour took ostrich leaps on the roof of the Hotel Comfort in
    Strasbourg.

These Surrealist moments cherished each roof a long time.

In the thickened weather of Surrealism the cathedral

is across the street.

Wise lettuces exaggerate their claim near the windows of the Hotel Comfort.

And you have sent your letter of explanation for the pleasure obtained

in the wooden jar. Speech-maker, you have sent notes of pleasure

in the glass jars.

Tasting of weather and cinnamon.

Index of Titles and First Lines